Accountability Frankenstein

Understanding and Taming the Monster

Accountability Frankenstein

Understanding and Taming the Monster

by

Sherman Dorn

University of South Florida

INFORMATION AGE
PUBLISHING

Charlotte, North Carolina • www.infoagepub.com

Library of Congress Cataloging-in-Publication Data

Dorn, Sherman.
  Accountability Frankenstein : understanding and taming the monster / by Sherman Dorn.
  p. cm.
  Includes bibliographical references.
  ISBN 978-1-59311-623-1 (pbk.) -- ISBN 978-1-59311-624-8 (hardcover) 1. Educational accountability--United States. 2. Education--Standards--United States. 3. Education--United States. I. Title.
  LB2806.22.D67 2007
  379.1'58--dc22
                                                            2007006371

ISBN 13: 978-1-59311-623-1 (pbk.)
        978-1-59311-624-8 (hardcover)
ISBN 10: 1-59311-623-3 (pbk.)
        1-59311-624-1 (hardcover)

To Elizabeth Griffith, Kathryn Dorn, and Vincent Griffith—a teacher and two students as well as my much-loved family.

CONTENTS

ACKNOWLEDGMENTS

Any professor owes a primary debt of gratitude to one's own institutional colleagues. Several current and former colleagues at University of South Florida (USF) have encouraged me, written articles and edited books with me over the years, and given me specific suggestions on accountability over the years: Kathy Bradley-Klug, Kathy Borman, Deirdre Cobb-Roberts, Michael Curtis, Erwin V. Johanningmeier, Larry Johnson, Howard Johnston, Harold Keller, Mark Klisch, Sister Jerome Leavy, Reginald Lee, Deanna Michael, J. Lynn McBrien, Christine Ogren, Kelly Powell-Smith, Terry Richardson, Tomás Rodriguez, Barbara J. Shircliffe, Stephen Turner, Will Tyson, and Roy Weatherford.

Several grants and other opportunities contributed to my understanding of accountability in Florida. In 2001, the Spencer Foundation provided a grant to create the Consortium for Educational Research in Florida, and in 2004 the Educational Studies Policy Laboratory at Arizona State University sponsored a set of briefs on Florida reform, two of which I wrote. In each case, the support was crucial in giving me the time and capacity to think about my own state's accountability system.

Other scholars and fellow citizens who have contributed ideas in response to specific questions or have made helpful suggestions on drafts include Paul Bielawski, Gerald Bracey, Art Burke, Dan Butin, Leo Casey, Kathy Emery, David Figlio, Bob Hampel, Charlie Heath, James Horn, Heather Lewis, Kathryn McDermott, Monty Neill, Michael Resnick, Jane Robbins, A. G. Rud, Bob Schaeffer, Mary Ann Stankiewicz, Stephen Turner, Wayne Urban, and Robert E. Wright. My master's class in the fall of 2007 read a complete draft and gave invaluable feedback. David Berliner graciously shared a set of page proofs from

Sharon Nichols and his *Collateral Damage* (2007) so that I could read it while revising my own manuscript.

Several educators and public officials in Florida with different perspectives on accountability have provided insight over the years on accountability, particularly Kathi Bateham, Tom Fisher, John Hilderbrand, Michael Monroe, Faye Pages, Gloria Pipkin, and Jerry Richardson. All of my children's teachers have helped me ground my ideas in the reality of everyday teaching.

My thinking about accountability as a focus of research began over a decade ago when I joined an e-mail list on education policy moderated by Gene V. Glass. As the founding editor of *Education Policy Analysis Archives*, Gene published two early articles on accountability, "The Political Legacy of School Accountability" (*Education Policy Analysis Archives*, 6(1), 1998, http://epaa.asu.edu/epaa/v6n1.html) and "America Y2K" (*Education Policy Analysis Archives*, 8(2), 2000, http://epaa.asu.edu/epaa/v8n2/), each of which has been cannibalized and passages rewritten for this book. He has continued to encourage my efforts over the years, including proposing this book to Information Age Publishers.

Finally, I owe my family my gratitude for their love and support. My mother and late father raised me with the sense that education was a right and an obligation. My oldest sister Liz Parker has repeatedly educated me on the perspectives of a school board member. And to Elizabeth Margareta Griffith and our children, Kathryn Dorn and Vincent Griffith I owe the greatest debt for their insights and forbearance while this book took shape over 7 months.

PREFACE

You seek for knowledge and wisdom, as I once did; and I ardently hope that the gratification of your wishes may not be a serpent to sting you, as mine had been.
—Victor Frankenstein (Shelley, 1818/1869, p. 25)

ANATOMY OF A POLICY FRANKENSTEIN

Our country's way of holding public education accountable is out of control. While the public goals of accountability are positive—improving the academic achievement of students and equalizing educational opportunities and outcomes—our politicians have allowed the goals of accountability to justify the mechanical uses of standardized testing and crude sanctions at both the state and national levels. The result is a technocratic disaster, uses of testing for purposes for which they are neither designed nor well-suited, with responses by schools that too often are both irrational and destructive of the broader goals of education. We have built an accountability Frankenstein monster in this country, one that distracts teachers from key tasks and dehumanizes education. We have built this monster out of the hope that a statistical formula can dramatically improve schooling and out of the fear that there is no other option to reduce inequality in the education of our children.

Those hopes and fears have misled us, and wiser heads have known of the dangers of this type of accountability for some time. More than 30 years ago, evaluation researcher Ernie House explained the dangers of confusing responsiveness with the exertion of bureaucratic power:

Most accountability schemes ... apply a mechanical solution, a power solution, to reform complex social organizations. The schemes are exasperatingly similar. First, a small number of prespecified goals are set. Second, some measure of output is established—often only one measure like achievement scores. Third, people with good results are rewarded, and people with bad results are punished. The output measures are maximized with little concern for limits or side effects. (House, 1975, p. 50)

House's warning in the early 1970s has gone unheeded, and we have ended up with a system that he feared, one that operates on autopilot instead of common sense.

At times, the rhetorical defense of our accountability system has been as out of control as our accountability by autopilot. In 2004, former U.S. Secretary of Education Rod Paige called the National Education Association a "terrorist organization" for its opposition to No Child Left Behind (Goldstein, 2004). A press representative of Florida's former Education Commissioner Tom Gallagher used a fairly common explanation: "Most Floridians do not want to go back to the poor state our schools were in" before Governor Jeb Bush's accountability system was put in place in 1999 (Fineout, 2006). The evidence on Florida's achievement since Jeb Bush became governor is mixed at best (Chatterji, 2004), but the rhetoric emphasizes a stark comparison of the past with the present. This defense of high-stakes accountability emphasizes the fact that *something* changed. It is what British satirists have called politicians' logic—something *had* to be done; this was something; therefore, we had to do it (Lynn & Jay, 1988). However, that argument obscures the technical and conceptual flaws of high-stakes accountability. As with Mary Shelley's Dr. Frankenstein, the defenders of high-stakes testing have worked for and created a creature that is neither natural nor wise.

I am certainly not the first to criticize No Child Left Behind or other versions of high-stakes accountability in various states (e.g., Meier & Wood, 2004). Susan Ohanian, Alfie Kohn, Marion Brady, and many others have come before. But, unlike some critics, I do not see standards or the goals of school accountability as evil. These critics of high-stakes accountability are in many ways like Mary Shelley—seeing the technocracy of accountability as unnatural in the same way that her monster was an object lesson in the evils of hubris.[1] For example, Ohanian calls advocates of high-stakes testing *standardistos* (e.g., Emery & Ohanian, 2004). For years, Kohn has railed against the philosophical assumptions of behaviorisms and using rewards and punishments at all in schools, either for individual students or for educators (e.g., Kohn, 2004). Brady has argued that standards themselves are inappropriate (e.g., Brady, 2000). I think I understand these humanistic critics of standards and accountability. To use technocratic tools to improve education threatens to remove the individualism, spontaneity, and joy of the best education many of us have experienced. To Brady and others, the real world is more complicated than our compartmentalized curriculum. To Ohanian and Kohn, good education relies on something more than scripting. Most of us have had our "aha" or eureka moments, where something a teacher said gave us a new perspective, or where we finally understood a concept we had struggled with. And in most cases, these moments did not come in scripted lessons or during fill-in-the-bubble tests. To many critics of high-stakes accountability, trying to improve education by standardizing it is an obscene marriage of technocracy and democracy. These opponents are frustrated with the irrationality of our current systems without crediting the possible value in accountability.

Like Ohanian, Kohn, and others, I am deeply troubled by the effects of high-stakes accountability on schools. There have been too many reports of rampant test preparation to ignore—and by test preparation, I mean spending weeks teaching third-graders how to take standardized tests, not teaching the curriculum (e.g., McNeil, 2000; Nichols & Berliner, 2007). My children have seen their own school time swallowed up by test-preparation. I have heard from teachers in one nearby school district how a *pacing calendar* is commonly used by principals to dictate where in a textbook the district's elementary teachers must be from day to day, allowing insufficient time for reteaching concepts where needed. For a school official to say blithely that elementary teachers should deemphasize -*ing* word endings in language arts because -*s* and -*es* endings are on the test but -*ing* endings are not on the test is letting the fear of test consequences drive instructional decisions (Tobin & Winchester, 2004).

Yet I disagree with the arguments that accountability is always wrong, essentially an argument against standards and accountability in the broader sense. For several reasons, the push for accountability is both a good thing in general and also deeply rooted in the recent history of schooling. If accountability has become a Frankenstein monster, it is not through evil intent, and we should not shy away from understanding the contradictions in education politics. Because the Boris Karloff *Frankenstein* movie dominates public knowledge of the story, we sometimes forget a crucial element of Mary Shelley's plot: Victor Frankenstein abandoned his creation, after being revulsed at the first sight of him:

> I had worked hard for nearly two years, for the sole purpose of infusing life into an inanimate body. For this I had deprived myself of rest and health. I had desired it with an ardour that far exceeded moderation; but now that I had finished, the beauty of the dream vanished, and breathless horror and disgust filled my heart. Unable to endure the aspect of the being I had created, I rushed out of the room. (Shelley, 1818/1869, p. 45)

Frankenstein wanders around the town until his boyhood friend Henry surprises him, and he finds himself too mortified to explain what he had done:

> I then reflected, and the thought made me shiver, that the creature whom I had left in my apartment might still be there, alive, and walking about. I dreaded to behold this monster; but I feared still more that Henry should see him. (p. 48)

He hides his work for years, until he heads home and discovers that his creature has killed his own brother.

> Two years had now nearly elapsed since the night on which he first received life; and was this his first crime? Alas! I had turned loose into the world a depraved wretch, whose delight was in carnage and misery; had he not murdered my brother? (p. 60)

Even then, Victor Frankenstein listens to the person he created and agrees to create a companion until he decides the risk of a second creature too great:

> I had before been moved by the sophisms of the being I had created; I had been struck senseless by his fiendish threats: but now, for the first time, the wickedness of my promise burst upon me; I shuddered to think that future ages might curse me as their pest, whose selfishness had not hesitated to buy its own peace at the price perhaps of the existence of the whole human race. (p. 131)

If Frankenstein's first sin was the hubris in his creation, others followed: too proud to acknowledge his errors, he did nothing until the consequences of his actions became too painful to bear, and even then, he chose poorly. The creation of a high-stakes accountability system is not the greatest error of its proponents. As I explain in this book, the political drive for accountability is strong and in many ways reasonable. The far greater sin would be to watch the consequences and do nothing or, worse yet, ratchet up the pressures without acknowledging the errors of the recent past.

Thus, I see the politics of accountability as far more complicated than the two-dimensional views of both accountability defenders and some opponents, each of which sees the other argument as proposed by a set of villains or fools. The problems of accountability are rooted in the contradictions of our democratic history. We want both a system that rewards merit and a system that generates equality. We have operated a society that insists on the value of technical expertise and also the value of public transparency. We can simultaneously insist on the public purposes of schooling and also value schools for their ability to promote the private interests of families and students (e.g., Labaree, 1997). That contradictory nature of education politics is reflected in the inconsistent views of the American public when polled, as respondents can simultaneously claim that both families and schools are primarily responsible for educational achievement (e.g., Rose & Gallup, 2005, 2006).

A Very Brief History of Test-Based Accountability

> *I doubted at first whether I should attempt the creation of a being like myself or one of simpler organization; but my imagination was too much exalted by my first success to permit me to doubt of my ability to give life to an animal as complex and wonderful as man.*
>
> —Victor Frankenstein (Shelley, 1818/1869, p. 42)

Today, children in the United States take more annual standardized tests than at any time in the past. Those tests are linked to consequences both for students and for educators. For students, the score on a state-mandated test may determine whether they proceed to the next grade or graduate. For teachers and administrators, the aggregate scores of students are commonly printed in the newspaper and used to judge the school's worth. Test scores determine the reputation of schools, the value of homes near a school, and the reputation of a community. In some states, test results direct money to high-scoring schools and shame to low-scoring schools. Signed in 2002, the federal No Child Left Behind Act makes some sanctions uniform across the country. For schools with concentrations of children from poor families—for schools that receive federal aid under Title I of the law that has become No Child Left Behind—the federal government mandates a specific sequence of consequences for the third, fourth, and following years in which a school does not meet federal standards: giving parents the choice to send their children to other schools in the district who have met federal standards, providing tutoring (using federal aid for this purpose), and taking more extreme action (by firing some or most of the staff, reorganizing the school, turning the school into a charter school, contracting management out to a private company, or having the state take over the management of the school, among other options). Today, public schools operate in a high-stakes accountability system, where the results of annual testing can dramatically changes the lives of students and their teachers.

Today's accountability systems for both students and teachers have higher stakes than at any other time in our country's history. As other historians have written, both testing and accountability have existed for many decades, but the combination of testing with consequences for both students and schools is recent (Beadie, 2004; Cuban, 2004b). Some version of standardized testing has existed since the nineteenth century, and much of that testing had high stakes for students—whether the tests determined admission to high schools, the challenge and quality of courses assigned in high school, or admission to selective colleges. The most (in)famous standardized tests in the first half of the twentieth century were crude so-called intelligence tests, administered in groups and whose results were used to slot students into curriculum tracks (Gould, 1996; Tyack, 1974). (The vast majority of high-school students were in nonacademic tracks.) Because the earliest tests had been constructed around the cultural norms of the psychologists who designed them, the results commonly confirmed social class, ethnic, and racial stereotypes of the time and rationalized a substandard education for millions of children. The testing industry also created tests that were supposed to measure academic achievement, and over time, those tests became more prominent. But stakes tied to the tests were primarily for students until the last third of the twentieth century. In the 1970s, some states started to link high school graduation to passing a standardized test or to promotion from one grade to another. For the most part, standardized testing has had a continuous presence in schools since the late nineteenth and early twentieth centuries. As Nancy Beadie (2004) points out, what is new since the late 1960s is the common practice of states' mandating annual standardized testing and linking the tests to grade promotion or graduation.

The history of accountability for schools and educators has taken a different path from the consequences of testing for students. As historian Daniel Calhoun (1973) and sociologist Robert Dreeben (1968) have noted, one subtle effect of testing students has been to displace responsibility for results from the school onto the student. That fact does not mean that accountability has not existed for schools, but it has been different from accountability for students. Until the early twentieth century, school governance (and accountability) was truly a local matter. For several hundred years, there was no such thing as a school system in the British colonies in North America and the young United States. There were private tutors and schoolmasters, charity schools, academies, seminaries, village (district) schools, dame schools, and grammar schools. The lines between the categories were fluid, and accountability was held in the hands of a local school committee, parents who paid tuition, and benefactors. As school bureaucracies grew in nineteenth-century cities, governance remained local. For example, the Philadelphia school board in the early years of the twentieth century had more than 60 members, each one of which was the chair of his or her own neighborhood school board, which hired and fired teachers (Issel, 1978).

That localization ended in the twentieth century, but growing centralization did not create a new form of accountability. Even as control over schools centralized in the first half of the twentieth century—with urban school boards shrinking in size, often appointed rather than elected, and with states forcing small rural districts to merge—testing remained the burden of students. As the first two chapters explain, administrators used standardized testing as part of their claim to insulated authority to run schools. It was not until the 1960s and 1970s that the first real moves to connect test results to schools began. That tentative effort at accountability was at both the federal and state levels. In 1965, the federal Elementary and Secondary Education Act required annual testing as part of the evaluation of school aid that the act provided in Title I. (The No Child Left Behind Act is the 2002 reauthorization of this program.) But though the evaluation of Title I programs created a precedent for test-based accountability at the federal level, most of the new testing in the 1960s and 1970s appeared at the state level. New York, California, and Pennsylvania created state-level testing programs in the 1960s, though only New York's program identified the results from individual schools (Wynne, 1972). Florida, Colorado, Maryland, and Mississippi passed laws in the early 1970s they called school accountability, and by the mid-1970s, 10 other states had (Cooperative Accountability Project, 1974; Wise, 1979).

Many states established a link between testing and school accountability by the end of the 1970s, though the local history varied. The shape of Pennsylvania's program was negotiated, as the legislature created statewide testing only after administrators lobbied to eliminate reporting by individual school and district. Michigan's program was initially championed by the state department of education without school identifiers, until legislators and the state board of education insisted on such labeling (Wynne, 1972). In the early 1970s, Florida's legislature and governor very clearly linked accountability to testing and created a statewide testing program explicitly for it and regularly tinkered with the design during the 1970s (Herrington & McDonald, 2001; Michael & Dorn, 2007). The one common feature of state-level testing programs was the business relationship between school systems and testing companies. When creating testing programs, state departments of education knew they did not have to write or administer the testing program itself, because the testing industry already existed from the decades-long relationships with local school districts. State officials thus became and remain contract managers, overseeing a private company assigned the responsibility of creating, printing, and scoring tests.

In the 1980s and 1990s, the nature of testing and the relationship between testing and accountability was in flux. In many states, graduation exams became the norm, though the vast majority of students easily passed the tests that became targeted at relatively low skill levels—thus the term attached to those requirements, *minimum competency test*. In some places, such as Chicago in the late 1990s, standardized tests were used as promotion gateways, leading to hundreds of children being held back in the same grade for 2 or more years (Nagaoka & Roderick, 2004). Starting in 1984, Texas began ratcheting up its testing program, the difficulty of tests, and the consequences attached to them (both for students and for schools) (Rhoten, Carnoy, Chabrán, & Elmore, 2004). And in 1991, Tennessee began an experiment with an accountability system built on complex statistics, what it called value-added assessment of the growth in student learning (Educational Improvement Act, 1992).

But that intensification of testing and consequences did not occur everywhere. Critics of standardized testing argued that fill-in-the-bubble tests were inadequate as assessment—too focused on compartmentalized skills to be meaningful. Lauren and Daniel Resnick (1992) and others argued for assessment of student performance on tasks that went beyond multiple-choice questions. They argued that if one built a test good enough, teachers would improve instruction. The goal was a test that was linked to clear curriculum standards, one that theoretically challenged students to go beyond rote memorization and provided a better picture of what students could do. California and Kentucky became laboratories for the performance assessment experiment in the 1990s. Kentucky's Supreme Court had ruled the entire system of public education unconstitutional, from financing to governance, and the legislature responded by creating a new funding formula for the state and an entirely new assessment system based on performance (Rhoten et al., 2004). California also attempted a largely performance-based test system until a growing controversy over the test items killed it (McDonnell, 1994).[2] Rhode Island experimented in the 1990s with an accountability system involving personal inspections of schools using teams of fellow educators (see chapter 1 for more details). One state—Iowa—had no high-stakes accountability system for either students or educators through the entire period that many of its peers were creating state testing programs and experimenting with accountability (Carnoy & Loeb, 2002). In the mid-1990s, testing and accountability practices diverged dramatically across the United States, with some states requiring multiple-choice tests linked to tangible sanctions and rewards, other states with performance tasks as part of state assessment, and some states with either no consequences or relatively minimal sanctions. Testing and accountability was in flux.

Florida's history of testing and accountability illustrates this flux during the 1990s and the quick intensification of test-based accountability at the end of the 1990s. In the 1970s, both legislators and governors agreed in principle on the need for accountability and for a statewide testing program as part of it. This accountability system included a clear consequence for high-school students—passage of a standardized test before graduation—and multiple-choice tests whose results were public information. The graduation-exam requirement was itself tested in a federal lawsuit, *Debra P. v. Turlington* (1983, 1984). The court ordered a delayed phase-in because high-school students in the late 1970s would have been in segregated schools in the late 1960s and early 1970s. Later, a federal appeals court ruled that the state program did not violate the Civil Rights Act of 1964, a decision that established legal standards for graduation exams. Yet, despite the court affirmation of high-stakes testing, Florida did *not* intensify its accountability system. Instead, the school accountability system varied in its reliance on testing. For example, in the early 1990s, the state attempted to decentralize school improvement efforts by creating school councils (including parents and community members as well as administrators and teachers) and requiring that the school councils write improvement plans—but without specifying the improvement plans' content (Herrington & McDonald, 2001; Michael & Dorn, 2007).

But also in the early 1990s, Florida legislators and state officials began to respond to the standards movement by writing a set of curriculum standards and authorizing the creation of a new set of state tests that they hoped would be closely tied to those standards. In creating this new system, the Florida Comprehensive Assessment Test (or FCAT), state officials created a hybrid test, partly multiple-choice and partly based on performance items, with testing of writing, reading, and math at three points in K-12 grades.[3] In the mid-90s, the state rolled out its new program, beginning with the writing exam, in which 4th-, 8th-, and 10-grade students had to respond to a prompt with an essay.[4] But the leadership of the state department of education had shifted from the decentralized approach a few years before, and the newly-elected Commissioner of Education Frank Brogan used the results of the new FCAT to put several dozen schools on a public list of "critically low-performing schools" (Herrington & McDonald, 2001; Michael & Dorn, 2007).

Four years later, Brogan was the new lieutenant governor, elected along with new Governor Jeb Bush, and in the first year of their term, the Florida legislature rewrote the state's accountability system (Fla. Statutes ch. 99-398, 1999). The new law required testing every year from 3rd through 10th grades in reading, writing, math, and now science. Third graders needed to pass the reading test to be promoted to fourth grade. The test results are used to assign each school a single letter grade from A to F.

Schools who are assigned an A grade or improve in their letter grade receive $100 per student as a bonus for the school. Public-school choice was offered to parents of students assigned to schools assigned an F 2 years out of 4. And, until the state's highest court struck down the program in January 2006 (*Bush v. Holmes*, 2006), the same parents could also use a state voucher to send the child assigned to a "double-F" school in a participating private school. In less than a decade, the state of Florida moved from a system that had a minimum competency test as a legacy of the 1970s and a decentralized accountability system, on the one hand, to a system that had far more intensive annual tests in eight grades and where the scores had higher stakes for students and high stakes for educators, on the other hand.

With the signing of the No Child Left Behind Act in 2002, the federal government pressed all of the states to create a system that was more intensive than either of the systems in Texas or Florida, where the new president and his brother had been governors, respectively. While No Child Left Behind did not change the nominal consequences for students, it dramatically raised the stakes for schools and the educators working in them. The key mechanism in the No Child Left Behind Act is a requirement for states to judge the performance of each school based on annual testing in Grades 3-8. Each school must be judged on whether its students are meeting Adequate Yearly Progress (or AYP) standards. The AYP standard essentially asks the following question: Do the students at the school meet the state's declared benchmark on the way to 100% of students' being proficient in math and reading by 2014? After the 2002 passage of No Child Left Behind, each state had to write a plan that the federal government approved, identifying the tests used, the threshold for each test that would mark proficiency, and the projection of increasing proportions proficient that would connect the existing performance in 2002 to 100% proficiency in 2014. Grade by grade and subject by subject, that projection created the benchmarks against which school performance is measured. To meet AYP, the proportion of students meeting the proficiency threshold has to match the benchmark for that year, not only for students as a whole but also subpopulations that the state identifies—students with disabilities, students on free- and reduced-lunch program rolls, and students in various ethnic and racial categories. The failure to meet the benchmark in any subpopulation group means that the school fails to meet AYP as a whole, a failure that triggers a set of mandated sanctions. This disaggregation of results by subpopulation and the establishment of a 100% proficiency target for 2014 are the most controversial mechanisms of the No Child Left Behind Act.

The Organization of This Book

Proponents of the No Child Left Behind Act have described it as both evolutionary and revolutionary (Hess & Finn, 2004). In one sense it is evolutionary since it followed an era of test-based accountability at the state level, and it is also revolutionary in the heavy hand of the federal government in test-based accountability. To understand the current moment in school accountability, one must understand the larger contradictions in education politics. While this book has some discussion of accountability for students—tests used as gateways for promotion or graduation—the book focuses on tests used to judge schools and educators. The goal of this book is to provide a broader perspective on the school accountability debate by exploring the contradictions inherent in high-stakes testing. As an historian of education, I see these contradictions rooted in the last century or more of education history in the U.S. changes in accountability over the past 10 years have accelerated long-term trends, and each of the first five chapters addresses one of those trends or legacies. One legacy shaping accountability is the rise and fall of administrative authority in the twentieth century. The decline of administrators' prestige and real power in the second half of the twentieth century, along with increasing demands for equality in educational opportunity and changed funding for schools, increased the expectations for accountability. This history is the subject of the first chapter.

A second relevant legacy has been the awkward relationship between expertise and democracy in the United States. Part of the politics of expertise has come from the concrete tools that require training and experience (whether designing bridges, performing surgery, or constructing and scoring achievement tests), but part has revolved around an incomplete buffering of expertise from lay criticism. The awkward use of tests and jerry-built statistics in accountability systems—and the harsh criticism of that use—represents a continuation of the politics of expertise in the United States and a century-long tension between expertise and popular participation in decision making. The second chapter explores the historical reasons for our reliance on test scores as the main measure used in accountability, and the third chapter explores the fragility of the test score statistics and formulae.

A third legacy has been the overly-broad expectations held for schools. Schools in the United States have long been expected to solve broad social problems, but political rhetoric in the past half-century has raised those expectations. Since the end of World War II, schools have been expected to help the nation fight the Cold War, fight the War on Poverty, fight prejudice, and fight for position in the global economy. The dynamic of school reform has established its own set of expectations—

most visibly in the set of educational goals established in a summit in 1989 and in the No Child Left Behind Act's dictum that all children shall be proficient by 2014. Unfortunately, the history and current debate avoids the real question of how to set appropriate expectations for students and schools. Goals are the subject of the fourth chapter.

A fourth legacy is the rhetoric of child saving and child protection. Since the late nineteenth century, reformers have often used the *interests of children* as a rhetorical trump card in policy debate, whether in the creation of juvenile and family court systems in the late nineteenth century or accountability systems in the early twenty-first century. The fact that any conception of a child's interest is *an adult's argument about children's interest* is usually ignored. Both high-stakes accountability's defenders and critics often assume that advocates of the other position are self-serving. But material self-interest is not the only potential motivation for individuals. It is time to step back from this destructive dynamic and acknowledge that the critical questions are adult questions, and that adults can have multiple motives. Motivation and the consequences used in accountability systems comprise the focus of the fifth chapter.

In the United States, we can construct a sane way of holding schools accountable, taming or rebuilding our accountability monster. Such a system requires acknowledging the political and policy needs for accountability and standards. A sane system of accountability would respect the technical limits of achievement measures. A sane system of accountability must replace symbolic rhetoric about high expectations with difficult discussions using real evidence. A sane system of accountability would create a system that works for the adults who are paid to teach our children and whose own material interests and identity are intimately tied up with how we define children's best interests. It is a missed opportunity as well as destructive that we have not yet constructed a sane system of school accountability. This book tries to help.

NOTES

1. Technocracy is setting social policy by technical methods, isolated from politics (e.g., Scott, 1933).

2. Some proponents of performance assessment called it (and continue to call it) authentic assessment. From a social-science perspective, there is no such thing as an authentic assessment of skills in the institutional environment of a school; the choice of terms here was largely political, to suggest that multiple-choice tests are somehow more inauthentic.

3. The new 10th grade exam also became the graduation test during a phase-in period in the late 1990s and early 2000s.

4. The fourth-grade prompts for the writing exam can also require a story.

CHAPTER 1

THE POLITICAL ORIGINS OF ACCOUNTABILITY

Accountability has a longer political history than we usually hear of in today's education debates. In addition, we sometimes take the existence of standardized testing for granted because of its recent history. One of the more important services that historians can provide is to eliminate misconceptions about the origins of accountability. These misconceptions appear in arguments on multiple sides of the accountability debate. For example, supporters of high-stakes accountability sometimes argue that tying test scores to sanctions is a natural extension of school reform efforts. Erik Hanushek and Margaret Raymond (2002) wrote:

> Accountability systems have been developed almost universally across the states to deal with the aggregate performance shortcomings that are now widely recognized. That history has shown that we do not know how to link programs, resources, and other inputs to student outcomes so that regulation of inputs cannot be assumed to satisfy outcome objectives. The sea change moving from a basic regulatory environment to one that emphasizes performance and outcomes can be interpreted as recognition that something else has to be done. (pp. 80-81)

Hanushek and Raymond are suggesting that high-stakes accountability is inevitable in a rational policymaking environment. Arguments about inevitability or a single rational choice are generally unconvincing to historians, who look for where events could have been different. In contrast to Hanushek and Raymond, opponents to No Child Left Behind and similar state policies have occasionally suggested that the current moment in accountability is based on a desire to ruin public education and feed money to private entities. Testing gadfly and former head of Virginia's student testing program Jerry Bracey wrote in 2004,

> NCLB sets up public schools to fail, setting the stage for private education companies to move in on the $400 billion spent annually on K-12 education ($500 billion according to recent statements by Secretary of Education Rod Paige). The consequent destruction or reduction of public education would shrink government and cripple or eliminate the teachers' unions, nearly five million mostly Democratic voters. It's a law to drool over if you're Karl Rove or Grover Norquist. (p. 63)

Bracey's argument here is focused on the federal No Child Left Behind Act and the interventions required, not *all* testing systems. (Bracey is skeptical of high-stakes testing in general.) But if Hanushek and Raymond were being simplistic, so was Bracey, who focused on one key characteristic of No Child Left Behind. If Hanushek and Raymond emphasize inevitability, Bracey emphasizes the destructive potential of testing, specifically for the political and financial survival of public schools. Both arguments lay claim to common rhetorical ploys—asserting inevitability for accountability, according to the supporters, or the ill intent of accountability advocates, for the opponents. But the stories implied here are misleading, and anyone looking at accountability policy should understand both the long-term trends that underlay high-stakes accountability policies and the contradictions involved.

One part of background information is the relatively recent history of using test scores to judge schools. School statistics have existed since the late nineteenth century, and claims to objective measurement of student achievement from the turn of the twentieth century. Achievement scores have typically been only for internal consumption within school bureaucracies until recently. In the wave of school criticism after World War II, ideological debates over progressive education and the needs of the Cold War were the explicit points of conflict. However, statistical evaluations were invisible in the 1940s and 1950s debates over schooling (Ravitch, 1983; Spring, 1989). The public debate over Scholastic Aptitude Test (SAT) score trends did not exist until the mid-1970s, even though the decline in mean scores began in the early 1960s. For example, the *New York Times* did not start reporting SAT scores annually until 1976 (Maeroff, 1976). No network news broadcasts between 1968 and 1974 reported test scores as the substance of the story; the first networks to do so after 1967 were ABC and CBS on October 28, 1975.[1]

I use this information largely to point out that we should be wary of various stories told about accountability. My skepticism of the political stories in education debates does not mean that I am a dispassionate observer. I have two children in Florida's public schools, and I expect schools to be accountable to parents and the public. At the same time, I have seen accountability run amok during Jeb Bush's two terms as governor. But knowing that something is wrong is not enough. We must understand the political underpinnings of accountability. Because of the recent history, we may gloss over the problems with explanations that high-stakes accountability is inevitable or ill-intentioned. Test-based accountability for educators was not inevitable, even though standardized testing existed for decades before the first inklings of accountability. Today, accountability for both students and schools is deeply-rooted. Whether using high-stakes testing or in some other form, accountability neither will nor should disappear in the foreseeable future. The rest of this chapter explains why. It explores the political roots of accountability, the flexible rationale for high-stakes testing, the relationship between accountability and other aspects of education politics, and the costs of high-stakes accountability. Though I will return to the high stakes for students on occasion, for most of this book, the issue at hand is holding educators accountable.

THE RISE AND FALL OF SCHOOL ADMINISTRATION

The roots of accountability needed somewhere to grow—conditions that did not fully exist in 1950. One precondition for the modern accountability era was the reduction of prestige that administrators held immediately after World War II. In the first half of the twentieth century, networks of administrators around the country worked hard to buffer their authority from outside pressures, pressures that they perceived as political interference. Only through the reduction of their prestige could the modern sense of accountability could grow. One of the historical ironies about accountability is that administrators are now judged by the same type of evidence that their predecessors used to buffer themselves from public scrutiny of school management 70 or 80 years ago.

Public education professionalized at the same time as law and medicine, in the late nineteenth and early twentieth century *zeitgeist* that historians call the Progressive Era. In the Progressive Era, teachers did not acquire recognized public expertise in a way that would lead to autonomy. School administrators did. School administrators deliberately built a set of bureaucratic institutions and professional networks in the early twentieth century to buffer themselves politically, in part by claiming the need for autonomy to exercise professional judgment and wield their expertise (Tyack, 1974; Tyack & Hansot, 1982). The autonomy that school administrators built in the first part of the twentieth century depended partly on a national trend to strip authority from local elective offices in education, such as the 60-odd precinct boards of education in Philadelphia that were replaced by a small board appointed by judges in 1911 (Issel, 1978; Tyack, 1974). But the autonomy also depended on administrators' making the case that they could manage schools scientifically. Education quickly came to rival chemistry in American doctoral education in the twentieth century. In 1930, the number of doctorates were similar, 248 in chemistry and 243 in education, and together the two fields comprised more than 15% of all doctorates in 1910, 1920, 1930, 1940, and 1950 (contributing 30% of all doctorates in 1950).[2] Would-be administrators were enthusiastic enrollees in statistics courses (Jonçich, 1968). One part of this claim to scientific management came through the hiring of university education professors to conduct management surveys of urban districts. These school surveys were not statistical test summaries but closer to the contemporary management consultant's report, a description of how a system looked to the survey head and a list of recommendations (Tyack, 1974; Tyack & Hansot, 1982). The second part of the claim to scientific management came through the expanding use of tests to make curriculum decisions about individual children. After World War I, psychologists who had tested English-language "IQ" tests on Army recruits discovered their largest markets in schools (e.g., Gould, 1996). By the 1920s, hundreds of districts were using group-administered tests to determine whether students would have access to a challenging curriculum in high school (e.g., Tyack, 1974). [3]

By mid-century, testing became one of the common tools of public-school management. Even though the use of testing restricted rather than opened up opportunity, few challenged the broad use of testing. Students took tests for their own classes and also to determine their opportunities in schooling. Teachers took tests, especially after 1930s court decisions striking down teacher salary scales that treated teachers differently by race—often the new use of teacher tests was to reconstruct unequal pay scales but without using race explicitly (Baker, 1995). When Southern school boards searched for bureaucratic tools to resist desegregation, pupil-placement laws and rules placed psychological testing at the heart of that bureaucratic resistance. For the Black students in Atlanta who applied in 1961 to desegregate the city's all-White high schools, each had to undergo 7 hours of psychological testing, and at the end of the process, the school system proudly announced that 10 of the 134 applicants had qualified to transfer (Dorn, 1996). Few challenged the broad uses of testing through the mid-1960s in large part because of the professional autonomy of school administrators.

That autonomy has waned since the middle of the twentieth century. The shrinking of administrative autonomy is neither a surprise nor harmful. After all, administrative autonomy had been used to reduce the academic opportunities for millions of American schoolchildren. After the second *Brown v. Board of Education* decision in 1955, courts' willingness to let administrators and school boards define appropriate desegregation plans led to token desegregation for more than a decade (e.g., Douglas, 1995; Patterson, 2001; Shircliffe, 2006). One of the reasons for the decline of administrative authority came from popular discontent with the arrogance of administrators. Resistance to desegregation was certainly one face of this arrogance. The civil rights movement had targeted schools as one public institution that was treating poor and minority children unequally, and the responses by both school boards and administrators reshaped educational politics. Ironically, the attack on school inequalities undermined the autonomy of administrators in multiple camps, both from those who thought that inequality is morally wrong and also from those who had relied on state and local control of education to preserve bastions of private privilege. But the impression of arrogance extended to other areas, as well. In the 1950s, liberals such as Arthur Bestor (1953) criticized administrators' and educational writers' willingness to water down academics for the majority of high-school students. In the 1970s, social conservatives unhappy with desegregation and arguments in favor of shifting schooling away from a highly-structured, "teacher-centered" classroom framed their concerns as a "back to basics" movement—part of a broader struggle over the meaning of education after World War II (Grant, 1988; Hampel, 1986).

Discontent with administrative arrogance was matched in the 1960s and 1970s by changing dynamics in politics in general. Even if administrators had not helped feed the decline of their authority, they would have faced a harder political environment by the late 1970s and 1980s as the political credibility of all public institutions deteriorated. The Vietnam War and Watergate created a credibility gap between what public leaders said and what most citizens saw happening (Schell, 1975). As a result, for police, the postal service, and public schools, their credibility eroded because those are the three government agencies whose employees are visible daily. The influence of national perceptions of government on perceptions of *local* public employees does not account for all of the erosion of administrative authority. Certainly, both police and schools provided plenty of reasons in the post-World War II world why Americans would want more accountability. But the erosion of trust in national political institutions helped undermine the legitimacy of school administrators as autonomous professionals and public schools as worthy of financial and political support (Tyack & Hansot, 1982). One would be hard-pressed to imagine high-stakes accountability with publicly-released test scores half a century ago, when the attacks on administrative authority had just started. Today, school administrators have relatively little protection from public criticism. Accountability has turned the use of educational statistics upside-down. Statistics bolstered the claims of administrators to expertise early in this century, but politicians and popular news media now use statistics to judge school systems. The primary power of school officials these days is not public respect of their expertise but bureaucratic authority.

Pressures on Schools

While school administrators were losing prestige in the middle third of the twentieth century, several other developments were creating pressures for accountability in the modern sense. One source of pressure was the growing substantive criticism of schools that the earlier part of this chapter describes. A second source of pressure was a nationalization of education policy debate sparked by the Cold War, antipoverty efforts in the 1960s, the civil-rights movement, and then the economic decline of the 1980s (Berliner & Biddle, 1996; Spring, 1989). As chapter 4 describes, arguments that schools should solve important social problems raised expectations, expectations that schools probably could never meet. A third source of pressure was a shift in education funding from local sources to state governments in the 1970s. Lawsuits inspired by the *Brown v. Board of Education* (1954) decision attempted to equalize funding by claiming that either the federal or state constitution forbade unequal distribution of school revenues. After *Serrano v. Priest* (1971) in California became the first successful funding lawsuit, others in different states and in the federal courts (*San Antonio v. Rodriguez*, where advocates of equal funding eventually failed in a 1973 Supreme Court decision). But even without a federal mandate for equalization, states faced equalization lawsuits based on each state's constitution. State legislators also confronted other reasons to anticipate spending more on education: special-education lawsuits, teachers-union activism, and inflation. No one should be surprised that legislators wanted some quid pro quo for spending more on education. Tony Morley, an observer at a gathering of Southern legislators in the Georgia Sea Islands in June 1972, explained what he had heard, a year after the *Serrano v. Priest* (1971) decision in California mandated a centralized collection and disbursement of school funds, and less than a decade after the modern teachers union movement had started:

> There was a lot of general talk by the legislators about the coming demand for "accountability." These legislators see both *Serrano* decisions and teacher unions bidding up the cost of state support for public schools. If lawmakers are going to be tagged for the bill, they want to have more assurance about what they are buying. They don't know how to get such assurance, however, and the educators they deal with don't know how to give it to them. Neither is clear as to what would be acceptable evidence.[4]

Funding-equalization demands and teachers unions were not the only sources of growing state involvement in education funding, but to legislators they represented the increasing demands for state revenues. The growing centralization of school revenues fed a growing interest in education at the state level, expressed at least in part in efforts to hold schools accountable (Resnick, 1980).

Both of these conditions were necessary to foster accountability. Because school administrators had lost considerable prestige and power, there was no check in the last 30 years on the positive demands for accountability. And there were definitely positive demands for accountability. As a result, schools became more vulnerable to criticism and came under greater scrutiny as they were criticized, expected to solve social problems, and drew more resources from states. When federal Associate Commissioner of Education Leon Lessinger published *Every Kid a Winner: Accountability in Education* (1970), he was feeding rhetoric into an existing political dynamic (Martin, Overholt, & Urban, 1976; Sirotnik, 2004). That there would be *some* type of mechanism sought to hold schools accountable is not a surprise. However, the word and the exact shape of accountability were not foreordained.

The Flexible Rationale for Accountability

In its first decade, modern accountability rhetoric and policies mixed three elements: a fiscal metaphor in rhetoric, the use of standardized tests, and the first attempts to hold students accountable for having some knowledge before graduation. All three of these elements were evident in Florida, which created an education law with *accountability* in its title in 1971. That year, Governor Rubin Askew called for "programs of accountability," and 2 years later, he described his vision to fellow Southern governors as "a comprehensive management information, cost accounting and educational assessment system" (Southern Governor's Conference, 1973, p. 51). The parallels to financial accounting in a corporation was neither accidental nor unnoticed at the time (Martin, Overholt, & Urban, 1976). During the mid-1970s, the Florida legislature fleshed out that ambitious but vague language with increased reporting requirements for school spending, the first statewide standardized testing program for students in Florida, tests for new teachers, and requiring that students pass standardized tests before receiving a high-school diploma (Herrington & McDonald, 2001; Michael & Dorn, 2007). One of the minimum competency tests created by several states in the 1970s, Florida's new requirement immediately spawned a federal lawsuit, *Debra P. v. Turlington* (1983, 1984), which delayed the implementation of the graduation test (see the description in the preface). But most of the other provisions were implemented without much argument. If Tony Morley was correct that legislators at the time did not know what they wanted in accountability, they were willing to experiment.

While legislators were experimenting, their actions clearly suggested a focus on education as investment. Among the three elements in the 1970s—a fiscal metaphor, standardized testing, and graduation tests—the common theme of accountability was a human-capital argument. Essentially, the argument for all three was that a state was investing in its children's education and should watch over that investment. That human-capital argument was neither new nor applied solely to accountability. For at least a decade, discussions of schooling and its problems were phrased in human-capital terms. The rhetoric has been used by liberals and conservatives alike, by Democrats as well as Republicans (e.g., Dorn, 1996; National Center on Education and the Economy, 1990; Purdum, 1999). When legislators and governors turned to the same concept when thinking about accountability, they were applying a familiar idea rather than making a dramatic departure.

But the rationale for accountability was not entirely about human capital in the 1960s and 1970s. A minority of accountability's proponents focused on testing to make sure that everyone receives a decent education. Today, civil-rights rhetoric is a dominant theme in the national debate over accountability, but that was not the case in the 1960s or 1970s. Nonetheless, a civil-rights rationale for testing did appear early in the discussions over the Elementary and Secondary Education Act. During legislative hearings in 1965, Senator Robert Kennedy pushed for annual testing as part of the evaluation of Title I programs:

> If I lived in the community where the $2 million was being wasted, I would like to know something about that. I would like—I wonder if we couldn't just have some kind of system of reporting either through some testing system which could be established which the people at the local community would know periodically as to what progress had been made under this program. (cited in Wynne, 1972, p. 42)

To some extent, Kennedy's comments were shared by grassroots and national civil-rights advocates. In the 1960s, Philadelphia activists used test scores to criticize the city's public school system (Dorn, 1996). In the early 1970s, the United Bronx Parents wanted to use tests to hold schools accountable, as did the (national) Poor People's Campaign (Wynne, 1972). When New York City's schools contracted with one of the major testing firms, Educational Testing Corporation, to run a local test system that would compare school test scores with those of schools with similar demographic characteristics, psychologist Kenneth Clark erupted in fury. He wrote that separate comparisons by demographic characteristics would lead to unequal expectations and "concretize class stratifications and ... racial distinctions." Clark saw separate expectations as a civil-rights issue and interpreted the New York City program as a "sham" (Buder, 1971, p. 25; Wynne, 1972).

To say that the civil-rights rationale for accountability appeared only in the late 1980s and 1990s is incomplete, though, for it omits the machinery of government from the story. While the rhetoric of accountability in the 1970s was firmly based in human capital, the policy mechanics of interpreting standardized tests were slowly but firmly focusing on policies whose goals were to equalize education. With the largest portion of federal education aid focused on schools with high concentrations of poverty starting in 1965 (with Title I of the Elementary and Secondary Education Act), federal policymakers wanted some way to gauge the success of spending. Robert Kennedy's push for testing became the starting point for additional efforts to keep Title I programs accountable. From 1976 through the 1990s, the most common use of tests in Title I came through a manipulation of standardized test scores called the normal curve equivalent, which some hoped would put different tests on an identical scale (RMC Research Corporation, 1976). The use of normal-curve equivalents became the standard tool in the evaluation of Title I and other poverty-related programs, sometimes to the consternation of observers who debated the methodological, use, and political issues involved (Barnes & Ginsburg, 1979; Linn, 1979; Stonehill & Groves, 1983; vanderPloeg, 1982; Vinovskis, 1999). But normal curve equivalents were not intended to be perfect; their use was a part of accountability's experimentation as Congress and the executive branch struggled to assess the effect of Title I and other programs (Cross, 1979).

As the Elementary and Secondary Education Act went through several reauthorizations, the emphasis on evaluation of the aid to schools with concentrated poverty intensified. In 1988, Congress emphasized that the goal of compensatory education was to improve achievement and required the identification of ineffective programs based on normal-curve-equivalent analysis (Davis, 1991; Jennings, 1991). In 1994, the reauthorization removed the requirement to analyze effectiveness by normal-curve equivalents but replaced it with a mandate to create academic standards, create annual assessments at key grades that would be aligned with standards, include schools in poor neighborhoods in state assessments, and define adequate yearly progress in a way "that links progress primarily to performance on the assessments carried out under this section while permitting progress to be established in part through the use of other measures" (Improving America's Schools Act of 1994, §1111(b)(2)(B)(ii)). The term *adequate yearly progress* thus appeared in the 1994 reauthorization, 8 years before the No Child Left Behind Act. At the time, the term was a flexible concept, requiring that states defined progress but not prescribing how they would do so.

The theory of action behind the 1994 reauthorization was that states needed to create academic standards, match assessment to those standards, and intervene in schools in poor neighborhoods using "primarily" test results to decide if the school had satisfied adequately yearly progress standards. The inclusion of most students in state assessments was a necessary condition. One purpose of the 1994 law was to fold compensatory education evaluation into the regular statewide assessment program in all states and push states to improve those assessment programs. The same principle could be seen in the reauthorization 3 years later of the country's special-education law, the Individuals with Disabilities Education Act Amendments (1997). States who received federal special-education funding had to include students with disabilities in statewide assessments and report on their performance. However, that mandate for including all students in state assessments was not as prescriptive as the No Child Left Behind Act in 2002. The precise decision making about what schools were making adequate yearly progress was left open, and states were allowed to consider evidence other than the tests mandated by the law. This flexibility was a political practicality given the rhetoric and politics of local control, but there was also a deeper trade-off behind the reauthorization:

> The *quid pro quo* for accountability is flexibility. School officials have considerable latitude in deciding how to use Title I resources. Dollars do not have to be tied to specific students. Title I funds can be combined with state and local funds in order to carry out comprehensive reform and upgrade the entire instructional program in schools with 50 percent or more low-income pupils. If they inhibit reform, most federal rules can be waived. (Independent Review Panel, 2001, p. 4)

As they had before, legislators experimented in accountability.

That history set the stage for the consent of key Democrats in Congress for the No Child Left Behind Act. Rep. George Miller (D-CA) and Sen. Edward Kennedy (D-MA) were key cosponsors of the 2002 law. When President George W. Bush proposed the No Child Left Behind Act in his 2000 presidential campaign and in his first year in office, he and his aides were drawing on both ways in which standardized testing had become intertwined with civil rights—both in the rhetoric and also in the developing machinery of regulation and oversight. It is inaccurate to say that No Child Left Behind was solely a coalition of liberals seeking greater funding of education with President Bush, who was more interested in high-stakes accountability (e.g., Gordon, 2005). The liberals were familiar with the human-capital rhetoric, and key Democrats in Congress had been keenly interested in the evaluation of Title I programs for many years (also see McGuinn, 2006).

Policy Feedback and Accountability

The story just told about the No Child Left Behind Act, civil-rights rhetoric, and federal regulation and oversight is an example of policy feedback. *Policy feedback* refers to a relationship between the mechanics of policy and later debates about that policy and related social issues. The money, regulation, practices, and oversight tied to policy help set expectations in the future. Those expectations comprise a political legacy of government policy that shapes the politics of that policy. Those who study government from a variety of disciplines recognize that public policies set in motion political dynamics that shape the contours of accepted political debate. Two parts of the original Social Security Act of 1935, pension insurance and Aid to Dependent Children (the former federal program most call welfare), demonstrate the way that policies can define the political landscape. The pension insurance part of Social Security is a universal program; anyone who pays into Social Security as a wage-earner and beneficiary is eligible for payments when older. The universality of the Social Security pension has made its basic features unassailable politically. By contrast, federal welfare was a means-tested program. Only poor people were ever eligible for federally-supported welfare programs. Unlike Social Security pension insurance, welfare was politically vulnerable because of its means testing. Since most people would like to live long, they think of Social Security as an important safety net. But most people do not want to be poor and may not think they ever will be poor enough to be on welfare. The universality of Social Security has protected it politically. Thus, when President Ronald Reagan suggested changing the pension program in the early 1980s, politicians rallied to support the system, and the reforms became incremental rather than dramatic. The most recent attempt at radical reform in 2005 failed miserably. The policy feedback from having Social Security in place protected its existence. However, without universality, federal welfare had a much less powerful base of support, and the Republican Congress and President Bill Clinton ended the federal welfare guarantee in 1996. The original outlines of the two programs shaped future debate over them (Skocpol, 1991, 1992).

The different histories of school desegregation in the South and elsewhere since 1954 are also results of political feedback. The fundamental paradox of desegregation is that the South had the most integrated schools in the country by the late 1980s (Orfield, 1993). Southern schools have been more integrated because of two policies vigorously pursued by white, racist politicians and officials before 1954: state laws mandating segregation and policies of school and local-government consolidation. Because state law and intentional acts by school officials were an obvious cause of school segregation, federal courts after 1954 had clear and convincing evidence of unconstitutional segregation in Southern systems and were willing to order far-reaching remedies in the late 1960s and early 1970s. In addition, Southern school systems are usually much larger than systems in many other states because of consistent success in consolidating school systems this century. For example, Mecklenburg County, North Carolina, has had one school district since 1965, so the suburbs of Charlotte are in the same school system as the city. In contrast, the suburbs of Boston are in school systems separate from the central city. Desegregation advocates in the South had two advantages stemming from consolidation. First, courts were still willing to order metropolitan desegregation plans in the South, after the *Milliken v. Bradley* (1974) decision required that judges find specific evidence of discriminatory intent to remedy metropolitan segregation in fragmented urban areas. Second, large systems made white flight more difficult. Because the South had both a history of state-directed discrimination and also large school systems, desegregation efforts in the region in the late 1960s and early 1970s were more vigorous and far-reaching than in the rest of the United States (Douglas, 1995; Orfield, Eaton, & Harvard Project on School Desegregation 1996). The political feedback of statutory segregation and school consolidation made extensive desegregation more feasible in the South.

These stories of government pension and welfare programs in one case and desegregation in the other demonstrate the relationship between the structure of public policy and later political decision making. One needs to be aware that policy feedback is not just a one-way dynamic. A government is not an empty vessel easily manipulated by electoral and other political forces. Instead, government agencies have their own interests, and officials often act in their organizational interests (Balogh, 1991b; Galambos, 1970). As other public agencies do, schools have their own professional and organization dynamics that mediate outside influences. Thus, political feedback in school policies is part of a larger negotiation over the role of public schools. Two facets of that constant bargaining are particularly relevant to understanding the current school accountability regime: the limits of educators' professional authority and the local nature of schooling. First, as explained earlier in this chapter, school administrators have tried to claim both bureaucratic autonomy and public acknowledgement of expertise involved in running schools. They have been far more successful in the former task than in the latter. In addition, schooling is a local, public service. As the next section explains, the rhetoric of local control today may mask considerable centralization, but the details of governance can vary across individual school districts. Local political control of schools and the close watch that one can theoretically keep over such institutions may be one reason why school administrators garnered autonomy earlier in this century. One can thus view statistical accountability systems as one way to resolve the dilemma between granting autonomy and authority to educators and keeping them under some political control.

The broad sweep of popular schooling gives an additional impetus to policy feedback in public education. Put simply, almost every adult in the United States went to school, and most attended public schools. Based on their own experiences, the vast majority of Americans have an idea in their head of what a "real school" is. The more that adults share in terms of their experiences, the more firmly grounded is that implicit definition of schooling. David Tyack and Larry Cuban (1995) described this phenomenon as the *grammar of schooling*, a shared definition and a political inertia resisting dramatic school reform. They saw this effect as generally beneficial, mostly restricting reforms to incremental changes (which they saw as the better path to improving education). Seen more broadly, however, the policy feedback between standardized schooling and education debates may not be as healthy as Tyack and Cuban describe. Inertia is not always productive. A common definition of "real school" led to inertia in the South's initial resistance to desegregation (which in the 1950s was a radical reform). Policy feedback in the case of schooling may also lead to an illusion of similarity. The common definition of school may provide a way for schools to conform to a common script of schooling even when the quality is dramatically different, as Mary Metz (1990) has argued. If two schools have 50-minute periods, bells, homework assignments, football teams, proms, and graduation, they both might be called high schools, even if the quality of instruction and the experiences of children are dramatically different. In such contrasts, the common script of high school can easily obscure the differences.

As the policy feedback that comes from adult memories, this common script shapes current debates over accountability. First, the fact that most adults in the U.S. share a common memory of taking math, English, history, and science classes means that there is a shared framework for what an appropriate curriculum is. Not only do those experiences in high school and college define a common understanding of disciplinary boundaries, but they *also* help establish priorities for what subjects are essential to test. No one clamors for high-stakes tests in psychology, anthropology, or philosophy, let alone fields such as environmental studies that we generally consider interdisciplinary, in large part because those are not shared memories for adults. We generally *do* remember taking (or suffering through) the classes that are most frequently tested.

We also remember taking tests, many tests, of all kinds. We remember grades. We remember being ranked, being judged by our academic performance, and having future opportunities determined by tests and grades (Dreeben, 1968). For that reason, increasing the stakes for *students* being tested is a change in degree but not a change in kind from the experiences of adults. If asked, many Americans would explain that if they took tests and were graded by it, then today's children can take them, too. From this perspective, the intensification of test-taking is an incremental change. That experience of being graded also creates a basis for using tests to judge *schools* as well as students. Florida Governor Jeb Bush used this explicitly in 1999 when he pushed and signed a high-stakes accountability law that assigned single-letter grades to schools based on test scores (Fla. Statutes ch. 99-398, 1999). *Grading schools* is but one step removed from grading students.

Other consequences of policy feedback are less directly tied to adult memories of schooling but are still important. The common tie of school reputation to property values dovetails neatly with the judgment of schools by test scores. Because part of property value depends on speculation, even if the current residents or buyers are childless, home buyers and sellers are keenly aware that some *future* buyer of a home may have children who will attend nearby schools. Thus, real-estate agents have an incentive to know the reputation of schools. Those moving to an area can look for Web sites that display a wealth of data about individual schools. And all of this data is intimately tied to real-estate values. Figlio and Lucas (2004) showed that in the first years of Florida Governor Jeb Bush's accountability law, a single letter-grade improvement for a nearby school was associated with a several-thousand-dollar rise in property values. Real-estate agents and homebuyers thus have a perceived need for and incentive to seek information about schools, as well as an assurance that school attendance zones will remain stable. The link between schools and property values inherently ties adults' material interests to the evaluation of schools.

A less tangible link from adult interests to the evaluation of schools is in our society's general assumption of a strict public-private divide in education. In the United States, the public-private divide became pronounced in the second half of the nineteenth century, and that divide is reflected in the current practice that accountability policies apply *only* to public schools. In the first half of the nineteenth century, public funds occasionally went to private schools, both nonreligious schools (as in New York's public aid to academies) and also to religious education (Kaestle, 1983). Through a long, drawn-out conflict, that blurry divide between public and private spheres of school organization slowly became more defined. In the early twentieth century, efforts to eliminate private education entirely stopped when the Supreme Court decided in the 1920s that parents had a constitutional right to important decisions about childrearing, including choosing to pay for private school (*Meyer v. Nebraska*, 1922; *Pierce v. Society of Sisters*, 1925). Those decisions implicitly recognized a categorical difference between public and private schooling. In reality, that dividing line has not always been so strict; special education has regularly blurred the line between public and private (Dorn, 2002). In the last 20 years, that dividing line has become even more blurred with two developments: the creation of voucher programs, where public funding is directed to private schools; and the creation of charter schools, which combine some aspects of public control and accountability with greater freedom to operate than most local public schools. Even with the recent blurring of public and private spheres, accountability policies have generally operated under the strict-divide guidelines: Whether charter schools are treated in ways similar to local public schools varies from state to state, and voucher programs are generally not accountable in any way similar to local public schools. One of the reasons why the Florida Supreme Court struck down the state's small voucher program tied to accountability is because the participating private schools were not held accountable in a variety of ways, including achievement (*Bush v. Holmes*, 2006).

One reason for the different treatment of public, charter, and voucher schools is the degradation of the public sphere in general, in political debates and policies. This degradation is related to the recent blurring of the public-private divide. As politicians have responded to growing distrust in government, they have turned to privatization as one option for providing government services. Privatization has involved several tactics: outsourcing some functions to private companies; outsourcing an entire public agency; providing vouchers for individual citizens to seek services from private providers; and eliminating the government activity entirely. In reality, schools and other public agencies have *always* had a close relationship with private providers. For example, textbook publishers have earned billions of dollars from selling their mediocre writing to school districts across the country (FitzGerald, 1980; Moreau, 2003; Ravitch, 2003). But the wave of educational privatization has not been matched by extending accountability to the quasi-public or private entities receiving public funds for education (Apple, 1996). Instead, many politicians from both major parties have referred to privatization and competition as tools to improve how governments operate. In their minds, privatization and accountability for only *public* entities are complementary policies because the problem is lack of quality in *public* schooling. That political definition of the problem as located in the public sphere creates a double standard, a double standard that many would not recognize because of the long-standing experience with a division between public and private spheres.

The double standard in accountability shows some of the power of policy feedback, but there is a danger in overestimating that power. In some cases, rhetoric does not reflect practices, or the language may mask a more complex history. Education rhetoric about *local control* is an example of such masking language. While politicians frequently refer to the concept of local control as a reason to limit federal-government intervention, the history has been more complicated. The different levels of government are important to policy feedback, but not in a simple way. In the nineteenth century, a debate raged when several northern states created the first, purely powerless state boards of education. Opponents of the persuasive bodies claimed that they were the first toehold of centralization. New York politician Orestes Brownson disagreed entirely with the notion of a unitary state. Instead, a state was a "confederacy of distinct communities," he said, each of which should control its own schools (Brownson, 1839). Then, one could truly say that there was local control of schooling. But that moment has long passed; Brownson and other opponents of even the mildest forms of centralization were prescient about the tendencies of centralization. In the twentieth century, cities and states successfully consolidated authority over more aspects of education, wresting them away from neighborhoods and small communities, respectively. Even a simple statistic such as the total number of school districts in the country reflects that centralization; while there were 117,000 school districts in the late 1930s, now there are fewer than 15,000 (U.S. Department of Education, 2005). If one looks at the structure of school governance, both state and federal laws restrict what local districts can do (and avoid). Some of that is good—we should not allow local school districts to segregate children based on race. Some is a little absurd, such as the statute in New York state that mandates schools teach the history of the Irish potato famine, an important topic in social history but an odd and idiosyncratic requirement to place in law.[6] But one would be hard-pressed to find any administrator or school board member who does not see state or federal requirements defining their tasks. In addition to state and federal mandates, occasionally centralization and standardization happens indirectly through the patterns of public-private relations. Because large states control textbook-adoption processes in a centralized fashion, what small states and individual districts find available is largely what gets approved in California, Texas, and a few other large states (FitzGerald, 1980; Ravitch, 2003). Thus, both public and private dynamics reduce the freedom of individual school districts. Furthermore, because educational politics are prominent features of state and federal campaigns, school board elections are less prominent in individual communities.[7] Today, it is legally, practically, and politically inaccurate to say that schools are entirely controlled at the local level. That tradition has shifted over the last century.

Today, the concept of local control often refers to state prerogative as much as local authority. In that redefinition, the *rhetoric* of local control has limited federal control over education. Thus, the No Child Left Behind Act mandates that states receiving Title I funding agree to assess children annually in Grades 3-8 in reading and math but not which test is used or what a test precisely covers. In the Clinton and both Bush presidencies, efforts to create national tests or curriculum standards foundered or were negotiated away. Manna (2006) explains this federal-state dynamic as one that allows actors at one level to "borrow strength" from the capacity or agenda of another level. State officials have been willing to encourage federal activism when it facilitated their education policy agenda, but only within limits. Whether framed as "national standards" or a "voluntary national test," both Democrats and Republicans fiercely defended the prerogative of states to define what a good education was. Any effort to create a national standard or test would run into the same political minefield (Mathews, 2006b).

Even defined at the state level, much of that defense of local control is more symbolic than practical. One would be hard pressed to find significant differences in the curriculum standards in math and reading among the states; though there certainly are meaningful differences in more politicized realms such as history or science, one generally finds elementary math standards to include basic arithmetic operations and secondary math including algebra and geometry. Many states first chose commercial, "off-the-shelf" norm-referenced tests to meet the federal accountability standards of the No Child Left Behind Act, making more than one cynical observer wonder what all the fuss about local control is about. One metaphor that might help here is sedimentation: The national educational discussion is a layer on top of and filtering down through older, local politics of schooling. Localism has remained a powerful force in some limited but important ways. It has controlled the politics of local and federal educational programs. For example, Southern members of Congress were critical in supporting federal vocational education programs early in the century because the federal government allowed Southern states to distribute funds disproportionately to White vocational programs and create different curriculum programs by race. The result was that vocational education programs served to reinforce the Southern caste structure (Werum, 1997). Traditional federal deference to state action also modified and limited Title VI of the Civil Rights Act of 1964, whose implementation helped force school desegregation in the South (Orfield, 1969). And opposition to federal intrusion has limited national action, including arguments in the 1990s for tests created and organized by the federal government. Politicians are willing for schools to buy textbooks from national publishers, but not to accept a publicly-decided set of standards or tests (Miller, 1997). Even if it is a shell of past practices, the rhetoric of local control helps shape debates over accountability.

The sedimentation of different layers of educational control may interact less in matters of principle than in political dynamics. Federal government decision making threatens more than local control of curriculum; it threatens local political networks and ways of doing business. Local political control of school policies and funding thus vie with the national debate. The result is frequently a set of variations on common practices, resulting in the illusion of local control in many school matters. Standardized testing and accountability systems comprise one example of that limited variation. For decades, most local school systems or states tested children in the spring using multiple-choice tests with scores that schools could compare against a population of children in the same grade, a group called the norming population. In the past two decades, many states and local districts have added real or reputational consequences for standardized tests, including publicly releasing score data. The result is a patchwork of high-stakes testing at the state level that covers most of the nation, in addition to the requirements of the No Child Left Behind Act. Despite theoretical local choice about standardized testing, one way of publicly judging schools has become dominant.

The same dynamic of policy feedback that shapes the debate over accountability has several consequences. One is the fact that the domination of standardized testing is partially self-perpetuating. States for many years have been accumulating testing requirements which their legislatures, state officials, or local administrators have chosen. Despite evidence that high-stakes testing does not provide stable information about school performance, test results have become the dominant way states, politicians, and newspapers describe the performance of schools. In less than 25 years, statistical accountability has become so ubiquitous that it appears inevitable. In retrospect, the speed of change has been both breathtaking and alarming. Political debate over the meaning of statistics has largely eclipsed other ways of describing what happens in classrooms. The dominance of educational test scores today hides the fact that we did not have to use test statistics as the dominant way of describing schools and their problems, and that in the past we have used many other means.

We must remember that the evaluation of schools by test score statistics is one among many possible ways of seeing education through both national and local perspectives. Whether we made that choice consciously or wisely is a different question, one that is hard to see because so many of us see high-stakes testing as the only option. Assuming we *must* use statistics as the primary means of gaining information about schools is dangerous.

In addition to the shared experience with testing, standardized testing has an institutional history. States have decades-long histories of managing contracts for standardized testing and managing accountability systems based on those tests. Switching to any other system requires considerable, visible political risks. In the late 1990s, Rhode Island created a system of school visiting—a more extensive version of what high school administrators would recognize as an accreditation visit, based on a now-extinct school inspection system in England (Wilson, 1996). The Rhode Island Department of Education designed the School Accountability for Learning and Teaching (or SALT) to push staff at all schools to examine their own practices before a 4-day visit of a team that follows students around. That team then combines their observations, their interviews with students and staff, and a state-conducted survey to describe the school and offer both praise and criticism where warranted. Rhode Island's Department of Education endured criticism over its student surveys, the staff time involved, and the cost of the system (e.g., LaPlante & Reddy, 1998; Rau, 1999; Steiny, 1998). Some of the reports praised schools, while others offered measured, mixed conclusions (e.g., Polichetti, 2000; Gedan, 2005; Gudrais, 2004) and yet other reports have been largely critical of schools for low expectations or dysfunctional cultures (e.g., Macris, 1999; Polichetti, 2003). As with any system change, the praise of the SALT review system was sometimes grudgingly given, even when those outside the state praised it (Rau, 1999; Steiny, 1998). Even though many teachers do not like the reliance on standardized tests, listening to an open, sometimes harsh criticism by peers and community members might make one long for the ability to hide behind statistics. But we sometimes forget that we have the choice of other ways of holding schools accountable.

Finally—and this is not to be underestimated—standardized tests have lower direct costs than any other system of accountability that might be politically viable. For fiscal year 2001, the total costs of buying commercial testing in the country as a whole was approximately $4.97 per student (estimating from industry revenues) (Hoxby, 2002). Because the National Assessment of Educational Progress relies on a sample of students in three grades, its costs were even lower: $0.85 for every student in the country. For the 25 states whose testing costs Hoxby (2002) estimated, the per-pupil costs ranged from $1.79 in South Carolina to $34.02 per student in

Delaware. Compared to the total costs of education, the most expensive system relative to total educational costs was that of Texas, which spent 0.29% on its extensive testing system for fiscal year 2001. In the United States as a whole, those expenses were about 0.06% of education spending. Standardized testing is relatively inexpensive if one only looks at direct costs.

The Costs of High-Stakes Accountability

Opportunity Costs

The direct costs of testing are only part of the picture; as Picus (1994) noted, one must consider both direct and indirect costs. Indirect costs or opportunity costs come in several guises. One opportunity cost of testing is the use of resources in the management of annual standardized testing. In every school, there are people whom a principal must assign to various functions, to store tests once they come from the publisher, organize individual booklets and answer sheets, distribute packets to teachers, remind or instruct teachers on test procedures, proctor the tests, arrange for make-ups, collect and repackage the tests, and keep the finished answer sheets secure before pickup. In the early 1990s, the Congressional Office of Technology Assessment (1992) estimated the indirect cost of test administration in one district as approximately twice the direct cost (also see Haney, Madaus, & Lyons, 1993). This indirect cost represents time that counselors cannot talk to children, teachers cannot teach, and volunteers cannot tutor. These opportunity costs are invisible in a school budget but very real.

A second opportunity cost is in the instructional time lost to testing itself. In high schools, this diversion of time is especially problematic, because testing interrupts teaching for one or 2 weeks for *all* students, even if they are not in tested grades. Several years ago, I listened to the complaints of several juniors and seniors at Leto High School in a public town meeting with Representative Jim Davis in Tampa, Florida, students worried that they would not be prepared for end-of-semester exams because the entire school schedule and assignments had been rearranged for Florida's annual testing. Even though they did not need to take tests, their teachers could not engage in any meaningful instruction if even *one* student in the class was a freshman or sophomore.[8] For students in Advanced Placement classes, this disruption is especially problematic in the spring and represents a waste of teacher and student time—an opportunity cost of high-stakes testing.

A third opportunity cost is in unnecessary test preparation.[9] I am speaking here of activities that are not justified as legitimate instruction, regardless of the label. If certain activities simply stop after annual testing or would not exist if the test were suddenly switched to a different format or emphasis (let alone if testing were removed entirely), then we can label that activity test preparation rather than instruction. Test-preparation takes many forms (Smith, 1991a). Creating quizzes or exercises in the same format as the annual test is one common example. In an environment with lower stakes than exist today, the Congressional Office of Technology Assessment (1992) estimated that teachers reported spending up to three weeks in test preparation, at a potential indirect cost up to 15 times the direct cost of the tests, an estimate consistent with other studies on how high-stakes accountability results in narrowing of the curriculum (Nichols & Berliner, 2007; Smith, 1991b). The purchase and use of test-specific preparation booklets is another example, one that is expensive for schools. There are thousands of middle and high schools today where there are certainly fewer copies of Shakespeare plays than copies of test-preparation booklets. Which is a better use of funding?

A fourth opportunity cost is in the change in the curriculum to emphasize tested subjects or to provide remedial work specifically targeted at the tests. A survey of principals by the Center on Education Policy (2006) documented that more than 70% of schools had reduced teaching in other subjects because of high-stakes testing—over 30% each for science and history. This survey is consistent with other studies (Jones & Egley, 2004; Nichols & Berliner, 2007; Smith, Edelsky, Draper, Rottenberg, & Cherland, 1989). As with the disruption of instruction during testing weeks, this is especially problematic in secondary schools, where teaching is more specialized and where reading and writing across the curriculum is insufficient for different subjects. We should understand what this survey shows and what it does not show: The narrowing of the curriculum from high-stakes testing does not mean that all schools had a broad or deep curriculum before the era of accountability (Toch, 2006a). However, the narrowing of the curriculum in response to high-stakes testing *does* prevent significant improvements in that area. Especially for adolescent students who are assigned remedial instruction in reading or entire schools which double-up instruction in tested subjects, the narrowing of the curriculum eliminates access to key subjects.

Even though they are identifiable trade-offs from an emphasis on standardized testing, opportunity costs of high-stakes accountability are discussed only in the margins of debate over standardized testing. But they are clearly understood by parents and the general public, ambivalent about the value of testing. Again, the results are not one-sided: Many parents and other adults still want accountability and see testing as important. But they also want some balance in the use of testing (Matus & Winchester, 2006; Rose & Gallup, 2005, 2006). Proponents of high-stakes accountability and some journalists are reluctant to discuss teaching to the test and on occasion misinterpret the concept (e.g., Mathews, 2006a).

Triage

There is significant evidence that schools under pressure to raise test scores engage in various strategic efforts to game the system (Jacob, 2005). One such effort is educational triage, focusing intervention on a limited set of students who "count" the most in the particular accountability system (Gillborn & Youdell, 2000). Booher-Jennings (2005) describes two forms of triage in a Texas elementary school. One form of triage was the identification and concentration of resources on students "on the bubble" of passing the state test, spending far less effort on students who were anticipated to pass easily and also removing resources and time from students whose skills were the weakest. A second form of attempted triage was the referral of students to special-education eligibility testing in hopes of excluding those students' scores from the teacher's and school's responsibility.[10] Booher-Jennings's work is consistent with other descriptions of and concerns about triage efforts (e.g., Figlio & Getzler, 2002; Hamilton & Strecher, 2002; Jacob, 2005; McNeil, 2000; Nichols & Berliner, 2007; Orel, 2003).

Long-Term Policy Costs

If the narrowing of the curriculum, test-preparation, and other costs are at the margins of discussion, some of the long-term costs of high-stakes accountability are invisible. Of these, the greatest is disconnecting our public debate over education from the real life of schools. Technocratic models of accountability threaten to turn public debate into a narrow, mechanistic discussion based on numbers removed from the gritty reality of classrooms. Over the past 20 years, the dominant method of discussing the worth of schools in general has been the public reporting of aggregate standardized test score results. Popular news sources typically distort and oversimplify such findings (Berliner & Biddle, 1995; Darling-Hammond, 1992; Koretz, 1992; Koretz & Diebert, 1993; Shepard, 1991). The reliance on statistics is not inevitable in national discourse, despite recent history. Whether one agrees with the goals of reform, one must acknowledge that prior waves such as concerns about math and science education in the 1940s and 1950s did not need test score data as motivation or evidence (Ravitch, 1983).

Test-score data and its use have pushed other issues to the margins. In 1983, the National Commission on Excellence issued a report called *A Nation at Risk* which claimed that mediocre schooling was threatening national economic well-being. The aftermath of *A Nation at Risk* eclipsed two major policy initiatives of the first Reagan administration. The early

1980s saw dramatic cutbacks in the support of the federal government for state and local public schools. At the same time, social conservatives both in and out of the Reagan White House were arguing for the creation of vouchers to support parents sending their children to private schools. Neither of these issues, however, were part of the central discussion of education policy after the release of *A Nation at Risk*. The dominant discussion in popular news media revolved instead around declining test scores, the presumed responsibility of schools for national economic decline, and how to tighten academic standards (Berliner & Biddle, 1995; Bracey, 1995). Few mentioned changes in the federal budget or privatization proposals, even though one was a concrete policy of the Reagan administration and the other was a radical proposal for changing the governance of schools. Ironically, the dominant discussion suppressed issues which concerned both liberals (upset at budget priorities) and social conservatives (wanting vouchers).

In the 1990s, former New Jersey Governor Christine Todd Whitman tried to argue that a standards-based accountability system alone could improve the state's schools. Her department of education responded to the state Supreme Court's call for equity with state-level achievement standards but no added resources, despite the state's history of vividly unequal funding among school systems. The argument by the executive branch was that standards, by themselves and despite existing funding inequities, would create school improvement. The assumption by Whitman was that test-based school accountability, a technocratic mechanism with threatened sanctions, would be sufficient to change schools, even schools with the worst records. The state court agreed with the governor in that New Jersey could have state-level standards but disagreed with the argument that funding was irrelevant. It then ordered the state to improve its funding of poor schools (once again) (*Abbott v. Burke*, 1997).

A danger of this narrowed focus is impatience with education reform. In the past several years, the release of test scores by a state or by the National Assessment Governing Board has usually provoked news coverage focused on whether the test scores *prove* the effectiveness of No Child Left Behind, a state's accountability system, or whatever the latest fad has been (e.g., Chaddock, 2005; Romano, 2005a). On a political level, impatience with reform and the cyclical reporting of statistics encourages the dominant myth of contemporary educational politics, that schools continue to decline in quality. That myth encourages a cynicism toward reform strategies. On the other hand, this cynicism is not absolute. Surveys regularly report satisfaction with local schools (e.g., Rose & Gallup, 2005, 2006). In addition, as chapter 3 explains, in states where accountability systems are jerry-built and provide rewards to a large proportion of schools, the accountability system can generate political buy-in at the local level. Whether that buy-in shapes national or state perceptions is a different question.

On a practical level, statistical accountability produces both undue impatience with reform and laxity toward incompetence. The yearly reporting of test scores creates an arbitrary schedule for judging schools: Do they improve by the next set of annual tests? The periodic nature of reporting school statistics drives the disposal of reform writ large, because policy changes cannot change classroom practices on a deep and fundamental level or become institutionalized in a short time (Lipsky, 1980; Tyack & Cuban, 1995). Yet paradoxically, the annual time-frame of standardized testing gives too much time for weak teachers to flounder without guidance or correction. Pinning personnel practices to annual testing may undermine the obligation of fellow teachers and administrators to keep a close eye on teachers without the necessary classroom skills. Principals may feel inclined to give poor teachers until the following cycle of annual tests to improve. For children, however, a year of being with an incompetent teacher can be extremely destructive. The problem is partly one of inappropriate time scales. Annual tests are too infrequent for appropriate guidance of instruction or evaluation of teaching, while they are too frequent to measure broader changes in schools.

The power of test scores to narrow discussion over education policy is not absolute, certainly. One can point to several topics of debate recently that are not necessarily tied to accountability or test scores: teacher qualifications, publicly-funded prekindergarten, class sizes, the teaching of evolution, vouchers, charter schools, and so forth. On the other hand, high-stakes testing reshapes the debate of these issues in two ways. It creates a hurdle to public visibility. There is limited space (or column inches) devoted to news in a newspaper and limited time in television news, and the devotion of significant space and time to test scores increases the competition for attention. All of the issues noted above have become visible in significant part because organizations with resources are able to publicize the importance of those issues.

In addition to creating an additional hurdle for public attention, the emphasis on standardized testing sometimes distorts public debate. One example of this narrowed evaluation of other topics is with charter schools. Charter schools are a relatively small but theoretically and symbolically important reform that started in Minnesota in 1991. While the details of charter schools vary from state to state, in general they are schools funded with public money, controlled by private, usually non-profit entities (though many charter schools contract management to profit-making "educational management organizations"), subject to *some* accountability provisions (depending on the state), and without the extensive bureaucratic controls local public schools have. The *charter* in the name refer to contracts between the school's founders and a public-school agency, giving the school the authority to operate in return for promises written into the contract. In most states, the primary category of charter schools allows open enrollment (or choice) by the parent or guardian of any child. Charter schools are thus quasi-public schools, a partial privatization and also a type of school choice, justified by the argument that a tradeoff of freedom from regulation for contractual accountability would encourage innovation and allow charter schools to forge closer ties to students and their families. The original arguments in favor of charter schools is a fascinating and ambitious goal. In general, both academic studies and news coverage of charter schools has been varied. In 2004, for example, major newspapers indexed by LexisNexis included 2,945 articles on charter schools, on a broad variety of topics.[11]

But on August 17, 2004, when the American Federation of Teachers released a report on the achievement scores of students in charter schools based on fourth-grade achievement data in the 2003 National Assessment of Educational Progress, debate over the report became both a headline issue and also quickly became distorted. The stipulated purpose of the report was criticizing the federal Department of Education for having buried the data instead of making it publicly available: "Frustrated by the repeated delays in the release of the NAEP Charter School Report and knowing that the data were collected in 2003, the American Federation of Teachers decided to try to unearth the basic NAEP charter school results" (Nelson, Rosenberg, & Van Meter, 2004, p. ii). The one-time collection had been authorized by the federal government, with a promised report, but the report had not been released. Immediately, though, defenders of charter schools focused on the substantive conclusion: There was no evidence from the 2003 NAEP data that charter-school students performed significantly better than students in local public schools. In public comments, coauthor Bella Rosenberg repeatedly emphasized that the teachers union supported the concept of charter schools but did not think they were a panacea. Charter-school defenders criticized the methods used in the report and emphasized that comparisons of test scores were not the fair way to judge charter schools (e.g., "Debating the Success of Charter Schools," 2004; Norris, 2004). As Carnoy, Jacobsen, Mishel, and Rothstein (2005) wrote in a report released by the Economic Policy Institute, a comparison of achievement in charter schools and local public schools *only* makes sense if one ignores the fundamental premise of charter schools, for in any innovation there is bound to be failure as well as success. Yet it had been charter-school proponents on the National Assessment Governing Board who had proposed the data collection effort in the first place, perhaps because they believed it would show that charter schools are somehow superior. Charter-school proponents had been misled by the domination of education policy debates by test scores and thereby distorted the fundamental issues central to charter schools in the first place.

High-stakes accountability has evolved from several political threads in the past half-century. Both human-capital arguments and civil-rights arguments have led politicians to want some system to hold schools accountable in terms of how they spend money and what children learn. This desire is both for transparency in what happens in schools—to make the outcomes public—and also to provide a mechanism that allows bureaucratic responses to those outcomes, to improve education generally and to reduce inequities. While accountability does not *need* to revolve around test scores, we currently have a system that does, a system that has real costs in terms of the lives of students and their teachers and also in terms of how we debate education policy. The political legacy of statistical accountability systems is complex because of the different possible aims of accountability and also because statistical systems will vary among different states and districts. Nonetheless, one can identify several broad patterns which stem at least in part from the proliferation of statistical accountability systems. Two legacies have seriously damaged our collective ability to have reasoned, broad discussion about the aims of schooling and reasonable public policy. Statistical judgment of school has narrowed the basis on which we judge schools and has also encouraged impatience with school reform. These costs have been ignored as defenders of high-stakes testing have placed their firm trust in a statistical machinery revolving around test scores. That trust is the subject of the next chapter.

NOTES

1. According to the Vanderbilt Television News Archives, the following broadcasts discussed standardized test score levels between 1968 and 1987: October 28, 1975 (ABC, CBS); November 17, 1975 (CBS); August 23, 1977 (ABC, CBS); August 24, 1977 (ABC, commentary); September 1, 1977 (CBS, commentary); September 21, 1982 (CBS); September 19, 1984 (ABC); January 9, 1985 (NBC); January 26, 1985 (CBS, NBC); September 22, 1987 (NBC). The search terms included "standardized and test*," "test and scor*," "SAT and scor*," and "SAT and (college or scholastic)." Excluded from this list are stories about the alleged discriminatory nature of tests.

2. Data taken from the ProQuest dissertations database; searches taken by calendar year and with subject words "chemistry" and "education," respectively. While the ProQuest database has numbers that are slightly different from how the U.S. Department of Education (2005) reports historical dissertation counts, the difference between academic and calendar year may explain part of the difference, and the numbers are comparable for the 5 years in question: 443 (USDOE) and 454 (ProQuest) in 1910; 615 and 705,

1920; 2,299 and 2,342, 1930; 3,290 and 3,387, 1940; 6,420 and 5,480, 1950. The greatest absolute and proportional gap (14.6% of the USDOE figure) is in 1950.

3. The academic curriculum came to be known as the "college prep" track, a label that was always a misnomer. In the late nineteenth century, when most enrollment was in academic classes, only a small minority of students ever attended college after high school.

4. Tony Morley, unpaginated observations from 1972 Seminar on Educational Finance, attached to Don Quinn to T. Terrell Sessums (n.d.), University of South Florida Special Collections, Tampa, T. Terrell Sessums Papers, box 20.

5. New York Education Law §801 reads, in part,

   [T]he regents of The University of the State of New York shall prescribe courses of instruction in patriotism, citizenship, and human rights issues, with particular attention to the study of the inhumanity of genocide, slavery (including the freedom trail and underground railroad), the Holocaust, and the mass starvation in Ireland from 1845 to 1850. (emphasis added; see Hernandez, 1996)

6. The growing prominence of education in political campaigns does not eliminate the importance of school board elections—they are stepping stones to other offices, frequently—or the way that local politics do determine many practices in schooling. The argument I am making is that local control is far more restricted than it was 200 years ago.

7. A news report of that meeting does not mention any specifics (Sandler, 2001).

8. Some argue that the costs of remediation should be included as an indirect cost of testing. I disagree, because one should instead consider those costs as part of appropriate instruction, not of a particular testing regime; see Center on Education Policy (2004) for the contrary view.

9. It is important to note that the principal of the elementary school resisted such referral efforts.

10. This total includes all those articles with "charter schools" in the headline, lead paragraph, or summary terms collected under the "general news/ major papers" category of LexisNexis Academic Universe. Of the controversy discussed in the following paragraph, there were only 46 articles published with "charter schools" in the headline or lead paragraph and that mentioned the American Federation of Teachers somewhere in the article, out of 1,173 published between August 17 and December 31 (or about 4 percent of all articles published in that period). The point is that even within a much broader discussion, the desire to show that charter-schools were generally superior to local public schools led to a public disconfirmation of that claim and a distraction from other issues.

CHAPTER 2

TRUSTING TESTS

I pledge allegiance to the myth that government knows what it's doing.
—John Brady Kiesling (2005)

While distrust of schools as public agencies is at the root of school accountability, the tools of accountability imply tremendous trust in the technocratic specifics of testing and derivative accountability measures. Almost every education accountability system today relies on test scores to make important decisions about the future of children and schools. That reliance on tests is a critical foundation of high-stakes accountability and the target of criticism. To defenders of high-stakes accountability, tests are sufficiently trustworthy that one can base crucial decisions on them. To some who oppose the use of testing, high-stakes standardized tests are anathema to real education. In almost no other area of political life are the technocratic details of policy the focus of debate. When we debate testing itself, we are making the role of technocracy in a democratic society central to accountability politics.

Statistical accountability systems are important because numbers have visible power in public debate. Anyone who listens to or reads politicians, journalists, and social critics will hear statistical references. Slowly over the last century, statistics have taken a prominent place in political culture. Whether the statistic is the official unemployment rate, poverty

Accountability Frankenstein: Understanding and Taming the Monster, pp. 29–57
Copyright © 2007 by Information Age Publishing

rates, poll results, or SAT scores, a specific number fills a niche in discussion. As Weiss (1988) wrote,

> The media report the proportion of the population that has been out of work for fifteen weeks or more, characteristics of high schools which have the highest drop-out rates, reasons given by voters for choosing candidates. These kinds of data become accessible and help to inform policy debates. (p. 168)

Starr (1987) explained that statistics do not just answer factual questions but imply which questions are most important:

> An average is not just a number; it often becomes a standard.... Many regularly reported social and economic indicators have instantly recognizable normative content. The numbers do not provide strictly factual information. Since the frameworks of normative judgment are so widely shared, the numbers are tantamount to a verdict. (p. 54)

A number connotes objectivity and importance. Because we perceive numbers and statistics as having a certain force on its face, we allow statistics to shape our perception of the world and the issues we perceive as important. They present selective information and thus center discussion on specific topics (silencing others). Nonetheless, we often yearn for the end of political uncertainty through statistics. Partisans in a conflict may heatedly argue that their methods are better, or their opponents' use of statistics is politically motivated, yet behind the veneer of cynicism lurks a desire for unquestionable statistics that will end debate. Maybe the official poverty line is arbitrary, but others have calculated alternative poverty estimates (Ruggles, 1990). The production and presentation of statistics is part of the fabric of public debate, and public policy that involves the heavy use of statistics must consider the long-term consequences of that use.

The political uses of statistics do not eliminate the ordinary judgments people make in life about technological expertise. That is usually healthy skepticism. Our lay skepticism is in tension with our everyday reliance on expertise and technology—taking medication approved by the Food and Drug Administration, driving over bridges designed by architects and engineers, even turning on electrical appliances with faith that the equipment will not explode. Each of those uses depends on techniques that are rooted in statistics, whether double-blind trials of drugs, the calculations of tensile strength for building materials, or electrical load in mains and household circuitry. We live knowing that there are consequences of basing innumerable details of everyday living on the judgment of experts and mathematical formulas. In general, professional expertise and math have been joined; the growth of government activity and regulation over the past 120 years has relied extensively on expertise and the increasing use of statistics. From FDA drug-approval processes to flood-insurance maps, from street designs to Social Security actuarial calculations, public policy depends on experts in different fields. This public use of expertise is sometimes challenged by those outside a field, challenged because ordinary citizens disagree with expert judgment or because the experts themselves do not agree on a matter of public importance. In other cases, politicians ignore the advice of experts, even when there is a clear consensus such as with global climate change. But even when contested, expertise is an integral part of our modern world.

The next two chapters focus on the public uses of achievement tests and the relationships among accountability, professional expertise, and test statistics. This chapter explores our reliance on testing with one question—*Why?*—while the third chapter explores it with another question—*Is it right?* This chapter explores the roots of our trust of testing in the development of professional expertise in testing early in the twentieth century and the modern reliance on this professional acumen for school accountability. The end result of a century of the standardized testing industry is in tension with transparency, but that end result is explainable. The first part of the chapter focuses on different explanations of the role of testing, while the second part of the chapter asks how inevitable that role is.

EXPLANATIONS OF THE TRUST IN TESTING

School accountability systems that rely on a test-based formula operate on policy autopilot (Starr, 1987). The existence of such a statistical autopilot is not unique to elementary and secondary school policy—Social Security cost-of-living adjustments depend on inflation measures, college student loans are tied to the prime rate, and so on. But there is a difference: Social Security payments affect millions in the same manner, while school accountability systems apply different types of labels schools in a nonuniform distribution. What is unusual about school accountability systems is the judgment of *local* circumstances through a statistical formula, typically without a step involving human judgment of an individual school. The rise of test-based school accountability has removed lay and professional judgment and substituted statistical formulae for discretion and democratic discussion (Meier, 2004).

The removal of administrative discretion has clear political roots—the fall of trust in school administrators. But statistical accountability was not inevitable; one could imagine a variety of ways that accountability could have turned out, and the past quarter-century has had several different ways of trying to keep schools accountability. The substitution of statistics for discretion therefore needs some explaining. This section explores several possible explanations without resolving which best accounts for the reliance on statistics. One explanation focuses on the administrative use of statistics a century ago and sees the reliance on test-score statistics as the cooptation of a tool of administration. A second explanation focuses on the status of psychology as a discipline and psychometricians as professionals peddling their expertise. In this view, the reliance on test-score statistics represents the successful marketing of status and expertise. A third explanation sees the statistical autopilot of accountability as the legacy of positivist philosophies of the nineteenth century, a belief in the triumph of fact-gathering that we may call naïve realism. In this view, our trust in test statistics is the logical end of a century of rhetoric about the objectivity of science and statistics. The fourth explanation focuses on the elimination of professional and lay discretion as a political function of accountability, effectively displacing hard decisions away from political arenas. In this last view, the reliance on test-score statistics creates a set of facts that then become the basis for a restricted political debate. In each case, this section describes the explanation and both its strengths and weaknesses.

Testing as a Coopted Administrative Tool

The current debates over measuring student growth are the end point of a century of standardized testing, an enterprise that began with crude assessments of a journalist in the 1890s and now runs to a multibillion-dollar industry. The history of the standardized testing industry parallels and intertwines with both the history of school administration and also the history of accountability. Administrators used standardized testing to claim managerial expertise a century ago, and now the successors to those tests undermine administrative. In the first half of the twentieth century, experts in creating standardized testing profited from racial prejudices of the day and also school administrators' desire to manage schools "scientifically." Probably the first comparative attempt at a standardized test in the United States was Joseph Mayer Rice's quizzing hundreds of students in several dozen U.S. cities in the early 1890s. In two articles in 1893, Rice laid out a broad allegation that urban schools were dull, stultifying places, full of drills that did little to improve students' knowledge. Many psychometricians identify Rice's (1893a, 1893b) testing as the first broadly-used standardized testing, albeit crude (e.g., Ayres, 1918; Engelhart & Thomas, 1966; Worthen & Sanders, 1991). The beginnings of sophistication in testing came in the early twentieth century, with the development of more explicitly planned tests in subject areas and also with the borrowing of intelligence tests from French educator Alfred Binet. Interest in developing standardized testing came both from those interested in mental disabilities (e.g., Henry Goddard, Director of Research at Vineland Training School for Feeble-Minded Girls and Boys in New Jersey, who translated Alfred Binet's test into English in 1908) and also those interested in academic achievement such as Stuart Courtis, who developed a best-selling series of math tests (Gould, 1996, Johanningmeier, 2004). By the end of World War I, there were more than 100 subject-specific standardized tests available for use in the United States (Monroe, 1918).

Lewis Terman (1930) combined those interests in both intelligence and achievement tests. After serving as a principal in an Indiana township, he studied at Indiana University and Clark University. Terman's graduate education came during the transition in psychology from its origins as an outgrowth of philosophy into what the new generation hoped would be a laboratory science. G. Stanley Hall began a large wave of qualitative studies of children in the 1890s and then became the first president of Clark University, a model of a small, graduate-only institution when Terman received his PhD in 1905 (Ross, 1972). Testing itself became a serious object of study from 1894 through 1904, culminating in the publication of major texts by Edward Thorndike (Jonçich, 1968) and the use of the new correlation statistic by Spearman (1904) to claim the existence of something he called general intelligence. Terman's subsequent enthusiasm for testing came as the leading edge of a new specialty, psychometrics, and that enthusiasm guided his career and in turn the education of millions of Americans. Despite having little training in statistics, Terman (1930) became interested in the growing field of mental testing at graduate school and continued those interests after obtaining a position at Stanford University in 1910. During World War I, he was one of the psychologists working with the army to test inductees with the Army Alpha and Beta Tests—the Alpha test for enlisted soldiers who could read and write English and the Beta test for soldiers who could not write or whose primary language was not English. Based on that work, he developed best-selling tests in the 1920s, both intelligence tests such as the Stanford-Binet Intelligence Test (an early IQ test) and also the Stanford Achievement Test series (claiming to assess general academic achievement).

While many historians focus on the history of IQ tests more than subject tests, school districts' use of testing made *both* types of tests profitable. While much of the historical literature on testing covers intelligence testing and its political and organizational uses, schools used intelligence testing and achievement testing in overlapping ways early in the twentieth century. According to Mazzeo (2001), before the 1960s schools used tests in a broad sense to justify guidance decisions for individual students—

that is, to select and justify academic programs for individual students.[1] Histories of testing have generally focused on IQ tests and their effects both in justifying stereotypes and also as tools for tracking and unequal access in schools (e.g., Cravens, 1978; Fass, 1980; Gould, 1996; Hanson, 1993; J. G. Richardson, 1999; K. Richardson, 2000, 2002; Selden, 1999). And psychologists at the time saw a difference between so-called IQ tests and achievement tests (e.g., Newman, Freeman, & Holzinger, 1937). From an organizational perspective, though, intelligence and achievement tests served overlapping purposes, both able to guide programmatic decisions for students.[2] The contractual relationships and the test-building schools overlapped considerably, whether the publisher was selling an intelligence or an achievement test. Those contractual relationships between schools and publishers developed and deepened over the twentieth century. The notorious use of the Army Alpha and Beta and subsequent intelligence tests to justify both immigration restrictions and the eugenics movement sparked criticism at the time (Bond, 1924; Franklin, 1991), but the criticism did not change a growing contractual relationship between schools across the country and various test publishers. Many test publishers earned their money early in the century by printing and distributing tests that would be scored locally. But over the course of the twentieth century, test publishers also developed businesses in the administration, scoring, and reporting of test results—probably best represented by the longstanding relationship between the College Board and Educational Testing Service. Today, standardized testing covers a variety of professional licensing exams as well as tests used in schools.

As other historians have noted, the use of standardized tests coincided with pressures to make schooling efficient (e.g., Kliebard, 1987; Tyack, 1974). Raymond Callahan (1962) argued that the spread of business-inspired efficiency studies was a cause of significant miseducation. Callahan was misled, however; administrators took up the ideas of inefficiency because they were *already* committed to what they thought was scientific management. Perhaps the battle for authority to manage schools led administrators to a greater zeal for scientific management out of defensiveness over their professional status. Perhaps the zeal for scientific management gave administrators a key tool to satisfy the urge for social efficiency.

If we look too closely at administrators' willingness to entertain efficiency as a goal, we may misunderstand the history of testing as the *cause* of ills instead of one of the *mechanisms* involved in tracking and prejudice. In particular, historians of testing have missed important dynamics by choosing one particular focus: IQ tests. As Gould (1996) and others have noted, a small group of psychologists legitimized intelligence testing by working with the Army to test all World War I inductees. The tests were culture-bound, the conclusions drawn by some of the psychologists were racist and xenophobic, and the successors of the Army Alpha and Beta tests were sold by the millions to school districts. And there is an important legacy of IQ testing for today, as described later: a distrust of testing by a small but significant minority of Americans. Yet it is misleading to describe the development of IQ testing as a cause of our obsession with testing. It instead served as one of several standardized testing that administrators used as tools. Before World War I, schools purchased hundreds of thousands of commercial tests in math, spelling, handwriting, and composition. Even if so-called intelligence tests had never existed, standardized testing would almost certainly have still guided the tracking of millions of students in schools.

Once administrators established testing as a bureaucratic routine, it continued, decade after decade, through the ups and downs of administrative authority. The testing routine and the commercial contracts between school districts and test publishers established testing as a technique available to any level of government. Thus, when Robert Kennedy suggested in 1965 that the federal government mandate annual testing as part of Title I, his knowledge came from more than half a century of testing conducted by local districts, and the same was true with state-level testing programs begun in the 1960s and 1970s. At least some of the current reliance on standardized testing comes from the administrative routines established almost a century ago. The strength of this explanation lies in the well-documented history of early standardized testing. A century ago, administrators used the existence of tests to assert managerial expertise, to claim that they managed schools scientifically and efficiently. Those tests survived even when the authority of administrators did not, and the next set of government actors at the state and federal levels to claim managerial control used the tools that local school systems had developed for their own purposes.

There is one significant problem with the explanation that relies on the cooptation of administrative tools: a substantial discontinuity in the testing marketplace and in the legal and professional context of testing in the 1960s and 1970s. If the cooptation explanation were true, one would expect continuity in the tools of testing, since the cooptation would rely on existing routines and contractual arrangements. But there were two critical discontinuities in testing practices in the 1960s and 1970s. First, the market for standardized testing began expanding dramatically in the 1960s, after the authority of administrators had begun to decline (Haney, Madaus, & Lyons, 1993). There was a sudden rather than a gradual change in the market. In addition, test publishers and psychologists faced increasing criticism of existing tests as culturally biased. This criticism came from both outside and inside psychology. With the passage of the

Civil Rights Act of 1964, private employers, public agencies, and schools faced the threat of lawsuits when key decisions depended on tests (Haney, Madaus, & Lyons, 1993). In addition, the landmark *Hobson v. Hansen* (1967) decision striking down the tracking system of the District of Columbia public schools threatened any student placement system that relied on tests. The decision also raised significant questions among education researchers about the use of IQ and other mass tests (e.g., Dunn, 1968). Within 15 years, there were two new bodies of literature on testing, one a set of court opinions establishing the rules under which employers and schools could use tests for important decisions, and the other a growing literature on test bias and techniques that test publishers could use to avoid bias and also to assert that tests were not biased (e.g., American Educational Research Association, American Psychological Association, and National Council on Measurement in Education, 1985; Berk, 1982; Flaugher, 1978; Linn & Werts, 1971). The adoption of standardized testing as an accountability tool of states was the cooptation of administrative techniques, but it was not a smooth process.

Testing, Expertise, and Professionalism

The other side of testing's early history is the development of psychology and psychological statistics. As Kurt Danziger (1990) notes, psychology's early ties to education in the United States probably influenced psychology more than public schools. The early laboratory studies in psychology became transformed as American psychologists first encouraged the study of children as a ready set of subjects and then started to market their expertise to administrators. The transformation of academic psychology into a professional network that peddled expertise paralleled the shift of other academic disciplines away from moral and ethical issues and toward an emphasis on technical competence (Brint, 1994; Furner, 1975). The relationship between academic psychology and school administration was symbiotic: each borrowed the needs of the other group to legitimate a set of activities and a professional identity tied to expertise. Behind the growth of standardized testing is a change in the management of large organizations and activities that stretch between organizations. The growth of standardized testing in the twentieth century is an example of interorganizational and intersector bureaucracy, or the management and protection of work that runs among more than one organization and between both public and private organizations.

Many historians tie the growth of expertise and professions to the Progressive Era at the end of the nineteenth and beginning of the twentieth—the belief in expertise as a key solution to the problems of urbanization and heavy industrialization (e.g., Bledstein, 1976; Furner, 1975; Starr, 1982; Wiebe, 1967). This professionalization was intimately tied to college attendance and involved professions that were both inside and outside the new universities. To a great extent the standard picture of professionalization is a Progressive-Era phenomenon where lawyers and doctors restricted entry into the profession, created publicly-recognized expertise, and thereby gained considerable prestige and autonomy from external regulation (e.g., Friedson, 1984; Starr, 1982). That picture of law and medicine frequently asserts the independence of such professions, as if lawyers and medicines practiced alone. And while many may have been in solo or small practices, neither law and medicine operate outside institutionalized environments. Lawyers operate in or depend on the existence of court systems, and in the early twentieth century, doctors became increasingly tied to hospitals. This interinstitutional environment is rarely discussed, but it is crucial to the professionalization of expertise.

In education, too, professionalization stretched between institutions—in this case, between K-12 schools and both academic psychologists and private test publishers. This institutional set of connections is rarely discussed in the literature on testing's history, which generally focuses on ideology and bias. Education historians typically describe the growth of testing as the dark side of Progressivism. The documentation is fairly clear that politicians used early intelligence testing to justify segregation and immigration restrictions and that school administrators used standardized tests in various ways to sort students and provide limited access to an academic curriculum. Yet the growth of testing also represented the growth of administrative autonomy and a growing collaboration between administrators and experts trained in testing. The growing power of superintendents was not just a reflection of the growth within school bureaucracies. Administrators developed their authority in a professional network that stretched among different organizations and different sectors. Within administration, superintendents and others began to maintain close communications and coordination with their peers. Superintendents also relied on university education professors to conduct school surveys; because these faculty had often been their graduate advisors, the consultant report recommendations could easily be predicted in advance (Tyack, 1974). And superintendents either created internal research offices or hired outside firms to create, publish, and score tests of all kinds. To understand the legacy of testing history, we need to understand the growth of expertise in professional networks.

For administrators of urban schools in the late nineteenth century, one of the great practical problems was the management of growing systems. While there had been several models of public-school organizations earlier in the nineteenth century, by the end of the century the die had been cast for bureaucracy (Katz, 1987; Kaestle, 1983). We can identify this concern with management in metaphors that educators used. Struggling for some way to think about huge school systems, educators, and others looked to the military and business, which were other large organizations clearly visible to schoolmen. Thus, John Dewey referred to the "army of teachers," administrators borrowed "to drop out" of ranks as a term for high-school attrition, and both educators and school critics referred to the need for business-like practices and efficiency (Dorn & Johanningmeier, 1999). The late nineteenth century consolidation of bureaucracies in urban schools did not mean that schools were following the military and business. Schools had experimented with the organization of large-scale work earlier in the century with the first steps toward bureaucracy and with Lancaster schools, where one instructor was in charge of classes of more than 100 students. In some cities, there were schools much larger than the small factories common in the early nineteenth century.

Yet schools eventually shared some of the language, organizational concepts, and the professional network arrangements of business managers. We need to be careful in retrospect to separate the similarities from causal explanations. Large organizations all have a need to manage information and control tasks, but the central purposes of an organization and the infrastructure will vary widely. In the case of monopolies, notable management changes came from attempts to internalize the tasks necessary to an enterprise from raw material to the management of demand (Chandler, 1980). The growth of mechanized industrialization and big businesses spurred the creation of new organizational structures, new occupations from accountants to typing-pool secretaries, and differently gendered work (e.g., Davies, 1982).

But that attempt of businesses to control their own fate was within the private sector, and the organization of work was less clearly tied to politics than in public education. The history of school bureaucratization is one of experimentation and then freezing, a layering of successive structures on top of or overlapping with each other—principals onto classrooms, then systems onto principals, then expertise in various areas (including testing) side-by-side with the system. The famous inertia of schools is a result of this sedimentation of institutional arrangements, with the end result that the web of control and interests make reorganization difficult (Tyack & Cuban, 1995). Yet, even with a different configuration, growing school bureaucracies needed management in some ways similar to other large tasks.

Thus, the Progressive-Era call for expertise did not invent a need to manage large enterprises. Businesses had discovered that need decades earlier, and armies and empires had done so centuries earlier. But the Progressive Era did see the rise of a new form of such management, management that stretched among different organizations. The twentieth-century phrase "the war effort" referred to national ideology but *also* to the multisector planning of a modern war. When such management has involved the apparatus of state, we call this regulation, and our common notion of regulation assumes a unidirectional flow of control, from regulatory body to the regulated industry. As many political scientists have described, that one-way picture of regulation is wrong. At the federal level, many industries developed an interdependent set of relationships among Congress, regulatory agencies, and the industry affected. Fund-raising support for elections flowed from industry to Congress, which sent money to the agency, which cooperated with the industry. This triangular relationship among the parties establishes a stable set of policies, or resistance to reform, depending on one's perspective (Rourke, 1957, 1984).

Expertise in professional networks is thus a creation of the Progressive Era. It developed concurrent with and in response to the needs of managing huge organizations. Expert professions relied on and contributed to the growth of universities and graduate programs in the United States (Bledstein, 1976). The rise of professional expertise overlapped with other changing class structures and the creation of a professional class—for example, with changing fertility patterns (e.g., Stern, 1987) and growing segmentation of labor markets in the United States (Gordon, Reich, & Edwards, 1982). The rise of expert professions also coincided with development of interorganizational and intersector management of tasks, associated with affiliation as much to profession as to an organization.

From the evidence of changing social-class structures, the era of mechanized industrialization was as much an information economy as the current one is. This changing social structure reshaped politics by adding an additional identity of *professional* to the choices that had developed in the 19th century (home or work) (see Katznelson & Zolberg, 1986, for an international discussion of social class structures). If there was anything coherent about Progressive-Era politics, it was the complication of older patterns by new identities—the drive for professional management of public policy, for efficiency, for rationalization. But in many ways both those impulses and our retrospective labeling impose an orderly transition on an inherently messy process. At the time, much of this professional impulse seemed logical in the face of corrupt politics, a level of corruption concentrated in growing central cities. As David Tyack (1974) has noted, state legislatures removed many city school boards from neighborhood electoral politics with the excuse that professional school management would somehow separate education and politics—and by this the advocates of such reforms meant corruption.

Notably, changes in school governance were not inevitable. The best counterexample lies in Chicago, where city politics were as corrupt as anywhere else. The reaction to corrupt politics came from a coalition that forced the city to collect taxes appropriately and use them to fund schools. In Chicago, the growing elementary teachers union (the Chicago Teachers Federation) allied with other local reformers such as Jane Addams to attack a corrupt system that did not collect the full taxes due schools from local corporations (Addams, 1910/1999). There was no guarantee in 1900 that small, corporate-style school boards would dominate urban education within two decades.

This early history of testing has influenced modern accountability in two ways, by denigrating the authority of classroom teachers and by building a pattern of professional business relationships rooted in and reinforcing the idea of professional expertise. The first connections between academic psychology and education grew between G. Stanley Hall and classroom teachers, with Hall's promotion of child study, a cataloguing of children's knowledge and interests (Ross, 1972). But those professional ties quickly shifted away from classroom teachers and informal child study and toward standardized testing and administrative control (Danziger, 1990; Porter, 1995). This shift in psychology's clientele from teachers to administrators created one institutionalized form of control over classroom teachers and a precedent for today's high-stakes testing industry. Today, teachers are largely eliminated from the business of high-stakes testing, either in the writing of items or the scoring of written answers (Nichols & Berliner, 2007). A few states are exceptions, either where teachers suggest items as in South Carolina or are involved in multiple steps of assessment, as in Nebraska and Maine. In general, however, the private testing industry is removed from classroom teachers, continuing a practice first established more than a century ago.

The second legacy is the continuity of business relationships from the early 20th century to the present, as local districts and then states built experience in managing testing contracts from the 1920s and 1930s (Toch, 2006b). Those relationships put significant authority for managing schools into the hands of an expert profession. Expertise has two tasks and corresponding advantages in interorganizational work. First, expertise contributes to task management directly, through knowing, supervising, and applying specialized techniques. Psychometricians know how to construct a test through item specification, supervision of item writing, and the process of winnowing down potential items to a set of plausible questions to include in a final published test. Psychometricians have developed a variety of techniques to ensure that the final scale sorts individual performances in a consistent manner and to ensure that items contribute to that consistency of sorting. All of these techniques are applied in coordination among different organizations—states and districts that write contracts, test companies that construct tests, and others involved in the test management process. The second task of expertise is to provide a rationale to filter participation in the management of key tasks. By acknowledgment of their specialized knowledge, experts have an automatic entrée into related discussions. Psychometricians are acknowledged as having the expertise necessary to discuss the technical qualities of tests and are accorded expert status in legislative hearings and courts when a hearing demands the description of the test production and scoring process. Teachers do not have those narrowly-defined skills, and so they are commonly excluded from the creation of standardized testing.

As with the cooptation of administrative tools, an explanation of high-stakes testing that relies on professional expertise has its greatest strengths in the early history of testing. If one were to describe the state of testing in the early 1930s or 1940s, one could have identified clear and lasting professional links among administrators, academic psychologists, and test-industry psychometrists. Once again, the major weakness lies in the 1960s and 1970s, with the first attempts by the federal and state governments to create accountability instruments. Neither local administrators nor academic psychologists were the primary actors in the earliest accountability efforts, nor were they behind the scenes, convincing politicians to use tests to evaluate Title I or to threaten the withholding of high school diplomas. Instead, politicians were at the forefront, experimenting with test-based accountability because they had the idea that tests were useful.

Objectivity as Folk Positivism

Because the cooptation of administrative tools and the assertion of professional expertise are not entirely satisfactory explanations of our trust in testing, we therefore must turn to the political arguments for accountability in the 1960s and 1970s, beginning with the statements of Senator Robert Kennedy and legislative observer Tony Morley:

> I wonder if we couldn't just have some kind of system of reporting either through some testing system which could be established which the people at the local community would know periodically as to what progress had been made under this program. (Kenney, 1965, as quoted in Morley, 1972, see note 4 chapter 1)

> If lawmakers are going to be tagged for the bill, they want to have more assurance about what they are buying. They don't know how to get such assurance, however, and the educators they deal with don't know how to give it to them. Neither is clear as to what would be acceptable evidence. (as quoted in Morley, 1972, see note 4 chapter 1)

There are two important ideas in these statements: the search for evidence and the uncertainty about what would count as evidence. But both Kennedy and the Southern legislators in the early 1970s did recognize testing as one potential source of legitimate evidence about accountability, and that continues today. The prime movers in accountability came from outside local school administration and academic and commercial psychology. That outside push both expanded the use of testing and threatened its technical integrity. As Haney, Madaus, and Lyons (1993) wrote, a variety of market and political pressures has led to the corrupt use of tests (e.g., one New York City principal who tried to decide on valedictorians via SAT scores), so much that trained assessment experts casually acknowledge that the uses of standardized tests commonly fall outside their validated purposes (e.g., Popham, 2004). Some trained in assessment are the harshest critics of much modern standardized test use, and yet their voices are largely ignored.[3]

Martin, Overholt, and Urban (1976) provide an explanation: It is the legacy of 19th century positivism that leads accountability advocates to believe that test scores are concrete and consequences will drive improved instruction in a behaviorist manner. Martin et al. point to Auguste Comte and other nineteenth century positivists, who asserted that the careful collection of facts would lead to the truth. Martin et al. assert that there is a direct line from Comtean positivism to the uses of testing in the 1970s. The psychologists who were building a claim for scientific expertise in the early nineteenth century relied on such claims, and one of the modern defenses of standardized testing is that it is objective evidence of student performance. In this view, the modern trust in test scores is a blind belief that there is an underlying reality of student achievement that tests probe with a reliable proxy measure.

The strength of this argument is in the relatively naïve defenses of test scores that one can hear from politicians and other defenders of high stakes testing. On the other hand, while I understand the appeal of this argument, this argument has both theoretical and evidentiary weaknesses. Theoretically, it is difficult to see how Comtean positivism would be more influential than American pragmatists such as John Dewey, who were confident that this new thing called science could be used to create beneficial social policies. But there is also little evidentiary weakness to tie positivism to today's defense of high-stakes testing. It requires considerable faith to believe that politicians and others who advocate high-stakes accountability are well-read in nineteenth century philosophy, know that much of behaviorist literature, or even can put forth anything more than bluster to argue the utility of test scores as a direct reflection of reality. What we see today is a folk version of positivism, the rough-hewn confidence that test scores must "mean something."[4] That folk positivism is less rooted in intellectual history than the political needs of the moment and circulating ideas about the utility of tests.

Testing as Displacement From the Political Arena

Those political needs suggest one last explanation of our trust in testing: Standardized testing and the broad publication of test scores serve a broadly political purpose. The function of technical expertise in a liberal democracy may be paradoxical, narrowing public debate by displacing the determination of facts away from political discussion. The politicians decide what counts as legitimate evidence, but they do not decide the facts themselves. That displacement of key issues away from public debate may be frustrating, but it also may fit into what Turner (2003) describes as a long-established pattern in liberal democracy of giving neutral arbitrating bodies important decisions, in significant part to narrow debate in the political arena. For example, courts often decide important issues by defining facts as well as law. In this view, test scores and other social instruments thrive less because of technical considerations than because they serve to define facts for political debate. The political role of standardized testing is less tied to supposed objectivity than to neutrality and distance from material interests. Thus, the standard arguments in favor of standardized testing and against the professional judgment of local teachers is not that tests are more *quantitative* but that they are *removed from the classroom*.

In this model of fact-finding and policy displacement, the quantification of test scores serves to boost the claims of neutrality and distinguish the independent definition of facts from more idiosyncratic judgments. Perhaps an honest educated politician might justify the reliance on test scores as follows:

> Look, I'd like to sit down with you and talk in depth about what we should be expecting students to learn, but I'm a busy guy/gal, and I'm willing to displace the hard decisions into some forum that has the patina of neutral disinterest. There are these folks called test publishers and psychometricians who can produce a set of statistics, from which civil servants can apply a formula to determine a label, and we can then use those labels to argue about what we should do with schools. But you're not going to get me to spend my time looking at DIFs or IRT graphs. I'd rather take the numbers and reports generated by experts and then decide what to do.

Turner's argument is that we have crossed the line into an expertise-managed society not by the usurpation of democratic principles but by the workings of liberal democracy itself. Society sometimes defers the decision of controversial issues to courts with the imperfect but workable assumption that courts are neutral forums insulated from interests that can create "facts" we call decisions (not that courts are objective in a quantitative sense). In a similar way, we defer important decisions about education with the assumption that tests are neutral opportunities to generate "facts" with which we can then make public policy decisions.

The strength of this explanation is that it matches the tendency of accountability systems to boil school judgments down to a few classifications. Florida's system labels individual schools each year with a grade from A to F, and those "facts" then become the grounds for other debates and judgments, from the determination of real-estate values to political decisions about how to respond to *failing schools*, itself a term that journalists use without much reflection (e.g., Ash, 2006). The displacement of fact-finding from the political arena also matches the interest-neutral forum to the professional interests of those defining themselves as experts. In an abstract sense, professional expertise welcomes the public to talk about the meaning of facts produced by a technical apparatus but not a challenge to that apparatus.

There are three primary weaknesses of this argument that test-based accountability serves the larger needs of liberal democracy to define facts prior to political debate. The first weaknesses is the assumption of inevitability, that the existence of interest-neutral fact-finding will triumph over political fact-finding and that the existence of statistical fact-finding will triumph over fact-finding by professional or lay judgment. There have been significant reversals in the use of statistical and formulaic fact-finding within education, most notably a rejection in the federal special education law of mass intelligence testing to identify students with disabilities (Education of All Handicapped Americans Act, 1975). The second weakness in this argument is the assumption that there will be a unique definition of fact-finding. With the simultaneous existence of state and federal accountability systems, states have already begun to experience a gap between the state labeling of which schools are failing and the federal label (e.g., Linn, 2005). What happens when there is a conflict in facts is something not explained by a liberal-democratic preference for interest-neutral fact-finding. Finally, that preference ignores the question of the content of factual judgments. As the statistical mechanism of the Adequate Yearly Progress standards grinds toward increasing proportions of schools labeled failing by the federal government, will the public accept the official judgment of the federal government that all schools are failing (Bracey, 2004)? I doubt that. Especially in wealthier suburbs, I suspect the majority of residents will make independent judgments of schools.

HOW INEVITABLE IS OUR RELIANCE ON TESTING?

The explanations described in the prior section each suggest very powerful reasons for basing high-stakes accountability on statistical formulas based on test scores. If one were to combine the explanations—seeing our trust in testing as a combination of administrators establishing a bureaucratic tool, psychologists establishing their expertise, the *zeitgeist* or popular sense of the usefulness of test scores, and the frequent liberal democratic preference for neutral arbitration of facts outside the political arena—one might get the sense that high-stakes accountability is inevitable. Such a conclusion ignores both the weaknesses of each explanation and the tendency for any causal explanation to emphasize broad explanations of change rather than historical contingency. The extent to which we are stuck with test-score statistics as the primary judgment of schools is an open question.

We can help decide how inevitable our reliance on high-stakes testing is by focusing on three related questions. First, we can assess whether important factual questions in education are generally resolved by neutral fact-finding or whether there is considerable debate and negotiation over how to decide what is true in education. If other important factual questions are frequently negotiated and debated, the existence of such debate suggests that accountability need not be test-driven. Second, we can look at the broader arguments over the role of expertise in society. Is the value of technical expertise as universally acknowledged as the earlier explanations suggest? Finally, we can look at the extent to which the American public has historically treated expertise, including reactions to the history of testing. For each question, the answer weakens the argument for inevitable use of test-score statistics. In the end, it is wiser to look for factors that shape the use of expertise and statistics rather than to see the current system of high-stakes accountability as carved in stone.

Are Education Facts Defined or Debated?

In deciding how much education politics accept the definition of facts by a neutral fact-finding process, we can think of three types of empirical questions that are important for education: facts which we teach students (i.e., what is in the curriculum), facts about the process of instruction, and facts about results. In each case, the determination of what is factual is crucial for the purpose and effectiveness of schooling. The patina of empiricism is so important in education debate that it is enshrined in the language of the No Child Left Behind, which has 119 uses of the phrase *scientifically based*. Yet in each type of empirical question, there are also important areas in which facts are debated and negotiated, not defined by a neutral process. The existence of the debates strongly suggests that facts are hard to agree on in education.

Currently, the most-contested fact we can teach students is the existence of evolution. Despite repeated court cases that have struck down the teaching of religious creation stories as science, opponents of teaching evolution have repeatedly tried to undermine its position in the science curriculum. These efforts have ranged from warning labels on science textbooks to the official approval of state science standards in Ohio and Kansas which openly questioned evolution as an accepted scientific theory and redefined science to include supernatural explanations.[5] In Florida, the state staff members are so skittish about evolution that while test items may refer to fossil evidence of evolution and the process of adaptation, but the Florida Department of Education (2002b) draft specifications for the high-school science exam explicitly states, "Items will NOT refer to evolution" (p. 93). The contesting of facts in science is not replicated everywhere in the curriculum—as Zimmerman (2002) points out, controversies about history have been resolved by including a variety of heroes in a triumphal narrative of the country's past. But it is an example of where facts that are settled in professional science are not necessarily settled where the K-12 curriculum is concerned.

Debates also exist over how we teach children as well as what we teach them. In the past 30 years, the proper instruction of reading has consistently been the most contested part of instruction, as advocates of phonics and whole-language have touted their preferred approaches as superior. In 1997, Congress authorized the creation of a National Reading Panel, which held hearings and issued a report in 2000 describing the best instructional approaches as including both teaching phonemic awareness and phonics and also teaching comprehension strategies. The rhetoric of the report is one of evaluating evidence, as each subgroup attempted to conduct meta-analyses (or quantitative syntheses) of the research base, but the process of selecting important topics and the tone of the report was one requiring negotiation. With more than 100,000 empirical studies of reading instruction, the panel had no choice but to be selective. The panel held five regional hearings, took testimony from more than 100 individuals and organizations, and decided as a group which topics required meta-analyses and how the final report should read. Even in an environment putatively focused on neutral evaluation of evidence, the selection of topics and the presentation was a matter of public input and negotiation—a matter of political tact as much as statistical analysis.[6]

If the National Reading Panel (2000) report was an attempt to create a scientific consensus through a negotiated as well as statistical process, the definition of graduation and dropout rates remains fiercely contested.

Calculating the proportion of students who graduate from high school addresses one of the key empirical questions about outcomes: how many finish? Yet there has never been a unique, satisfactory definition of either a dropout or graduation measure. Those proposed and used for two decades a 1988 federal law requiring an annual report on dropping out measure fundamentally different questions and have technical problems (Hauser, 1997). More recently, several researchers have proposed new measures of graduation, statistics that are different and highly disputed (e.g., Greene, Winters, & Swanson, 2006; Mishel & Roy, 2006; Warren, 2005), and the National Governors Association attempted to agree on a definition after Education Trust revealed that official state definitions of graduation dramatically and artificially inflated graduation statistics (Hall, 2005). What appears to be a simple question of counting students is far from simple either from a technical or political standpoint. Whether the question is about what we teach children, how best to teach them, or what is the end result of teaching them, in each case claims about education facts are contested.

What Arguments Exist About the Role of Expertise in a Democracy?

In addition to arguments about education facts, there is considerable debate over how much sway expert authority should have over public policy. In some ways, the debate has existed since the 1920s, when journalist Walter Lippmann and philosopher John Dewey argued about the capacity of a large democracy to make informed decisions. Walter Lippmann (1922/1957, 1925) was skeptical of the knowledge and skills of the general public and assumed that they would be easily swayed by propaganda. Morever, he thought the manipulation of symbols such as the flag was a necessary requirement of political action:

> [A symbol] enables people to work for a common end, but just because the few who are strategically placed must choose the concrete objectives, the symbol is also an instrument by which a few can fatten on many, deflect criticism, and seduce men into facing agony for objects they do not understand. (Lippmann, 1922/1957, pp. 235-236)

Far better, to Lippmann, was a system of independent experts who would advise the political elite of the country, make visible to them the broader social patterns of the day in an objective way and thus contribute to well-informed public policy:

He [the expert] represents people who are not voters, functions of voters that are not evident, events that are out of sight, mute people, unborn people, relations between things and people…. he can exercise force by disturbing the line up of the forces. By making the invisible visible, he confronts the people who exercise material force with a new environment, sets ideas and feelings at work in them, throws them out of position, and so, in the profoundest way, affects the decision. (Lippmann, 1922/1957, pp. 382-383)

Lippmann's argument is one in favor of an intellectual class serving a political oligarchy, an expertise-driven indirect democracy.

John Dewey respected Lippmann's criticism of democratic flaws—he had argued for years that social science could make important contributions to public policy. On the other hand, he disagreed with the assumption that the use of expertise had to come through elite institutions (Westbrook, 1991; Westhoff, 1995). He had four main counterarguments to Lippmann and other democratic realists. First, rule by experts would be impossible if the population were as ignorant and vice-ridden as the advocates of expertise indicated, and "rule by experts could not be covered up" (Dewey, 1927, pp. 205-206). Second, rule by expertise assumed the existence of preexisting general policies, not their creation from whole cloth. Third, experts had to have some contact and knowledge of popular concerns or lose touch with social reality, "shut off from knowledge of the needs which they are supposed to serve" (Dewey, 1927, p. 206). Most importantly, Dewey argued, democratic decision making forced the general public to confront the wisdom or folly of existing policies: "The man who wears the shoe knows best that it pinches and where it pinches, even if the expert shoemaker is the best judge of how the trouble is to be remedied" (Dewey, 1927, p. 207). Dewey thought the public is educable about public matters and should be respected enough to be educated by the experts:

It is not necessary that the many should have the knowledge and skill to carry on the needed investigations; what is required is that they have the ability to judge of the bearing of the knowledge supplied by others upon common concerns. (Dewey, 1927, p. 209)

Lippmann and other democratic realists won the debate, or at least the reality of government aligned more closely with Lippmann's arguments than with Dewey's. Lippmann correctly understood that public policy was created and implemented in a growing government structure, exemplified vividly in the growth of the federal government during World War I. In contrast, Dewey had only a minimal description of how governments operated or should operate (Westbrook, 1991). The democratic realists were more prescient than they realized, though more about the mechanics of state than the wisdom of its actions. As Snider (2000) explains, the public administration profession that developed in the 1920s and 1930s included largely atheoretical training in techniques of administration, and practitioners were largely ignorant of Dewey and the broader debate over expertise. The die was probably cast decades before the Lippmann-Dewey debate, when academic social science disciplines turned away from early efforts in the late nineteenth century to influence public policy and instead turned toward a narrower, more technocratic definition of their worth (Furner, 1975). Instead, the debate in the 1920s represents concerns over the growth of government and its intrusions into life during and after World War I (Westhoff, 1995).

One should avoid the temptation to overgeneralize from these examples. Professional expertise resides in human beings, not robots. Professionals tend to protect secrets and obscure technical details as a daily part of their work, but that tendency has not created a hermetic seal around testing knowledge. Several state departments of education are committed to releasing test items, even in Texas where the Texas Education Agency created a high-stakes environment earlier than most other states. Another piece of evidence that testing is not a hermetically-sealed profession is the fact that critics of testing often come from assessment backgrounds. Education gadfly Gerald Bracey is a former Virginia Department of Education director of research, evaluation, and testing. University experts in assessment are among the most vigorous critics of high states accountability, including Gene Glass (1978, 1990) and Robert Linn (2000, 2005). This type of insider criticism exists in other areas, as well. As Balogh (1991a) points out, the first criticisms of the nuclear energy industry came from within, from experts, and not from wild-eyed radical environmentalists. Yishai (1992) noted, "Civil service professionals greatly contribute to melting the iron" in iron-triangle relationships" (p. 106). No basis for identity is immune to the particular pressures of a context or time, and professionals can effectively contribute to our skepticism toward technocracy because they have access to all the strengths *and flaws* in the techniques they know.

The debates about expertise still go on, with proponents of participative decision making (Fischer, 1990, 2003) and the political delimitation of experts' authority over their subjects and methods (Turner, 2003). On a superficial level, today's concerns about the politicization of science (e.g., Lahsen, 2005; Mooney, 2005) look remarkably like those of Lippmann. As with Lippmann, critics of politicization of science today are concerned with the propaganda and the potential for lies to warp public understanding of issues such as global warming and stem-cell technologies. On the other hand, Lippmann's vision of a well-funded group of disinterested, independent experts was as much of a utopia as Dewey's idea that a large democracy could become a Great Community with enough effort and education. Because professional expertise grows and survives within and between institutions, the mundane matters and the politics of organizations often determine the scope of authority bestowed upon self-anointed experts. In real life, those who want to claim the mantle of expertise often have as much of a political battle on their hands as a professional discipline (e.g., Centeno, 1993; Evans, 2006).

The common picture of professional expertise when criticized is of the broad authority conveyed by expertise (e.g., Fischer, 1990). Entrée provided by expertise extends beyond the narrow areas that experts are trained in. Multiorganizational tasks require assignment of control over the work and management of different organizational interests, as well as the technical tasks that one typically assumes is the heart of an expert's education. The reliance on technical expertise often bleeds into areas of management and policy making—what one may term authority spillover. And in the slippage between the technical qualities of a test and the broader management tasks and values embodied in decisions, technical expertise provides psychometricians with an advantage in the uses of standardized tests. The legacy we inherit today is the assumption that there *is* a smooth, technocratic way to implement political demands for accountability. The long-term effect of expertise's rise in education has been less about the legitimacy of professional expertise than the legitimacy of a specific tool, the test score. In relatively few places today is the assertion of psychological authority direct. In decision-making meetings for individual students, where federal law requires a multidisciplinary approach in making eligibility, placement, and program decisions, this advantage can manifest as teachers' and parents' deference to school psychologists (e.g., Harry, 1992; Smith, 1990).

But in most cases, the greater danger of authority spillover is the assumption that tests exist or can exist to serve an accountability system on an autopilot basis. At the state level, legislatures commonly mandate a new test or a test-based requirement and then leave the implementation and the inevitable balancing act of priorities to staff who advise political appointees on final regulatory decisions. In departments of education with sufficiently expert staff, the state manages a process that ties the tests and outcome statistics in theory to some standard-setting process. In Florida, for example, tests are based on item specifications that come from a list of domains recommended by a select group of educators based on grade-level expectations written in a similar process derived from standards that themselves were drafted by a similar process (Florida Department of Education, n.d.a). This set of links is a recursive chain, using a set of consultative processes to build actual tests out of a politically understandable but vague demand for standards. This recursive chain is entirely within the administrative realm of a state department of education, not in the political realm. The choices made here may be reasonable, but they are not the only way to set priorities among the universe of what we want students to learn. By removing those choices from political discussion, Florida's legislature has repeatedly obscured the choices and inevitable trade-offs. In those states without such staff expertise, where a state chooses an off-the-shelf commercial standardized test, the state does not even pretend to have local standards. Until recently, Tennessee and several other states outsourced key decision making about academic priorities to a commercial company, accepting the company's judgment of what is important in reading, math, or other subjects.

One could see the continuing reliance on standardized testing as evidence of shrinking influence of statistical expertise in making policy and a more politically calculating use of statistics. Observers of environmental policy politics are more concerned with the politicization of research than the assumption of power by self-anointed experts. Lahsen (2005) is concerned with the blurring of scientific debate with propaganda in issues such as global warming. Observers of one environmental debate in Europe noted acerbically,

> When stakeholders connect their own meaning to information it often leads to convincing strategies in which stakeholders try to inflict their truth on others. Knowledge is often used as ammunition in trying to reach [their] own goals and interests. In this way knowledge doesn't facilitate but rather frustrates the policy-making process. (Van Buuren, Edelenbos, & Klijn, 2004, p. 22)

With high-stakes accountability, the problem for transparency is not so much the practical authority exercised by civil service managers and psychometricians as the assumption politicians and news reporters make about the utility of test scores. I have some concerns about the process of setting curriculum standards and cut-score test thresholds—a lip-service to participation that Parkinson (2004) said is a "technology of legitimation" (p. 389). But the primary concern we should have is the blithe assumption that test scores mean something concrete or are a useful proxy for student performance. This assumption is a statement about the authority of a tool more than the professional expertise. It is a referential authority, there for politicians and others to use in asserting the factual condition of schools. And in high-stakes accountability systems, the statistical autopilot assumes the reality of scores.

Today, the spillover authority of expertise today resides in the instrument, the tool, and the assumption that a test score is an accurate proxy for what children have learned. In some ways, one may think of folk positivism as the cultural legacy of expertise. For several reasons, the authority given standardized tests is not a matter of conveying policy authority to a priesthood of statisticians, a theoretical delegation of policymaking. Importantly, education statisticians are not a monolithic group; as mentioned earlier, there is vigorous debate in academic circles about the limits of test results, giving some statisticians the role of testing critic, sometimes as whistle-blower (also see Balogh, 1991; Dzur, 2003; Jones, 2004). Whether politicians and administrators understand and use that debate is a different question. But the debates over the social role of professional experts may not be as relevant to the use of testing as it would have been in the first third of the twentieth century, when the professional networks of administrators and psychologists made the recognition of expertise a far more critical part of test use.

Do People Trust Expertise and Technocracy?

While the philosophical and political debates about professional expertise may not be especially helpful in determining how inevitable high-stakes testing is, public attitudes are. As noted at the beginning of this chapter, there is considerable ambivalence about technology and the extent to which we rely on unexplained expertise. Our ambivalence has multiple sources, perhaps tied to our modern dependence on the infrastructure of technology and expertise. Maybe because we *must* have faith in technology, we are sometimes painfully aware of its weaknesses. So we can simultaneously revere and castigate experts. On the one hand, the high prestige of certain occupations and reliance on expertise in the United States is well-known. Over 28 years of polling, the Harris Poll has consistently found that respondents mark scientists and (medical) doctors as having the greatest prestige (Harris Interactive, 2005). Maybe it comes from what Potter (1954) called the optimistic attitude of Americans or our general romance with technology (Nye, 1996). On the other hand, however, there is a lingering distrust of expertise and specialized knowledge, as historian Richard Hofstadter (1963) identified an anti-intellectual heritage in the United States.

There are several identifiable sources of cynicism about the role of experts. As explained earlier, the management tasks intimately tied to expertise has frequently led to the conflation of technical expertise with authority over related political issues, or authority spillover. An expert in public health or testing may be asked about a host of nontechnical and political matters, and such an expert must also be a vocal professional advocate in a policy or political realm to guard her or his projects. Authority spillover can obscure the political and value judgments inherent in public policy. The battle against sexually-transmitted diseases in the

early twentieth century illustrates such a conflation and the two-way negotiation over the role of expertise. As Brandt (1987) has described, the
public health efforts to combat sexually transmitted diseases were consistently intertwined with moral judgments of those efforts and of individuals at risk of contracting gonorrhea, syphilis, and other diseases. The
"magic bullet" of expert guidance over health policy was inevitably a matter of moral and political judgment. A second cause of cynicism and distrust is in the history of exclusion of different voices and interests from
participation in public affairs. Professional experts do not operate in a
social vacuum, and where professional networks are exclusive, they can
ignore different perspectives on social problems. In the early twentieth
century, graduate education was a predominantly male, overwhelmingly
white world, and thus the professional works of those with graduate
degrees was demographically limited (for a synthesis of gender and
higher education history, see Dzuback, 2003).

In education, authority spillover and the social definition of professional networks led to the legitimation of scientific racism through intelligence tests early in the twentieth century and an exclusion of community
voices that reinforced a lasting distrust of expertise in education. Early
advocates of intelligence testing such as Henry Goddard and Lewis Terman believed that their new science confirmed existing social prejudices
about inequality of races and nationalities. The new school bureaucracies
reified those prejudices, using standardized tests to justify denying a full
academic opportunity to millions. If the history of intelligence testing and
tracking were not enough to solidify mistrust of expertise, the predominately white male world of administration until the last few decades
excluded the voices of most teachers from discussion of education policy
(Tyack & Hansot, 1982; Strober & Tyack, 1980).[7] This exclusion extended
to organizations that seeded today's teacher unions. While teachers
formed the majority of membership in the National Education Association, the organization was led by males until the 1970s, and gender has
always played a significant role in union politics (Murphy, 1986; Urban,
2000). Delpit's (1995) argument that teachers from minority cultures are
largely ignored in education circles resonates because of a long history of
such exclusions.

One legacy of educational experts' history is significant ambivalence by
teachers toward nonteacher judgments, including the use of outside standardized testing. This history has created a set of conceptual landmines
scattered throughout the education policy trenches. Can the same tools
that were used to justify inequality be used for the opposite result today?[8]
Some of the visceral opposition to standardized testing by opponents of
high-stakes testing starts with this historical legacy and the belief that
standardized testing must inherently be a tool of inequality, will always be

culturally biased, a "lunacy of ... [high-stakes] testing policy and the conscious intellectual and emotional genocide that is being waged against children of poverty" (Horn, 2005). Those who defend the uses of standardized testing in high-stakes contexts may be tempted to view such judgments as ignorant anachronisms, given the changes in test-construction procedures and different ideologies a century later. On one internet e-mail list, Art Burke, a former staff member in the accountability office of the public schools in Vancouver, Washington, responded to Horn (2006) as follows:

> Drawing a straight line from the abuses of IQ testing in the 20s to the use of reading and math tests in today's public schools, as if there has been no history in between and as if understanding and uses of the results have not changed, is bizarre, reckless, and irresponsible. (Burke, 2006)

Burke is correct in one sense—there is a substantial difference between today and a century ago in the techniques of test construction, the professional standards, and the uses of standardized tests. However, that scorn misunderstands the distrust as a feature of testing, while it is as much a distrust of expertise, many of whose characteristics remain the same today. Close to a fifth of teachers think that standardized testing does far more harm than good (Johnson, Arumi, & Ott, 2006). Even if tests today are not constructed by racists, they still contain some of the same features as the early era of tests—as explained in the next chapter, test scores are composite, circumscribed, comparative, and consistent. There is still a professional network of psychometricians who construct tests and the resulting scales. Today, the process is different from the past, certainly. Both the process of standardized testing and the derivative accountability processes that rely on it distance us from a real sense of what children can do. Horn is wrong in his extrapolation of history, but his distrust of testing is a useful illustration of a broader distrust of testing as expertise-driven (also see Smith, 1991b).

From this distrust, one might reasonably conclude that high-stakes testing is not inevitable or necessarily permanent. On the other hand, there is also danger for those who would use the distrust of expertise for political purposes, because such distrust cuts in more than one way. The risk is especially true for educators who might both claim to be professionals with expertise in their area while simultaneously distrusting those who claim expertise from outside the classroom. In his speech to the annual convention of 9,000 delegates, National Education Association President Reg Weaver (2006) staked a claim to teacher expertise: "We have the experience and the expertise, and we should be the vanguard innovators of education reform." And yet he also relied on skepticism about expertise:

> Dr. So and So, says that thus and so, is what needs to happen.... And, somehow, miraculously, we have a new theory about how children and students should be educated.... The practice of let me get my theorist, and you get your theorist has done nothing for decades, but made our children and our students pawns in a dangerous game. And guess what, we all lost! You want to hear my theory? Dr. So and So needs to get his so and so inside a classroom before he espouses thus and so about how a classroom should be run!... A group of individuals who haven't seen the inside of a classroom— much less a classroom like those that many of you work in—making decisions and developing theories on the direction for public education, that should be unconscionable or inconceivable, my friends! Our nation should be outraged!

In some ways, the attempt to pit different notions of expertise against each other is understandable—it uses the ideas available over the past century, both expertise and the distrust thereof. Yet this use of existing ambivalent attitudes toward expertise does not help us find a saner way to approach expertise. It is a diversion of efforts away from a more creative approach to expertise, one that would be consistent with democratic principles and transparency. At the moment, the ambivalence toward expertise is evidence that the way accountability systems rely on test-score statistics is not inevitable, not that the best argument is to argue against expertise.

Contested Determination of Facts

Given the debated nature of facts in education and deep public ambivalence about expertise in general and standardized tests specifically, it is inaccurate to see test-based accountability as carved in stone. The use and nature of statistics and expertise is shaped by the contested nature of facts and how we determine what facts are. But the contest itself is also shaped by other issues, from the history and nature of political expertise to the political nature of education and the administrative capacity of systems. As an example, one might consider the difference in the history of psychology between the United States and Germany. Danziger (1990) notes that German psychologists saw classroom teachers as an audience, and they were driven far less by the marketing of services for education than were U.S. psychologists, who quickly shifted their clientele from teachers to school administrators. Danziger argues that the restrictive, explicitly class-based system of education in imperial Germany gave teachers more social status, while the mass system of public education in the United States had become bureaucratized by the late nineteenth century. In part because education had become associated with citizenship in the nineteenth century (Katznelson & Weir, 1985), classroom teachers had lower social status in the United States than in Europe, and the feminization of teaching in North America created a sex segregated hierarchy in cities and later all schools: elementary teachers were primarily women, while administrators were predominately men (Strober & Tyack, 1980). The expanding use of tests helped solidify this hierarchy as well as buffer the mostly male administrators from political pressures.

Today, at least four factors are likely to shape the tools used to hold schools accountable. One is the status of expertise broadly and specifically in education, as described in various ways throughout this chapter. The status of expertise is as applicable to classroom teachers as psychologists and other education researchers, and if the question is which profession's expertise is respected less, teachers will generally lose … and high-stakes testing will be more likely to win on a permanent basis. A second factor is the existence of alternatives that meet the liberal-democratic incentives for neutral fact-finding. Relying on the judgment of *local* classroom teachers and administrators is politically unacceptable, given the roots of accountability. But the existence of alternative judgments can open up debate about how we hold schools accountable and judge whether each school is meeting its obligations. A third factor is the administrative feasibility of potential alternatives. In the 1990s heyday for performance assessment, what became quickly evident was that state-level performance assessment was expensive (e.g., Aschbacher, 1991; Hardy, 1995; Picus, 1994). In addition, because the evaluation of performance assessment can be inconsistent, large-scale performance assessment may not meet the political requirements of accountability that are tied to the goals of a neutral, trustworthy definition of facts (i.e., student performance) (Linn, 1994).

This chapter has explained the drive for statistical school accountability as the result of four historical developments—the rise of administrative professionals who used standardized tests to gain respect and autonomy, the networking between school administrators and professional psychologists that raised the prestige of testing and psychology at the same time as it raised the status of administrators, the continuation of some level of trust in tests as neutral indicators of school performance, and the political need for disinterested, neutral methods of determining facts. At the same time, however, these developments did not make high-stakes testing inevitable. We still debate what a fact is in many areas of education, and one of the legacies of more than a century of standardized testing is deep distrust of testing among a significant minority of teachers and the general population. The status of expertise, the existence of alternatives to high-stakes testing, and the administrative feasibility of such alternatives are likely to shape the future of high-stakes testing. What our current trust in testing and its future does not explain is whether we *should* trust the judgments that come from high-stakes testing.

NOTES

1. Many school districts also used achievement tests to indicate the relative success of their programs, but that use did not eliminate the use of such tests for guidance purposes.

2. Even the name of the most famous college admissions test, the SATs, illustrates the ambiguity involved in the test specifics, changing from Scholastic Achievement Test to Scholastic Aptitude Test to just the SAT (Owen & Doerr, 1999).

3. Nichols and Berliner (2007) argue that most high-stakes accountability violates the professional guidelines for testing described in the American Educational Research Association, American Psychological Association, and National Council on Measurement in Education (1999) standards. See Phelps (2003) for a contrary perspective.

4. Philosophers would probably use the term *naïve realism*.

5. The most active source of news on this controversy is the Panda's Thumb Web site, http://pandasthumb.org/

6. This discussion excludes the question of how accurate the National Reading Panel's conclusions were.

7. See Blount (1998) for a discussion of female superintendents early in the rise of administration.

8. See chapter 3 for an extensive discussion of formative evaluation and curriculum-based measurement.

CHAPTER 3

HOW TRUSTWORTHY ARE TEST SCORES?

The political drive for high-stakes testing and the political questions about its future do not answer a fundamental question: *Should* we trust the statistics that come from high-stakes testing? In contrast to most other areas of expertise, the core purposes of school accountability are transparency and equity. The political impulse to accountability dictates that we should know what children are doing. Yet the routine of testing makes such knowledge less trustworthy than one might expect, creating one or more layers of abstraction between what children do and what state governments say children do. To the best of my knowledge, there is no state or federal test that reports the proportion of 9-year-olds who have memorized their multiplication tables. So we cannot use evidence to debate whether such an expectation might be appropriate, whether children meet it, or what to do if either answer is no. We are lost in a morass of abstract measures with only relative meaning.

In addition, the pressures that are put on tests add another layer that divides the test scores from student performance. Nichols and Berliner (2007) have collected convincing evidence that documents distortions that affect high-stakes testing, from the narrowing of the curriculum and narrow test preparation to educational triage and outright cheating. They argue that the organization pressures inherent in high-stakes testing create the distortions. The end result is that test scores say much

Accountability Frankenstein: Understanding and Taming the Monster, pp. 59–86

less about the performance of students than the dry reporting of mean test scores suggest. Linn (2000, 2003, 2005) and Popham (2004) point out that in addition to the technical weaknesses of existing state-level assessments for report *individual* scores, the statistical manipulations used to summarize school and district performances are frequently untenable.

The end result is a federal accountability policy that is untrustworthy for the task, based on nothing concrete, and runs on formula. In contrast to the stated aims of accountability—transparency and a focus on clear expectations—the Adequate Yearly Progress standards of the No Child Left Behind Act are recursive, abstract, isolated from the political judgments of what we should expect from students, and inherently polluted. Many state accountability systems are no better, jerry-built statistical algorithms that live at or beyond the margins of each system's technical capacity. The advocates of high-stakes accountability have built and defended systems that are too fragile to sustain the expectations of accountability.

That conflict leads many to ignore an uncomfortable fact: In school accountability, both the details and the broader policy issues matter. But the importance of each part of that pair is too often ignored. The antagonism over accountability has led to the treatment of testing and statistics as a black box, for good or ill. The defenders of high-stakes accountability are wrong to assert that almost any test or statistical algorithm is better than nothing. And critics are wrong when they assume that the technical machinery of testing is inimical to decent school reform. But there is no chance of effective and humane school reform without facing the fragility of testing.

A composite scale that ranks individuals in a consistent fashion has a variety of useful technical qualities, and psychometricians are practiced at constructing such instruments. But such a scale distances us from what student learn. Concrete information is buried inside the composite scale, and those who established the legitimacy of such tests long ago tacitly or actively agreed that such concrete information was less important than the technical qualities of a composite scale. Whether the abstract composite scale is of use in a world that demands transparent accountability has never been a topic of open debate.

The first section of this chapter explains the fragility of tests and accountability systems, identifying key characteristics and how those characteristics undermine the accountability purposes of high-stakes testing. The second section discusses the broader systems that rely on post-test statistical manipulations, or the judgments that are derived from a score-based formula. The third section of the chapter focuses on a common rationale for accountability system: It changes behavior. While a broader discussion of motivation is in chapter 5, we can address some philosophical issues in this chapter. The last section of the chapter is a case study of growth or value-added measures as a paradigmatic example of the tension between technocracy and democracy. This last section describes both the technical difficulties with value-added measures and how the holy grail of value-added measures has obscured the political questions involved: how we set expectations for schools and students.

THE FRAGILITY OF MEASUREMENT

Perhaps one reason for distrust of standardized testing is the failure to have a sufficient public discussion about the documented limits of testing as a technology. Even with the historical ambivalence toward expertise and standardized testing, there is still enormous trust that policymakers place in testing technologies as a tool for accountability. The limitations may be vaguely acknowledged in passing, but there is still the assumption that a test score says something concrete about a child's academic achievement and that accountability statistics derived from test scores are similarly accurate, meaningful, and easily classifiable. The Adequate Yearly Progress standards of the No Child Left Behind Act rely on the existence of such trustworthy mechanisms. Yet the foundations of such assumptions are questionable.

Composite, Circumscribed, Comparative, and Consistent

Some general principles in assessment are accessible to anyone with a minimum of statistical training, and the various shifts in test theories over the decades change the details but not the outline of test construction. As with most writings on assessment, Heubert and Hauser (1999) and Popham (2004) focus on the terms *reliability* and *validity*, which refer to the stability of measurements and the reasonableness of inferences drawn from those measurements. As an historian, I look at testing less with the lens of an assessment and more with a social-science perspective: What key traits of testing determine its use in a social and political sense? For that reason, my description of test characteristics is organized around the political use of testing for accountability purposes. Four common characteristics of modern standardized tests are important in discussing how tests are used in accountability systems. They provide both the strengths of standardized tests as an expert tool and also key limitations.

Composite

The most important characteristic is the composite nature of most standardized test scores. A math test that fourth-graders take is not about a single type of item such as multiplying two-digit numbers. Math tests combine a variety of items from different categories, so that a 9-year-old child might see several one-step multiplication and division problems, some estimation problems, a few two-digit multiplication problems, others on decimal points, and yet others on adding or multiplying fractions, reading graphs, common units of measurement, geometry concepts, and so forth. The exact process used to transform raw scores into total scale scores for an individual test is of less importance than the fact that either the raw score or a scale score represents composite information about student performance on the test.[1] In this way, a scale score for almost any standardized test with multiple items will not indicate anything specific about particular skills. Instead, the existence of a composite scale score assumes that there is some general skill level one can approximate with a test.

The composite nature of test scores has one primary technical advantage: efficiency. If one were to construct a test that accurately identified the performance of a child in even a handful of skills, the test would require several hours to administer. To busy teachers, efficiency has an immediate practical value. In special education, the literature on *curriculum-based measurement* focuses on such efficiency after more than a decade of researchers' efforts (primarily in the 1970s) in making instructional decisions based on more detailed analysis of strengths and weaknesses (Deno, 1985). But such detailed assessments are time-consuming, and if a teacher must administer such assessments without help, a child could only be assessed a few times in an academic year. When a teacher should make adjustments more frequently and for individual students, efficiency matters, and a growing literature suggests that a teacher can effectively decide on instructional strategies based on weekly-gathered short tests (Stecker, Fuchs, & Fuchs, 2005). For classroom teachers, time constraints make efficiency valuable.

Yet composite scores have significant weaknesses when used for annual tests. Being neither frequent nor specific, an indicator of a general skill level once a year has minimal utility for instructional decisions. For high-stakes purposes, the composite nature of test scores is also problematic. While the distribution of items in a standardized test is often reasonable in a *prima facia* manner, there is no uniquely optimal distribution of domains or items in a test. Most people could look at the distribution of items and find that they represent a rational sample of skills in math or reading, but they could make a similar judgment about alternative test compositions. At some level, test construction itself is an exercise in creating a serviceable if arbitrary instrument. Florida's history of state testing illustrates that arbitrary nature. At occasional points since the late 1960s, the state's teachers and other educators have been involved in either prioritizing parts of the curriculum to be tested or judging individual items. As a process, this inclusion is admirable. But the results also suggest how any group of educators could nominate any reasonable objective as a priority for testing. After the passage of the state's Educational Accountability Act in 1971, committees of curriculum supervisors and teachers were allowed to nominate objectives from a list as priorities for testing. The state department of education discovered that every single learning objective from the list had been nominated by at least one such educator committee. In the end, the state used a single reading-curriculum consultant to identify the priorities for the state, ignoring the work of the committees (Florida Department of Education, n.d.a). As in many state departments of education, Florida improvised during the selection process to maintain feasibility, even at the cost of the process's inclusive qualities. The nonuniqueness of test construction specifics in most cases may not change test scores in dramatic ways, but as discussed later, small shifts can have meaningful implications either for individual students or for accountability-system outcomes as a whole. The high-stakes nature of modern testing magnifies the importance of small shifts from arbitrary decisions.

Circumscribed

In addition to being composite, most tests are circumscribed, covering only a limited part of the official curriculum in a subject. A test cannot assess everything that a teacher addresses in a year. The directions to test publishers often describe a sampling technique for what a test covers. For example, Florida's high school science test targets 50 mid-level standards (or benchmarks, depending on the terminology) (Florida Department of Education, 2002b).[2] But of those 50 standards, only 15 are included in every test. The other 35 are included in some tests but not others. As the item specification document indicates, "While some benchmarks have been identified for annual assessment, most benchmarks will be assessed using content-sampling methods (sampled across different years of the test)" (Florida Department of Education, 2002b, p. 4). Nichols and Berliner (2007) and Popham (2004) both note how this sampling of the curriculum limits the information that any test score provides. The circumscribed nature of all tests limits any inference we draw from test scores. A test score gives absolutely no information about the parts of a subject that are not sampled in that year's test.

Comparative

For accountability purposes, the third important characteristic of tests is the comparative nature of scores. It matters not for this purpose whether a test nominally provides relative information (how well a student performs in comparison with some benchmark population) or absolute information (how well a student performs in comparison with some abstract benchmark achievement). Test scores directly or implicitly rank student performance (see Wilson, 1998). In a technical sense, the accuracy of a test is the accuracy of the student's placement in a real or theoretical ranking. That comparative nature of testing extends to item selection. Because of the widespread use of a common set of test-construction tools, potential items are selected or rejected based on a measure of difficulty that is relative and recursive: Difficulty is determined by performance on the item and on a set of larger items (Baker, 2001).[3] In line with the goal of efficiency that also encourages composite scales, items that all students mark correctly or incorrectly do not help with the ranking process and comprise a small portion of most professionally-reputable standardized tests. Because the vast majority of students might get most questions right on a topic covered well, test construction techniques can omit topics just *because* teachers teach it well (Popham, 2004).

Consistent

The last test characteristic of note for our purposes is consistency. Here, consistency means more than the technical term *reliability*, which refers to the score that a test produces. To be commercially successful, any test will produce reliable scores. But a test publisher must consider consistency in a much broader range of issues. A set of tests in successive grades generally looks familiar, even as they cover somewhat different material. A test publisher will try to equate scores of a new test with an older version, so they behave in similar fashions. Some aspects of consistency fall into the area of *validity*, or the relationship between test scores and the abstract concepts behind the test construction. But consistency is also useful in a political and marketing context: Many administrators and educators look for tests that behave in ways that they have seen before. In contrast, tests that behave very differently from previous tests would arouse the suspicions of educators and administrators.

Test Preparation

The combination of comparison and consistency leads to one of the key weaknesses in standardized testing: One can predict and therefore prepare for tests. The best-documented test-preparation technique is that of Princeton Review, founded by John Katzman in 1981 based on a tutoring technique devised by Adam Robinson (Owen & Doerr, 1999). Because tests are constructed in a similar way to produce consistent rankings, someone with only a little knowledge of tests can dramatically increase her or his own performance without knowing more subject matter. The Princeton Review technique relies on the choice and placement of questions based on difficulty and the fact that a difficult question is one that few test-takers answer correctly. If a test-taker can correctly gauge the difficulty of an item and identify the answers that would attract an "average" test-taker (i.e., one that is likely to answer "difficult" questions incorrectly), then she or he can quickly eliminate the attractive wrong answers and increase the odds of answering the question correctly. Robinson created the character of Joe Bloggs as the "average test-taker," whose instincts on easy questions are usually correct and whose instincts on difficult questions are usually incorrect. If one can identify a question as difficult, the concept of errors as Joe Bloggs's intuitive choices helps one eliminate wrong answers, as Katzman explained in an interview about the SAT college admissions test:

> *In the figure above, what's the greatest number of non overlapping regions into which the shaded region—a doughnut—can be cut with two straight lines?* ... So what Joe Bloggs does is, he'll just cross lines.... The easy answer there is four.... What are the odds that on the toughest question on the SAT that you've done enough work?... And again, a good test taker's sitting there. And he answers *four* and goes, *God, there must be* [a] *tougher* [answer] *than this*.... So you cancel four. And of course, since you're able to get four, you cancel three and two also.... The answer's got to be five or six ... and you say, *What else would Joe Bloggs do?* He'd say, *Well, they want the greatest number possible. So maybe it's six. Maybe it's the greatest number.* So it's not that either. The answer's got to be five. (Chandler, 1999)[4]

Katzman and Robinson developed their techniques for college and graduate admissions tests, where the clear purpose of the test is to make fine distinctions in ways that colleges and universities could use to make admissions decisions. While Robinson created the Joe Bloggs approach for paper-and-pencil tests, where the difficulty level generally increases within each section, they have tailored it for computer-adaptive tests, where any two test-takers will see very different questions based on their performance on the first few questions (e.g., Martz & Robinson, 2007). The existence of effective test preparation has an important consequence: the proliferation of test preparation as an activity in and of itself to raise test scores and game the system (Koretz, 2005; Nichols & Berliner, 2007). A later section will explore the human consequence of such test preparation. But there is a second consequence of the existence of effective test preparation: If one can raise test scores without knowing more of the supposed content, how accurate can the test scores be? Even assuming the best reliability and imagining the impossibly unique composition of a test, a score is inevitably the result both of the test-taker's knowledge of a subject and the test-taker's test-wiseness.

The Organizational Capacity of the Testing Industry

If test preparation reduces the trustworthiness of test scores in one way, there are other problems both with the accuracy of individual tests and the statistical bridge constructed between individual tests and accountability policies. The most obvious flaw is with inaccurate test scores. As the number of tests have skyrocketed in response to state accountability policies and the No Child Left Behind Act, errors in the construction and scoring of tests have multiplied (Nichols & Berliner, 2007). After public pressure in 1999, McGraw-Hill acknowledged that programming errors had resulted in artificially lowered test scores in Indiana, Nevada, New York City, South Carolina, and Wisconsin (Rhoades & Madaus, 2003). In 2000, National Computer Systems misscored the tests of more than 45,000 Minnesota students (again through programming errors), resulting in the incorrect denial of high school diplomas (Draper, 2002). Test companies have had to acknowledge more recently that students have been incorrectly denied diplomas in Ohio, and eight states reported on a 2006 survey that they have experienced significant errors in test results in the last few years (Toch, 2006a). As with the arbitrary nature of test composition, scoring errors may have a small effect on a student's test score or a school's averages, but because many accountability policies are tied to students' meeting a specific threshold or cut score, small errors in even a single question can have lasting consequences for individual students and the evaluations of schools. One significant problem with the nature of test errors is that we only know about the errors that are publicly reported. In some cases, test publishers report errors, but others only come to light because of complaints or lawsuits (Rhoades & Madaus, 2003). But in a system with increasingly high stakes, the secrecy and obscurity of test-score errors is a significant conflict between the technocracy of accountability and the democratic expectations of transparency (also see Henriques, 2003).

One significant change in the practices of the testing industry is the proliferation of a variety of tests—state-specific annual testing, mid-year assessments that districts hope will provide useful information about students, and so forth. This proliferation of tests stretch the technical skills of test publishers (Toch, 2006a). In this way, the current focus on testing puts student assessment beyond the capacity of the system. Toch (2006a) suggests that this is an exception in the history of the testing industry: To him, No Child Left Behind disrupted a system that had been in relative equilibrium for decades with a regular system of norm-referenced commercial tests, where test publishers could reuse tests and invest less in test development. While it is true that norm-referenced testing dominated annual testing until the last decade or so, it is inaccurate to claim that these problems have only occurred recently. Rhoades and Madaus's (2003) documentation of testing errors come largely from events before passage of the No Child Left Behind Act, and the 2003 and 2006 headlines on SAT scoring errors are only the most recent in a series of stories that stretch back several decades (Arenson, 2006; Owen & Doerr, 1999). Errors are an inevitable part of testing, even if they are more frequent in a system under stress.

DECISIONS BASED ON TEST SCORES

If the testing industry is currently under the stress of rapid growth, the fragility of many accountability systems comes from two different sources: the complexity of accountability's statistical machinery and the arbitrary nature of any cut score or threshold. With the exception of a handful of individual districts with local accountability systems, accountability policies are enacted and implemented at the state level. Even the No Child Left Behind Act leaves the setting of proficiency cut scores and the adequate yearly progress in proficiency percentages as state decisions. Several states have had experiences with accountability for several decades, and the fragility of these systems is not new. Consider first accountability systems with complex formulae or sorting bins, such as those in use in North Carolina, Florida, or California. In each of those states, information from different tests and (for California) the demographic profile of the school are combined to determine an overall evaluation of the school.

Formulaic Accountability

A formula-driven accountability policy inherits the weaknesses of its information sources as well as carrying its own technical vulnerabilities. Whether one speaks of a label in California and North Carolina such as "schools of distinction" or letter grades in Florida, the identification of a simple label with a school obscures the assumptions made in the mechanics of the system. In Florida, the system used to label individual schools changed several times between 1999 and 2003, so that the "A" label in

1999 had entirely different criteria from the "A" of 2006 (Florida Department of Education, 1999, 2000, 2001, 2002a). The details of each system illustrate the potential complexity and the distance from discussions of student performance. California and Florida have point-based systems, where a school's evaluation is additive based on several categories. For each California school, its Academic Productivity Index since 1999-2000 has depended on the number of students in each norm-referenced quintile for each test, adjusted by different weights for the quintile and test (Thum, 2002). Currently, Florida's schools earn points for every percentage point of students in different categories (achieving at least the middle performance level in reading, math, and writing; fitting into Florida's definition of students making progress; and the percentage of students in the lowest reading quartile performance the prior year who fit into Florida's definition of students making progress) (Florida Administrative Code 6A-1.09981). Until recently, North Carolina's system was based both on the proportion of students reaching the middle performance level on tests and also a growth formula based on a prediction equation from early 1990s data (Goldstein & Behuniak, 2005). Starting with the results from 2005-06, North Carolina's system depends on changes to grade-specific student performance when compared to state test-score distributions from a benchmark year. Technically, the school's academic-change index is the mean difference for all students and tests between a student's z score for the current year and test (measured against the benchmark distribution) and the predicted z score taken from prior tests (North Carolina Public Schools, 2006).

While the details from these states vary, the complexity of systems adds a level of abstraction to the accountability system that puts the interpretation of the labels beyond most public discussion. The complexity exists for several reasons. First, staff members in each state department of education are bound to the statutes that legislators write, statutes that may not be possible to implement in a clear fashion. Second, staff are well aware that the statutes may change in the near future, or test contracts may change, and staff members thus have an incentive to devise a system that can accommodate minor changes (such as additions or changes in tests— California's system can clearly accommodate such changes). More fundamentally, states at the margins of high-stakes accountability systems are inherently inventing new systems and trying to balance the feasibility of system development and the legislators' intentions against the political consequences of the system.

The complexity of an accountability system can also help muffle opposition to accountability if it gives a reasonable chance for students or schools to be successful in the system's labeling. There is a technical reason to avoid systems that focus on extremes of any distribution: Some evidence of volatility of test scores in smaller schools implies that reward or punishment systems may disproportionately identify small schools in a system that focuses on distribution extremes (Hamilton & Strecher, 2002; Kane & Steiger, 2002).[5] But the political potential to muffle opposition within a system may be more important than the technical qualities of a system, for schools typically trumpet any positive label on any Web site, pamphlet, or streetside marquis. All three of these states provide evidence of the capacity for complex systems to muffle dissent. In every year of its accountability system's history, the majority of North Carolina's schools has received some recognition award (North Carolina Public Schools, 2005). In Florida's system, 13% earned recognition in its first year, 1999, but that proportion rapidly grew, and a majority of schools received recognition awards in each of the years from 2003 to 2006 (Florida School Recognition Program, n.d.). In California, 47% of California's schools earned statewide recognition in 2002, and two thirds of the schools in the Los Angeles Unified School District earned recognition (Campbell, 2002; Edwards, 2002). While California's budget crunch in the following year eliminated the program, news reporting at the time suggests that the money associated with the program gave administrators a reason to buy into the accountability system; even if items that the money provided could have been purchased by regular appropriations, administrators associated purchases with the accountability system (Campbell, 2002; Edwards, 2002; Portner, 2002; Tong, 2003).

If the complexity of accountability systems can muffle dissent even as they make accountability obscure, the dependence of many accountability measures on simple cut-scores is a different weakness. These cut-score policies include laws in many states that require individual students to meet a certain score threshold on each of multiple tests to graduate with a standard diploma. But accountability policies targeting schools also use cut scores, and No Child Left Behind Law requires their use—to meet the law's adequate yearly progress standard, schools have to have certain percentages of students who each pass score thresholds on math and reading tests, thresholds established by each state. One weakness of policies that focus on thresholds is that a threshold mechanism magnifies the consequence of small errors. For individual students very close to a cut score, an error in the scoring of one question can erroneously push the student over or under the cut score. These errors may come in the random variation associated with individual student test scores or in flaws in the construction or scoring of tests. As described earlier in this chapter, the composite nature of test scores create an additional source of uncertainty around test scores—one can never know how much a score might change with a different item specification.

Cut Scores

Finally, the entire enterprise of setting performance thresholds is inherently arbitrary. Glass (1978) and Wilson (1998) have pointed out that there is no statistical procedure to establish a bright-line standard that declares the cut score as basic, proficient, or advanced, and a score just under the threshold as inadequate. Any cut score or threshold is arbitrary, with no inherent meaning. The arbitrary nature of such attempts flows directly from the characteristics of standardized tests discussed earlier in the chapter. Test scores emphasize gradations, not absolutes. Constructed to make distinctions between performances that are very close, tests imply that small distinctions reflect similar performances. In addition, the composite nature of standardized testing prevents anyone from tying common-sense notions of performance to test scores. There is no state test with a clear cut score indicating when students can round a number accurately to the nearest ten or hundred. Test scores might make clear distinctions between students who generally perform very well and who generally perform very poorly in the subject, but the establishment of a cut score implies that there is a categorical distinction between adjacent test scores. Glass pointed to evidence of wide discrepancies in different methods of synthesizing judgment on such a categorical distinction; to him, the inconsistency in such judgments was clear evidence that setting cut scores could never meet the basic professional requirement of consistency—in this case, the consistency of how test scores were used to make high-stakes decisions.

Respondents to Glass (1978) in a special issue of the *Journal of Educational Measurement* danced around the political context of Glass's argument: Arbitrary judgments become capricious when tied to high stakes such as high school graduation, and an assessment expert or public official is making a pretense at legitimacy with any claim that cut scores are objective and absolute. The responses of Block (1978), Hambleton (1978), Linn (1978), Popham (1978), and Scriven (1978) together presented four broad counterarguments. First, they suggested that Glass's objections to the techniques then in use did not preclude the development of some better method in the future. Second, they pointed to existing instructional uses of even arbitrary cut scores and thresholds, uses such as decision-points for intervention and remediation which the respondents felt were eminently justifiable. Third, they argued that there was a difference between an arbitrary decision that was based on reasoned judgment, on the one hand, and capriciousness, on the other. These were nontechnical arguments, and the best defense of arbitrary standard-setting remains nontechnical. As Kane (2001) noted, Glass's technical criticisms of cut scores have retained considerable force over the years, despite the various attempts to improve on the techniques that existed at the time (also see Shepard, 1995). The techniques currently used to condense various judgments into some single cut score cannot eliminate the essential elements of testing that make scores comparative—and undermine the logic of classification.

DO THE ENDS JUSTIFY THE TESTS?

The defense of cut scores thus depends entirely on their use, not their technical adequacy. Can imperfect, arbitrary thresholds nonetheless be serviceable? The respondents to Glass in 1978 justified cut scores in part by the consequence of inaction—or, as Scriven argued, sometimes establishing even an arbitrary cut score "is very much better than nothing, and somewhat better than anything else" (p. 275). Scriven was discussing the minimum value of cut scores by reference to alternatives in the case of admissions tests (i.e., that the predictive validity of the underlying measure was minimally sufficient to make decisions). Popham (1978) focused specifically on state graduation tests, which were in their infancy at the time:

> But what if Glass, however convincing, is completely wrong? Thousands of youngsters, no longer obligated to display minimum proficiency in basic skills, may end up with a decisively worse education than would have been the case if they were in an instructional system where minimum competency was sought. (pp. 297-98)

Popham was saying that the *possibility* of a defensible cut-score definition should be magnified by the potential loss of educational benefits from going without the policy, in the case of state graduation tests. A common element of both Scriven's and Popham's remarks was the claim that the justification of cut scores depends on consequences. On the one hand, the use of a particular accountability mechanism is a critical context. On the other hand, however, this argument is a slippery slope if separated entirely from technical issues. If the use of a cut score improves education regardless of the technical merits, then the process used to set the cut score does not need to meet high professional standards. The test and the accountability mechanism can be a black box, unknown and irrelevant. Legally, federal courts have ruled that tests used as graduation criteria must meet professionally technical standards (*Debra v. Turlington*, 1983; American Educational Research Association, American Psychological Association, & National Council on Measurement in Education, 1999). Politically, however, Scriven and Popham have been closer to the mark. The survival of graduation tests and other cut-score policies has depended more on the perception of utility than on the technical qualities of policy implementation. For many policymakers and observers, the push that results from testing and accountability is what is important, and the details of the test and statistics are of minimal relevance.

Problems with the Rationale

There are two problems with the argument that the ends justify the test: It undermines the logic of evaluation based on evidence, and it also undermines democratic processes. The first problem is that focusing on the ends guarantees the irrelevance of test specifics for accountability purposes. All that matters is whether there is external pressure put on schools to improve achievement. If the ends justify the test, then the quality of the test would be irrelevant. One could use a norm-referenced or criterion-referenced test; one could use a test completely disconnected from the curriculum; one could pick cut scores out of a hat; half or more of students' tests could be scored erroneously. If the ends justify the test, none of those issues would matter. As long as the black box of testing and accountability produced politically-sustainable pressure on schools to improve, the criterion is satisfied. The utility of testing then is not in improving instruction through accurate information about student performance but in providing a politically legitimate formal process for the identification of school failure. Given the potential for a test system that is substantively empty and serves only a formal purpose, justifying a technically flawed approach based on the consequences displays a profound distrust of transparency. Should we reform a public institution through deception, deception abetted by expertise? Here is a dangerous potential for direct contradiction between the reliance on testing as a tool and the democratic rationale for transparent accountability.

We can move back from the brink of testing as empty formalism, turning instead to Popham's (1978) distinction between capricious benchmarks and rational judgments. He wrote:

> But while it can be conceded that performance standards must be set *judgmentally*, it is patently incorrect to equate human judgment with arbitrariness in this negative sense. There are instances galore in which human beings exercise their judgmental skills to reach highly consistent and defensible conclusions.... If sophisticated standard setters comprehend the nature of their task, and have access to information relevant to that task, then there is no reason to assume that they too cannot exercise nonarbitrary judgments. (p. 298, emphasis in original)

Popham's argument is philosophical: At least in theory, there exists the capacity to make rational judgments, judgments that classify a continuous range of performances into a set of categorical bins. Schools and educators make such judgments regularly, from deciding who is admitted to an academic program to marking grades. Popham argues that the fact that such judgments frequently divide a continuous spectrum into classifications does not automatically render those judgments invalid. In abstract, we can accept the institutional necessity of and the plausible rationale for such judgments, especially where the stakes involve distribution of scarce resources (e.g., funds for remedial intervention).

The abstract possibility of rational judgment does not guarantee either that the judgments currently being made about performance are justifiable or that the uses of such judgments are necessary or wise. Both the need for making such judgment and the potential cost of mistaken judgments are inevitable considerations in the practice of potentially flawed categorical judgments (Linn, 2003). There is no reason to limit the numbers of schools identified in different ways, except to target resources.[6] A marginal use of thresholds when there are better approaches is not sensible. And even when thresholds are essential, there is no guarantee that the judgment will be sound. Consider the triage process in hospital emergency rooms. In an emergency room, triage performs an essential function to prioritize cases and target scarce resources (especially the time of physicians and nurses). For the last third of the twentieth century, a three-level acuity index became the dominant triage method in U.S. hospitals, and two-thirds of U.S. hospitals at the turn of the millennium used a three-level system (MacLean, 2002). Emergency room triage is a case where there is a clear mandate for classification, if there could be one— the need to distribute scarce resources and potentially fatal consequences of inaction. Emergency-room care is also a context where one would expect "sophisticated standard setters [who] comprehend the nature of their task and have access to information relevant to that task," as Popham (1978, p. 298) described. Yet a study of emergency-room nurses and certified EMTs found reliability rates for the common three-stage acuity index to be poor (*kappa* = .35) (Wuerz, Fernandes, & Alarcon, 1998). The five-stage acuity index used in Canada and a new five-stage acuity index developed in the United States both result in more reliable ratings (Beveridge, Ducharme, Janes, Beaulieu, & Walter, 1999; Wuerz, Milne, Eitel, Travers, & Gilboy, 2000). However, the problems with accuracy in triage in the 1990s should be a cautionary tale about the difficulty of forming appropriate judgments of categories. Even where lives are on the line and highly-trained personnel are available and focused on the task, agreement on categories is elusive. It is only because of the essential function of triage that we can excuse hospital emergency departments for their past behavior, and only if the reliability of triage judgments improves.

High-stakes accountability policies have no parallel rationale for the use of cut scores or threshold judgments. No children have died because there was no high-stakes accountability in a time or place. The abstract possibility that the cut scores might be rational is insufficient. When the consequence of a classification judgment is the denial of a benefit or other penalties, such decisions require evidentiary support of considerable weight. Reference to a recursive process such as the statistical consolidation of individual judgments is insufficient for a system whose core rationale requires transparency. When teachers are fired or students are denied diplomas because of marginal differences in performance, transparency requires that the basis for those judgments be set openly, not behind the screen of expertise or a seemingly oracular process. The burden is on those who advocate the use of such cut scores to demonstrate openly both the logic and the substantive soundness of such judgments. The desire to improve education does not justify capriciousness.

Cudgels, not Scalpels

We can look beyond the arbitrary qualities of cut scores to the questions about test-score use raised by Scriven (1978) and Popham (1978). How various institutions and individuals use test scores is critical to the defense of high-stakes accountability. While chapter 5 explores the issues of motivation in detail, some remarks about test uses are relevant here to the assumptions of technocratic competence. The explicit theory of action behind arguments for high-stakes accountability is that schools and students respond to consequences in ways that improve education. But that is *not* quite true; the only lever for change in high-stakes accountability is to drive behavior that anticipates test scores rather than responds to them. We may usefully divide the use of test scores into three types: *formative, responsive,* and *anticipatory. Formatively,* schools may use test scores to identify strengths and weaknesses of individual students or groups and devise appropriate instructional responses. At its best, formative use of student performance data is what the term *data-driven decision making* refers to. As explained earlier in this chapter, the typical annual standardized test provides relatively little information for formative use with regard to individual students. At best, assuming all test data is accurate and meaningful, a school may identify general areas of the curriculum that deserve scrutiny the following year. The types of tests commonly used for high-stakes accountability do not lend themselves to targeted intervention in a timely fashion.

A school or system may also *respond* to test scores with rewards and punishments. The responsive use of test scores is primarily a retrospective control on school quality, by providing rewards to confirm the accountability system's judgment of quality and by sanctioning students, schools, or educators when the accountability system judges the effort to be poor. If there is an intervention that is responsive, it is in mandated consequences such as those laid out in the No Child Left Behind Act—options to transfer to other schools, the provision of tutoring by outside agencies, or the reorganization of a school. While some analyze these provisions separately, it is important to note that all of these responses are retrospective, not timely. The lives of children move at a pace different from the scale of school reform. There is no retrospective consequence that can save a child's lost year. At best, retrospective use of test scores can drive system efforts the *next* year. As with formative uses, responsive use of test scores represents a blunt mechanism for change.

It is only in *anticipation* of tests and their consequences that the theory of action for high-stakes accountability includes changing instruction at the level of the individual student or within a school year. The arguments of voucher proponents in part rely on this anticipatory effect with claims that competition will drive improvements in schools (e.g., Friedman, 1955). And there is significant evidence that school systems and individual schools *are* changing instruction in hopes that such changes will improve test scores (Center on Education Policy, 2006). But we know very little about the rationality of such anticipatory changes or whether all anticipatory changes are effective or ethical. Consider the effectiveness of test preparation of some spheres (such as college and graduate-school admissions tests). The existence of test preparation is well-known, and it is both plausible and rational for any teacher or principal to believe that one can raise test scores through test preparation, without students' knowing more about the subjects tested. The existence of such drilling is well-documented, even if the current extent of it is unknown (e.g., Abrams, Pedulla, & Madaus, 2003; Madaus, 1988, 1991; McNeil, 2000; Nichols & Berliner, 2007). The diversion of instructional time into test preparation does not serve the long-term interests of young children—what third-grader could possibly need to know the test-wiseness necessary to succeed on the SATs? And in many cases, attempts to drill for tests do not even raise test scores. But if there is an accountability-related superstition for educators, it is in the belief that finding the right test preparation can raise test scores without improving instruction. Is this the path that defenders of high-stakes accountability wish educators to take?

In some ways, this division between formative, responsive, and anticipatory uses of testing is artificial. Ex-post facto justifications of minimum competency exams in the 1970s and 1980s referred both to responsive and anticipatory effects in claiming that the first graduation exams pushed school systems to target remediation at students who might not earn a standard diploma because of the tests—such actions both responded to evidence that some students were having difficulties with the tests and also acting to head off future failure (Dee, 2003; Frederiksen, 1994; Reardon, 1996). Yet in a fundamental way, that bundle of responses to a policy was still blunt systematic behavior, behavior that could have been mandated rather than indirectly prompted. High-stakes accountability is policy as cudgel, not scalpel. Is this bluntness the best that a test-based accountability system can offer?

THE MISMEASURE OF GROWTH

If annual testing technology limits high-stakes accountability to being more of a cudgel than a scalpel, many also see accountability mechanisms as insufficiently sensitive to important background factors that schools cannot control (e.g., Rothstein, 2004). Schools cannot determine whether children are fed, whether anyone takes them to pediatricians or dentists, whether they have a roof over their head, or whether adults read to them and love them when young. Schools cannot determine the language of origin for children or the presence and nature of disabilities. Many educators thus complain that rote accountability mechanisms do not credit schools with what they accomplish with children once in the building. As one Florida middle-school principal told me several years ago, she was sure she could have an "A" school if she could just pick the parents. A more involved discussion of these expectations will have to wait until the next chapter, but one must acknowledge that arguments about the proper attribution of achievement have driven one part of the debate over accountability. Given these arguments, many have suggested looking at achievement growth as a measure of school effectiveness. Over several decades, researchers have debated whether measuring growth is better than status and the difficulties of measuring growth (e.g., Cronbach & Furby, 1970). There are both technical and political issues involved in so-called growth models of achievement. Of these, the political issues are the more troublesome.

There are several statistical techniques whose goal is to parcel out changes from original status. The simplest is the difference between scores at two points in time; a slightly more complicated method is linear regression that uses some baseline measure as a covariate. But there are also more complicated, technically-demanding techniques, from repeated-measures analysis of variance to multilevel modeling. In the past two decades, these techniques have begun to filter into accountability models. Tennessee's Value Added Assessment System (TVAAS) has been in place since 1992, and in 2006 the federal Department of Education approved pilot projects in Tennessee and North Carolina to use growth in determining adequate yearly progress under the No Child Left Behind Act (Educational Improvement Act, 1992; U.S. Department of Education, 2006). The attempts to model growth have roots in several areas. In the 1980s, statistician and then Tennessee resident William Sanders convinced state legislators that there were statistical tools available to evaluate teachers fairly, through growth analysis, and they chose his workgroup to run the TVAAS. Some teachers union officials have also been attracted by growth analysis as a way to reduce some of the external factors teachers commonly feel they are held responsible for (e.g., American Federation of Teachers, 2006; National Education Association, 2005). More recently, a broad coalition of school officials and other groups responding to No Child Left Behind mandates have seen growth modeling as a way to improve No Child Left Behind (Forum on Educational Accountability, 2006; also see Callender, 2004). The impulse to use growth modeling illustrates the inevitable intersection between technical skills and democratic expectations. There are political questions at the heart of the debate over growth models, but any statistical algorithm is technically complex. To ignore either the statistics or the politics would be foolish.

Technical Issues

We begin with the technical issues, because they are easier to resolve, or at least grasping the limitations is easier. This discussion assumes knowledge of multivariate regression—a way to show the relationship between an important result such as an achievement test score and other information through a linear equation (independent variables or predictors). The regression equation shows how much the change in one of the predictors is associated with the predicted value of the outcome and how much the variation in the key result can be related to the predictors.[7] Readers who understand the last two sentences should understand the discussion that follows.

One should be aware that *growth modeling* and *value-added analysis* are generic terms; several statistical tools can model growth. Among education researchers, the tool of choice for measuring growth is multilevel modeling (Bryk & Raudenbush, 1992; Goldstein, 2003; Snijders, 2003). In ordinary regression, each record or data point has a set of information tied to the variable of interest. A student's test score would be matched up with information about the student's prior test scores, the student's age, sex, race or ethnicity, the presence/absence of a disability, language of origin, and so forth. For analytical purposes, information about the general environment of a record—for example, the average test scores of a student's class peers, or the extent of poverty among the school's students—is treated in the same way as information that is specific to a student. It is that similarity of treatment that can cause problems, for no child is an island. In real life, my own children are affected by their classmates and by the environment of the school. Modeling test scores without including such interrelationships can misstate the underlying relationships and also the accuracy of statistical estimates. The different varieties of multilevel modeling allow a statistician to model those cross-level relationships. A multilevel model can assume that test scores for students in a single classroom might cluster around a central point, that the scores for a school might cluster around a central point, and so forth. Multilevel statistical packages can partition out the variation in the key indicator of interest into that part statistically accounted for by one level from another—for example, differences among students accounted for by individual variation from the variation associated with their attending different schools.

In addition, multilevel modeling does not have to view the effect of any variable as fixed. Maybe the effects associated with poverty vary by which school one attends. Multilevel models can include variables whose effects are random. At least in theory, multilevel modeling allows a variety of accommodations to the real life of schools, where students are affected not only by a teacher but a classroom environment in common with other kids as well as the school and their own characteristics, and where the effects of those individual and environmental differences may differ in quality. The holy grail of multilevel modeling is the implicit and sometimes explicit promise that multilevel modeling can accurately portion out responsibility among different actors. If one plugs in the right variables, perhaps, one can find out the variation in achievement accounted for by prior achievement, by external factors, and by the school or classroom—that is, identify what schools add to student achievement.

Multilevel modeling is now possible on desktop computers anywhere in the world. Thanks to the growing power of microcomputers, standard statistical packages such as SAS, S-Plus, and SPSS include a variety of modules when consumers have sufficient interest, and all of these now include multilevel modeling components. There are also standalone programs such as HLM that focus entirely on multilevel modeling. And yet the statistical millennium is not here. The new vistas opened up by multilevel modeling do not eliminate the specification choices that all statistical work involves, it does not eliminate the caveats one must use with achievement data in general, and it has its own methodological vulnerabilities and caveats. Neither multilevel modeling nor other tools for modeling growth are the holy grail of achievement statistics (Goldstein, 1997).

Below, I explain some of the issues of concern specifically for at least some multilevel packages.

Specification Issues

The existence of multilevel models does not eliminate the need to make choices about what contributes to achievement. These involve both theoretical and political matters. Omitting important factors that affect education can distort the results of any statistical procedure. William Sanders has consistently argued that one need only include test scores from prior years (e.g., Ballou, Sanders, & Wright, 2004), while other researchers are highly skeptical that one can omit issues such as poverty or home language and have consistent, fair results (e.g., McCaffrey, Lockwood, Koretz, Louis, & Hamilton, 2004; Raudenbush, 2004; Tekwe et al., 2004). The interpretation of such effects is also in dispute: Would adjustments based on socioeconomics be a matter of fairness, or could it mask inequalities in the distribution of resources and teaching talent? More broadly, in any statistically-based accountability system, model specification is a political statement as much as a research matter. The attribution of achievement to schools versus other factors becomes entangled in the statistical algorithms used for accountability. Should race or poverty be included as a factor? If social background is included, some schools might be seen as better performing after adjusting for social background. But including social backgrounds might set different expectations for students already coming into school with disadvantages. The question remains, and the existence of multilevel modeling does not remove the problem that makes growth models appealing to many in the first place.

Vertical Scaling

In some statistical packages, there is a need for a uniform metric where the achievement of students at different grades and ages are on the same scale. That way, a score of a student who is 7 can be compared to an 8-, 9- or 10-year-old's achievement. This is not necessary with packages that use prior scores as covariates, but anything that looks at a measure of growth in some way strongly begs for a uniform or vertical scale. There are two problems with such vertical scaling, stemming from the fact that it is difficult to perform the type of equating across different grades and equivalent curricula that is necessary to put students from different grades on a single scale. Learning and achievement is not like weight, where you can put a 7-year-old and a 17-year-old on the same scale. To simplify dramatically, equating is a type of piecemeal process of pinning together segments of separate scales (each more closely developed) (Goldschmidt, Choi, & Martinez, 2003; Leung, 2003; Yen, 1986).

At least two consequences follow from the process of equating tests from different grades. First, the plausible errors in individual test scores or measurement errors in a vertical scale will be difficult to gauge, a fact that test publishers rarely identify, in contrast to errors in a single-grade scale which test manufacturers have far more experience scaling (and far more data on which to rely in establishing the scale) (Bielinski, Scott, Minnema, & Thurlow, 2000). In addition to the larger measurement errors, the interpretation of differences in a vertical scale will be even more difficult than the interpretation of differences in a single-grade scale (Martineau, 2006; Reckase, 2004). One reason is that academic expectations among different grades differ. Third graders generally have not been introduced to decimals in the same way that fourth and fifth grade students have exposure to decimals. A scale that tries to bridge achievement among different curricular expectations is a leap of faith at some level. Martineau (2006) points out that shifts in the concepts covered in a test will distort growth or value-added measures derived from a vertical scale. The other reason for interpretive difficulty is more subtle: The construction of a vertical scale can only be guaranteed to be monotonic, not linear. Higher scores in a single-grade test will map to higher scores in the cross-grade, vertical scale, but there will almost inevitably be some compression and expansion of the scale relative to single-grade test statistics. That nonlinearity is not a problem for estimation (since models of growth can easily be nonlinear). But the compression/expansion possibility makes interpretation of growth difficult. Does 15-point growth between ages 10 and 11 mean the same thing as 15-point growth between ages 15 and 16? These interpretive difficulties add additional layers of abstraction between student performance and public accountability.

Inconsistencies in Ranking

As Lockwood, Louis, and McCaffrey (2002) point out, models of growth can lead to highly uncertain estimates of performance. Part of this uncertainty lies in the complexity of models that swallow a substantial part of the available variance before estimating the statistical residuals associated with individual schools and teachers. Regardless of the cause, it has serious consequences for using growth models for accountability purposes. It erodes the legitimacy of such accountability models among statistically-literate stakeholders, who see that most variance is accounted for by issues other than schools and teachers.[8] In addition, the process leaves the effect estimates for individual teachers and schools very close to zero and each other. Thus, with William Sanders's model used in Tennessee, the vast majority of effects for teachers are statistically indistinguishable (e.g., Ballou, Sanders, & Wright, 2004). Because of how multilevel modeling packages treat variance, this tool is not inherently a powerful tool for making clear and large distinctions among individual schools and teachers.

Convergence Difficulties

Researchers who attempt to use multilevel modeling know that their algorithms require as much craft as science. The models do not always converge in stable parameter estimates, given the data. Researchers with specific, focused questions will often fiddle manually with equations and the variables to achieve convergence (e.g., Hox, 1995; Stoel, 2003). Resetting initial conditions or eliminating a level of analysis to gain convergence is acceptable in research because the goal is to squeeze as much new information out of the data as possible. But technical standards are different with accountability. Making idiosyncratic adjustments to a model violates the transparency principle of accountability, and nonuniformity violates the reasonable expectation that an accountability system behave in a stable fashion.

Bureaucratic Translation of Growth

From the prior discussion, one may assume that most states considering growth models use the most sophisticated tools available. But while many states may have considered complex multilevel models, only a few have used the more advanced tools. The General Accounting Office (2006) reported recently that only seven states calculated some measure of individual-level growth in their accountability systems, while 19 states used school-level aggregate data to calculate growth. Even among those seven states, the sophistication of methods varies. In Florida, the state simply determines whether a student has met the state definition for adequate growth on a test: leaping an achievement level, maintaining an achievement level as long as it is the middle or one of the higher achievement levels, or having a gain in the test's vertical scale that is equivalent to the median of differences in grade-specific cut scores (e.g., the median of the differences in the vertical-scale equivalent of the cut score for level 2 in third and fourth grades, level 3, level 4, and level 5) (Florida Department of Education, 2006). Currently, the clear majority of states that claim to use some measure of growth do so only on a haphazard basis.

Omissions of Student Data

In any accountability system that allows exemptions, there are concerns about which students count for the judgment of a school. Many states eliminate students who move between schools during the year, receive special education services, or are still learning English, and such concerns become magnified with any model of growth that omits students who move between test dates. There are both technical and political reasons to be concerned with such omissions. Technically, the removal of students from calculations reduces the accuracy of estimates and can bias the statistics if the students who move do not have achievement characteristics similar to those who stay (Little & Rubin, 2002; Rubin, Stuart, & Zanutto, 2004). The removal of students from accountability systems also provides a powerful incentive for schools to remove students from instructional intervention and even enrollment. Every year, there are anecdotal reports and rumors that some high schools push 10th graders out of enrollment before testing, supposedly to raise average test scores in a perverse educational triage (e.g., Nichols & Berliner, 2007; Orel, 2003). But even apart from the incentive for triage, one is hard-pressed to claim that any accountability system targets the most vulnerable when those are frequently the students who move between schools, systems, and states. The more years included in a model, the less that the most vulnerable students count in accountability.

An Additional Layer of Abstraction between Accountability and Student Performance

Whether the particular implementation of a growth model is multilevel modeling or a jerry-built state system, growth models tend to create an additional layer of abstraction between student performance and public discussion. In Florida, there are three layers of abstraction. One is the creation of an individual student's scale score on state testing. A second layer of abstraction is the state's awkward classification of annual student growth, defined as adequate if the student improved in the grade-specific achievement levels or maintained a certain rank place within the same ordinal achievement level in separate grades. A third layer of abstraction is the algorithm that bases the state's accountability label on the percentages of students in different categories (performing at a certain achievement level, performing at a certain achievement level for students in certain categories, or maintaining or improving in the state's perspective on growth) (Florida Administrative Code 6A-1.09981). The holy-grail appeal of growth models is seductive. Assessing growth is a deceptively easy choice for lawmakers who may be looking for a technocratic model whose putative characteristics appear beneficent and whose technical details can be left to staff members. But such abdication of hard choices is not consistent with transparency.

Proprietary Software

One mixed-model statistical package has a unique conflict with the transparency we associate with accountability. William Sanders's mixed-model approach (which appears in a modified form in the SAS statistical software package) shares many general characteristics with HLM and other packages, but the algorithm itself is secret, held as proprietary information. When Sanders's team analyzes data for states or districts, the detailed internal workings are thus unknown (Fisher, 1996; Kupermintz, 2003). Even though it is used as public accountability mechanisms in several jurisdictions, Sanders's work is not susceptible to independent review. The lack of independent review makes an accountability system based on Sanders's system especially problematic for a high-stakes system, because it removes any option for substantive appeal of Sanders's value-added measures based on errors in programming or other matters inside the algorithm's black box.

Policy Issues

To focus on the technical issues involved in modeling achievement growth would ignore the broader policy issues at stake. Since the announcement in November 2005 that the Department of Education would allow some states to pilot so-called growth models of accountability, there were a number of reactions, many of which were skeptical (Citizens' Commission on Civil Rights, 2005; Education Trust, 2005; Rotherham, 2005). Each of these reactions were grounded in concerns about the potential for growth models to weaken accountability standards. The U.S. Department of Education mollified these concerns in part through choosing William Taylor of the Citizens' Commission on Civil Rights and Kati Haycock of Education Trust as two of the pilot proposal reviewers (U.S. Department of Education, 2006). The review process considerably assuaged these advocates of high-stakes accountability, and the moves to include advocates in the reviewing should confirm the fact that a substantial part of growth modeling lies in the political realm (Haycock, 2006; Rotherham, 2006a, 2006b, 2006c). Focusing on political questions is perfectly appropriate given the political nature of accountability, as I explained in chapter 1. The political questions are the important ones, ultimately, and one cannot have a purely technocratic solution to political problems—as long as one does not ignore the technical issues.

Judging Status Versus Growth

At one level, the debate over growth models represents a larger dilemma between the desire to set absolute standards, on the one hand, and focusing on improvements, on the other. As Hochschild and Scovronick (2003) have pointed out, the two goals are in tension. On the one hand, there are concrete skills adults need to be decent citizens. Even if setting criteria for composite achievement test scores is problematic, the simplicity and absolute nature of status standards is appealing both to those who want schools to create a certain amount of human capital and also those concerned about the inequality of schools. On the other hand, many argue that focusing entirely on absolute standards without acknowledging the work that many teachers do with students with low skills is unfair to the teachers who voluntarily choose to work in hard environments. For children who begin a year far below the skills of their peers, making significant progress toward their peers is an accomplishment both for them and their teachers. Which goal should an accountability system emphasize? There is no easy path out of this dilemma. Focusing entirely on growth risks denying children skills and knowledge that they will need as adults. On the other hand, focusing entirely on achievement status risks incorrectly and unfairly punishing or stigmatizing some teachers as lazy even when the evidence clearly indicates otherwise.

Expectations of Growth

A second issue is the question of how much growth we should expect. It is especially important not to let statistical models obscure the political dimensions of this question. Sanders has consistently claimed that his technique sets the standard as an average of 1 year's growth per year in school (e.g., Sanders & Horn, 1994, 1995). The statistical reason for his default approach is clear: By comparing growth of one student to all students in that grade, Sanders need make no value or educational judgments about what we should expect in terms of growth. There are two problems with such an approach, however. First, Sanders's norm-referenced definition of appropriate growth is dependent on the behavior of the general educational system and only picks up differential growth. If somehow the annual residual of a student's status for the latest test is equal to the grand mean residual for all children in that grade, given the prior year's (or years') data, then the student has learned enough. If *all* children in the system learn very little, then learning very little is defined as appropriate growth in such a system. The second problem with Sanders's definition of growth is a matter of equity. For students who are significantly behind where you or I think they should be, or well behind their peers, an average year's growth is not enough. The Education Trust (2005) expressed that concern when the U.S. Department of Education announced it would allow pilots of growth models. There are technical studies of appropriate growth within a year (e.g., Fuchs & Fuchs, 1993), but the principle extends beyond instructional decisions. By any measure, uniform growth in any dimension of achievement keeps achievement gaps intact.

The appeal of growth models illustrates the fragility of testing described in this chapter. We want schools to be transparently accountable, but accountability systems distance us from knowing what students can actually do—and growth models add to such distance. We want accountability because we distrust public schools, but accountability systems trust the technocratic mechanisms of testing—and truly individual growth models are more complex than other accountability systems (secret in one instance). Legislators commonly mandate vague general goals for accountability, leaving the details to staff in a way that obscures central choices. Growth models comprise the ultimate lure to such abdication of open debate, promising to be fair while resolving none of the hard choices involved in what we truly expect from children.

NOTES

1. The composite nature of a test score is also true for graded essays, which receive global scoring in almost all cases.
2. While the Florida Department of Education indicates that the published item specifications are drafts from 2002, their public placement indicates that they are operative, and there is no later version.
3. Item response theory addresses the severe dependence of classical test theory on population samples with the construct of ability (θ) that is assumed to be sample-independent. Nonetheless, the measurement of item difficulty is dependent on knowing the characteristics of the sample.
4. To end up with five pieces, one slices the doughnut so that the cuts intersect in one side of the breading but also intersect the hole:

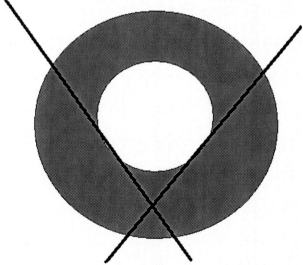

5. For a counterargument, see Rogosa (2005).
6. There is also no reason why we need to limit the students graduating from high school, just to limit the numbers, but this book focuses on accountability at the school level. One important difference between graduation

exams and accountability based on annual tests is that students have multiple opportunities to pass the graduation exams, while the evaluation of schools is based on a single round of testing.

7. In general, one should not assume that linear regression is predictive; it is more technically a model of statistical associations.

8. This swallowing of variance is true whether one sees it as a causal or noncausal model.

CHAPTER 4

SETTING UP
GOALS AND FAILURE

If growth models illustrate the unresolved tensions between technocracy and democracy, they also show the gap between the accountability debate and the inevitable political trade-offs of education policy. For a moment, assume schools can close the achievement gap between children in families with more resources and social capital and children from families with fewer resources and advantages. We can phrase this goal as a proposition for public consideration:

> Resolved, that students with considerable built-in advantages will learn in school but at a far lower rate than students without those advantages, so that by the time they leave school as adults, the students from advantaged households will entirely lose any advantages that their families spent 18 or more years to provide. The primary goal of school reform shall be to negate the competitive advantages of those efforts in gaining access to postsecondary education and in the labor market.

Stripped of the technical detritus school reform has created, this proposition is starkly egalitarian. It is perfectly consistent with measuring growth (if the growth targets for lower-achieving students would close existing gaps). But closing the achievement gap is also politically unsustainable in its complete form. Middle-class and wealthy parents will generally accept

Accountability Frankenstein: Understanding and Taming the Monster, pp. 87–121

some closing of the achievement gap, and some advantaged parents would welcome complete egalitarianism. On the other hand, many parents can and have responded harshly to serious compensatory efforts in schools. As Hochschild and Scovronick (2003) and Labaree (1997) point out, the egalitarian, collective goals for education are in constant tension with the desire of parents to use public schools for the *private* purposes of individual social mobility and economic success.

How much would the achievement gap have to close before there is some form of backlash? Probably none—the perception that No Child Left Behind neglects children in gifted-education programs has already prompted complaints (e.g., Winerip, 2006). Goodkin (2005) framed the issue as one of ignoring the developmental needs of children labeled as gifted:

> Not surprisingly, with the entire curriculum geared to ensuring that every last child reaches grade-level proficiency, there is precious little attention paid to the many children who master the standards early in the year and are ready to move on to more challenging work. (p. A5)

In Goodkin's comments, we see a potential defense of maintaining inequality; access to and participation in gifted programs are skewed by social class, race, and ethnicity (Donovan & Cross, 2002). Whether one is discussing tracking, education funding, or desegregation, the political defense of unequal education limits efforts to close gaps in access to a public education. Why should we be surprised at a backlash to efforts to close the achievement gap?

Some advocates of high-stakes accountability are now backing away from the argument that accountability will close the achievement gap. Petrilli (2006) recently wrote:

> NCLB's "adequate yearly progress" measure is ... not about progress. It's about getting a certain percentage of students from all subgroups over the "proficient" bar. Nor do schools have to close the gap in the average performance of subgroups. And for good reason. No one would support a policy that gave schools an incentive to hold down the performance of White students in order to show gains in closing the achievement gap. (¶¶ 9-10)

Acknowledging the political limits of egalitarian rhetoric, Petrilli reduces the goals of No Child Left Behind to providing a minimally adequate education. There can be some reasons for such a target—targeting a minimally adequate education dovetails with the most recent wave of education funding lawsuits, which focus on adequacy (e.g., Augenblick, Myers, & Anderson, 1997; Nickerson & Deenihan, 2003). However, such rhetorical backpedaling detracts from the civil-rights justification for accountability. Part of why we debate whether schools or society is more responsible for the achievement gap is because we have failed to talk openly about schooling as part of a broader welfare state (Cohen, 2005). In general, we rely on schools to substitute for the ameliorative efforts that other industrialized countries make with transfer programs (e.g., Hochschild & Scovronick, 2003). The debates over whether accountability hinders gifted education and whether it can close the achievement gap illustrates one fundamental fact: Accountability has obscured rather than helped resolve the political tensions between treating education as a public good and treating it as a means for assuring individual success. The choice of a particular target for achievement does not erase that tension.

This chapter focuses on tensions in one area: the political dynamics of expectations. The first section of this chapter explores the history of expectations for schools more broadly, from the panacea for social problems over several centuries to the twentieth-century aid to fighting whatever foreign or domestic conflicts were at hand, and how that history has made it difficult to distinguish between reasonable and unreasonable expectations of schools. The second section narrows the focus to the expectations of school reform, emphasizing the development of America 2000 and No Child Left Behind's goals as the most recent example of goals. The third section illustrates the concept of *politically acceptable failure* with three case studies: the collapse of the Arizona graduation test policies in 2000 for political reasons, the relatively weak standards of teacher qualification tests, and the dissent of former Florida Governor Jeb Bush from the federal Adequately Yearly Progress standards supported by his brother, the president. The fourth section explores alternatives to the absolute goals of America 2000 and No Child Left Behind; are incremental expectations politically viable? The end of the chapter introduces an alternative framework for both educational expectations and accountability.

The broader argument of this chapter is that the contemporary use of the terms *goals* and *standards* have conflated several separate topics in two important ways. The first type of conflation is the confusion between our expectation of schools' central purpose with our expectations of what students will learn to do. The current reform rhetoric assumes that there is a clear, direct path between cognitive development and economic productivity. There is scant evidence of a specific link between academics and economic productivity (e.g., Levin, 1998), and the rhetoric ignores the history of multiple purposes for public support of schools. This chapter separates the two topics—expectations of schools as a type of institution and expectations of what students can learn. The second conflation is the confusion among the different goals we might have for students' academic achievement. The No Child Left Behind Act and many state accountability systems have a set of policy triggers which imply that all educational problems are the same and that all problems are crises. This chapter ends with an explanation of why that assumption is neither wise nor necessary.

HISTORICAL EXPECTATIONS OF EDUCATION

We begin with expectations of schools as a set of institutions. Over the past 400 years in North America, schooling has carried a broad range of expectations, from socialization and conformity to changing society and liberation—often at the same time! The following survey is brief, with views selected to emphasize the range of expectations. Like Cremin (1990) and Tyack and Cuban (1995), most historians conclude that schools have never had the capacity to meet all of the expectations laid on them. We should still hold schools responsible for what is reasonable to expect. But our history of education rhetoric and school politics makes the division between reasonable and unreasonable more difficult.

Colonial Range of Expectations

From the beginning of European and African migration to North America, the goals of education were diffuse, except for a general sense that education should support the social order. Historians usually focus on the early history of Massachusetts Bay colony, perhaps because of three unique documents in the colony's development. A decade after the 1630 establishment of the Massachusetts Bay colony, the colony's general court issued several decrees urging the effective education of youth. In 1642, the court declared that the elders of each town had the authority

> to take account from time to time of all parents and masters, and of their children, concerning their calling and employment of their children, especially of their ability to read and understand the principles of religion and the capital laws of this country, and to impose fines upon such as shall refuse to render such accounts. (Cohen, 1973, p. 393)

Three years later, the court urged the education of young men in firearms in a second decree. Then in 1647, the court made a slight shift in its tactics for ensuring education and order:

> [E]very township in this jurisdiction, after the Lord hath increased them to the number of 50 householders, shall then forthwith appoint one within their town to teach all such children as shall resort to him to write and read,

whose wages shall be paid either by the parents or masters of such children, or by the inhabitants in general,... and it is further ordered, that where any town shall increase to the number of 100 families or householders, they shall set up a grammar school. (Cohen, 1973, p. 394)

Historians have tended to read these three acts as a way to bolster family and apprentice-based education as well as a response to the turbulent early years of the colony. (The dissents of Roger Williams and Anne Hutchison led to their expulsions from the colony in the mid-1630s—an earlier passage of the 1647 act refers to "false glosses of saint seeming deceivers.") Certainly, the explicit purpose of all three decrees is to support the order that the colony's leaders were hoping to establish. But the mechanisms were different. In 1642, the court declared that families and masters were responsible for education. Five years later, the court said that towns were responsible. In 1642, the purpose was mass education, so everyone could read the Bible and understand the society's expectations. In 1647, larger towns were also responsible for creating a secondary level of schooling, grammar schools, that would prepare the better-educated boys—and only boys—for Harvard College, the intended training ground at the time for ministers and colonial leaders (Axtell, 1974).

As European and African transplants spread through the Atlantic coastal plains, the purpose of education became more diverse, if frequently overlapping with religious and civil purposes that motivated the Massachusetts Bay Puritans. By the American Revolution, residents could identify a broad range of private tutors, *dame schools* run by town women in their homes, *district* or village schools, and public and private secondary institutions calling themselves academies, grammar schools, seminaries, and colleges. The purposes included literacy for religious study, day care, transmitting culture, leadership preparation, and the private advancement of one's sons (and daughters, on occasion). One should also view formal and informal apprenticeships in the colonies as part of the colonial repertoire of child rearing and education—providing for shared child raising and socialization into adult roles (including working) (Axtell, 1974; Kett, 1977; Rorabaugh, 1986). There was no educational monolith in 1776.

Revolutionary Arguments?

Even without a coherent set of institutions or goals, the educational infrastructure and expectations were sufficiently developed by the end of the 18th century that social critics in the new United States could and did propose new models of education for a new nation. The range of these proposals illustrates the variety of expectations that the new nation's cultural elite held for its schools. In the 1780s, Thomas Jefferson urged his state's legislature to create a hierarchical system of schooling for White males, to educate all in character and proper citizenship and also select the brightest poor White boys to send to grammar schools and, eventually, William and Mary College: "By this means twenty of the best geniuses will be raked from the rubbish annually, and be instructed, at the public expense, so far as the grammar schools go" (Jefferson, 1787/1954, p. 146). The broad education should be to

> teach [students] how to work out their own greatest happiness, by showing them that it does not depend on the condition of life in which chance has placed them, but is always the result of a good conscience, good health, occupation, and freedom in all just pursuits. (p. 147)

But the higher aim would be to protect his notion of a yeoman republic: "But of all the views of this law none is more important, none more legitimate, than that of rendering the people the safe, as they are the ultimate, guardians of their own liberty" (p. 148).

Fellow Continental Congress member Benjamin Rush (1786/1965) had a very different goal for education: creating a nation of Christians. Like Jefferson, Rush thought that education was critical to the survival of the new nation: "The principle of patriotism stands in need of the reinforcement of prejudice" (p. 9). But in contrast to Jefferson, whose proposed curriculum would eschew religious texts and instead be full of ancient and modern history, Rush thought the focus of schooling should be religious: A Christian

> cannot fail of being a republican, for every precept of the Gospel inculcates those degrees of humility, self-denial, and brotherly kindness, which are directly opposed to the pride of monarchy and the pageantry of a court. A Christian cannot fail of being useful to the republic, for his religion teacheth him, that no man "liveth to himself." And lastly, a Christian cannot fail of being wholly inoffensive, for his religion teacheth him, in all things to do others what he would wish, in like circumstances, they should do to him. (Rush, 1786/1965, p. 11)

Rush's version of Christianity is one of humility and collective effort. He wanted students to have a Spartan diet, have physical work, and learn how to sing, leaving foreign languages and other advanced subjects in what he called a collegiate curriculum.

Though he also argued for the use of history and religion, Noah Webster argued that language would cement the new nation. In his 1789 essay on the need for a standard system of spelling, he wrote,

[A] national language is a band of national union. Every engine should be employed to render the people of this country national; to call their attachments home to their own country; and to inspire them with the pride of national character. However, they may boast of Independence, and the freedom of their government, yet their opinions are not sufficiently independent; an astonishing respect for the arts and literature of their parent country, and a blind imitation of its manners, are still prevalent among the Americans. (Webster, 1789, quoted in Malone, 1925, p. 27)

His focus on the details of spelling and pronunciation seems quaint today, but he was deadly serious, worried about the fractious nature of a newly-independent country:

The body of the people, governed by habit, will still retain their respective peculiarities of speaking; and for want of schools and proper books, fall into many inaccuracies, which, incorporating with the language of the state where they live, may imperceptibly corrupt the national language. Nothing but the establishment of schools and some uniformity in the use of books, can annihilate differences in speaking and preserve the purity of the American tongue. A sameness of pronunciation is of considerable consequence in a political view; for provincial accents are disagreeable to strangers and sometimes have an unhappy effect upon the social affections. (Webster, 1789/1992, p. 34)

For Webster, one goal of schools should be a cultural unification of the nation. All three wanted education to help maintain the new nation, but the paths and the implicit "theories of action" were very different, from mass education in history and culture to a Christian education to creating the new nation through language.

Nineteenth-Century Reformers

School reform efforts in the early nineteenth-century were part of a broader social reform impulse, an attempt to address the social dislocations and perceived social disorder of early industrialization (e.g., Kaestle, 1983; Katz, 1987). This social reform movement spurred the creation of institutions such as asylums, hospitals, and prisons, places that were supposed to be curative and specialized. Only in schooling were reformers trying to change an existing institution rather than create new ones. But that perspective may be unfair; the common-school reform movement also was concurrent with the flowering of a Sunday-school movement (Kaestle, 1983). What *was* true of the early nineteenth century school reformers is that they greatly expanded the responsibility of schools to address social ills. This expansion of the role of schools began early in the century. In 1805, issuing an appeal for funds for the New York Public School Society (a private organization, despite its name), the new society's trustees emphasized the consequences of failing to support education:

> [T]here still remains a large number [of poor children] living in total neglect of religious and moral instruction, and unacquainted with the common rudiments of learning, essentially requisite for the due management of the ordinary business of life. This neglect may be imputed either to the extreme indigence of the parents of such children, their intemperance and vice; or to a blind indifference to the best interests of their offspring. The consequences must be obvious to the most careless observer. Children thus brought up in ignorance, and amidst the contagion of bad example, are in imminent danger of ruin; and too many of them, it is to be feared, instead of being useful members of the community, will become the burden and pests of society. Early instruction and fixed habits of industry, decency, and order, are the surest safeguards of virtuous conduct; and when parents are either unable or unwilling to bestow the necessary attention on the education of their children, it becomes the duty of the public, and of individuals, who have the power, to assist them in the discharge of this important obligation. (New York Public School Society, 1805, quoted in Bourne, 1870, pp. 6-7)

The trustees promised to emphasize instruction in morals and to avoid competing with other private schools (by targeting the poorest children in the city). While the desire to teach morality was consistent with the goals of Puritan education almost two centuries before, there was something new in the promise that education to prevent children from becoming "the burden and pests of society." During the early nineteenth century, in early industrialization, concerns about dependency became a significant motivation for would-be school reformers. At the same time, concerns about class tensions also created concerns.

In the late 1840s, tensions that had roiled several European states for years finally boiled over. While many Americans at the time viewed their country as a new start, far from corrupt Europe, others paid close attention to European affairs. In 1848, the same year as several springtime revolutions in Europe and the publication of the *Communist Manifesto*, Horace Mann wrote, "According to the European theory, men are divided into classes,... According to the Massachusetts theory, all are to have an equal chance for earning, and equal security in the enjoyment of what they earn" (Cremin, 1957, p. 84). Later in the report, Mann explained the reasoning at further length:

> [N]othing but Universal Education can counter-work this tendency to the domination of capital and the servility of labor. If one class possesses all the wealth and the education, while the residue of society is ignorant and poor,

... the latter, in fact and in truth, will be the servile dependents and subjects of the former. But if education be equably diffused, it will draw property after it, ... for such a thing never did happen, and never can happen, as that an intelligent and practical body of men should be permanently poor. Property and labor, in different classes, are essentially antagonistic; but property and labor, in the same class, are essentially fraternal. (Cremin, 1957 pp. 86-87)

Mann's message was both optimistic and a warning: Education can improve our society, and without education class tensions will rip society apart. Mann and other common-school reformers were not universally approved; many of their efforts were disputed vigorously (Kaestle, 1983; Katz, 1968, 1975). Essentially, Mann was claiming in this report and others that education could save society. In that assertion, Mann was hardly alone in utopian rhetoric.

Americanization and Vocationalization

More than half a century after the common-school heyday, a new set of reformers asked schools to respond to a new wave of industrialization and a new wave of immigration from Europe. As with earlier reform efforts, one should not characterize reformers of the late nineteenth and early twentieth century Progressive Era as monolithic and uniform (Filene, 1970). As Tyack (1974) noted, progressives such as Jane Addams wanted schools to respond to the needs of immigrants and children. But others whom Tyack called administrative progressives sought to rationalize schooling, aided by the first educational psychologists. In the long run, the new educational psychology helped administrators acquire the patina of science discussed in chapter 1, along with the extensive use of the new standardized tests and tracking. As Lagemann (1990) explained the outcome, educational psychologist Edward Thorndike won and philosopher John Dewey lost. With the Progressive Era, public schooling acquired two new purposes: Americanization and vocationalization.

Americanization in the early twentieth century meant the socialization of immigrants and their children into what reformers and school officials thought were cultural and political norms. Children were expected to speak English and were punished for speaking their home languages at school, even on the playground, and nineteenth century versions of bilingual education were often eliminated by states (e.g., Blanton, 2004). School officials frequently ignored the desires of parents in immigrant communities in the creation of tracking and other endeavors which limited their children's opportunities (Tyack, 1974). With World War I came an explicit effort to create cultural uniformity. Schools which often taught

German as an academic subject stopped German instruction with the U.S. entry into the war. The pledge of allegiance, written by socialist Francis Bellamy, became mandatory in many schools (Davis, 2005). From those who advocated Americanization, the broader expectation was that the schools would smoothly incorporate immigrant children into the broader society.

Many historians point to the growth of vocational education in this era as part of administrative progressivism, part of tracking and a watering down of the high school curriculum (Angus & Mirel, 1999; Tyack, 1974). That picture is true in many ways, but there are a few problems with the argument. Some of the more humanistic progressives such as John Dewey saw some potential in vocational education, if carefully structured. He acknowledged the impetus toward vocational education:

> The manufacturer, banker, and captain of industry have practically displaced a hereditary landed gentry.... The great increase in the social importance of conspicuous industrial processes has inevitably brought to the front questions having to do with the relationship of schooling to industrial life. No such vast social readjustment could occur without offering a challenge to an education inherited from different social conditions, and without putting up to education new problems. (Dewey, 1916/2004, pp. 252-253)

Yet he thought there was tremendous danger in training children for specific jobs based on their social class background:

> The problem is not that of making the schools an adjunct to manufacture and commerce, but of utilizing ... industry to make school life more active, more full of immediate meaning, more connected with out-of-school experience.... Any scheme for vocational education which takes its point of departure from the industrial regime that now exists, is likely to assume and to perpetuate its divisions and weaknesses, and thus to become an instrument in accomplishing the feudal dogma of social predestination. (Dewey, 1916/2004, p. 254)

Dewey's ambivalence toward vocational education was mirrored in the politics of specific practices. Katznelson and Weir (1985) described the local political struggle in Chicago over whether vocational education would be part of comprehensive high schools or whether there would be a separate vocational-education school that could shunt some students off into a limited set of opportunities. Chicago's nascent labor movement successfully opposed a separate vocational school, concerned that city manufacturers would use an isolated vocational school to train docile workers and strikebreakers. Yet they did not oppose vocational education when part of a comprehensive education.

In addition to the ambivalence many expressed toward vocational education, vocational education did *not* become the dominant track in high schools. What became known as "general education" was larger at mid-century than either a clearly academic program or vocational education. Moreover, the behavior of some school systems early in the century suggests that the growth of vocational education was partly a defensive maneuver by public schools. As Kantor (1988) points out, California high schools responded to the growth of proprietary commercial schools by creating parallel courses in the public schools. Because the equipment was expensive, and because most school funding at the time was local rather than driven by a state formula, the reason for expanding vocational education and matching the demand of students in those California districts could not have been to gain more revenues through student enrollment. Instead, the schools were protecting their cultural and political legitimacy as the institution of adolescence.

As Kantor (1988) and Lazerson and Grubb (1974) have observed, the long-term legacy of vocational education was *not* the direct training of youth for specific jobs or careers. Instead, the vocational-education movement created a new role for schools: to support economic aspirations of both individuals and society. This economic purpose of schooling and the political purpose of Americanization became additional layers over the legacies of other eras: schooling for morality, for conformity, for democracy, for cultural transmission, for character and independence, and for easing social tensions.

Post-War Themes

After World War II, the recurring calls for education to solve various social problems became a cascade that still has not subsided. From the 1940s through the early twenty-first century, various critics of public schools have called on public education to fight various ills and enemies. In every decade from the 1940s through the 1980s, national politicians have asked schools to help win real and constructed wars. In raising the expectations for public schools even further, these nationalized debates helped set the stage for accountability. In the 1940s and 1950s, national policy emphasized the role of selective education in fighting the Cold War. These policies included the system of draft deferments as well as direct debates over the role of schools in providing *manpower* for the Cold War.[1] As Spring (1989) has explained, high military officers such as Admiral Hyman Rickover chastised high schools in the 1940s for allegedly lax standards, when the critics saw a crucial need for schools to provide scientific and technical training for military and diplomatic needs. When the

Soviet Union launched Sputnik in 1957, the political reaction launched from a decade-long foundation of rhetoric. The National Defense Education Act of 1958 promoted selective higher education as well as training for teachers in critical fields. One title paid for counselors with the explicit intent that high school counselors would encourage selected students to attend college in scientific and technical fields (Dorn, 1996). In that selective education, public schools were to help fight the Cold War.

Within a decade, national politicians were calling upon schools to help fight the War on Poverty (e.g., Spring, 1989). After the assassination of John F. Kennedy, his successor Lyndon Baines Johnson pushed through landmark legislation in areas of both poverty and civil rights. In 1964, Johnson signed his key War on Poverty bill, the Economic Opportunity Act, which included the beginnings of the Head Start preschool program and the Job Corps' public-service jobs and job training for adults as well as the short-lived Neighborhood Youth Corps, which included programs both to keep students in school while working part-time as well as programs for those who had dropped out. A year later, Johnson signed both the Higher Education Act and the Elementary and Secondary Education Act, which together represented the single greatest year of expansion in federal aid to education—to college students in the Higher Education Act and to states and local schools in the Elementary and Secondary Education Act. In all of these cases, Johnson touted the power of education to transform individuals and a society, with the explicit aim of eliminating poverty.

Transforming society was also a goal in Johnson's signing of the Civil Rights Act of 1964 and the Voting Rights Act of 1965. Two provisions of the Civil Rights Act touched on education. Title VI prohibited the use of federal funds for programs that discriminated based on race, and although its enforcement was slow and inconsistent, the threat of a federal-aid cutoff helped move Southern schools to desegregate schools in more than token amounts in the late 1960s (Patterson, 2001). The other provision of the Civil Rights Act to shape debate over schools was a mandate in Title IV for a study "concerning the lack of availability of equal educational opportunity by reason of race, color, religion, or national origin in public educational institutions at all levels" (Civil Rights Act, 1964). Coordinated by sociologist James Coleman and published 2 years later, *Equality of Educational Opportunity* became a landmark study for its claim that the most powerful influence on student outcomes were families and peers in the classroom—and thus, the demographic composition of schools (Coleman, 1966). At the same time, the Supreme Court was finally following through on the promise of *Brown* a decade later by declaring invalid a set of bureaucratic tools that schools had used to resist desegregation (Patterson, 2001). *Brown* represented more than a promise of desegregation, however, as others sought to use it as both a moral and legal precedent for other battles over school equality, whether fighting unequal education based on gender, disability, or wealth. Schools became both a target of efforts to eliminate desegregation and a lever with which many hoped to eliminate discrimination in society more broadly. From the mid-1960s through the 1970s and beyond, many argued that schools should help fight a war on prejudice.

By the mid-1980s, though, the national debate had shifted from a war on domestic social ills to economic battles in the world economy. Several decades of Keynesian economic policies supported by both parties, access to inexpensive oil, solid growth, and public support of a growing suburban infrastructure were ending just as the peak of the Baby Boom reached adulthood in the 1970s. After several recessions and energy crises, a decade of stagnation in real wages, and double-digit inflation, adults in the United States began seeing the national economy as under threat. That political environment welcomed the *A Nation at Risk* report by the National Commission on Educational in Excellence (1983), which blamed the country's economic woes on allegedly declining schools, "a rising tide of mediocrity." *A Nation at Risk* blamed schools for economic woes in the midst of a broad trend toward deindustrialization that we now call economic globalization (Harrison & Bluestone, 1988; National Commission on Excellence in Education, 1983). Despite some serious flaws with the argument that education is entirely responsible for economic productivity—corporation decisions and government economic policies might be related to it!—the economic argument dominated education policy debate in the 1980s (see Berliner & Biddle, 1995).

EXPECTATIONS OF SCHOOLS AND SCHOOL POLITICS

The economic justification for school reform is still the dominant rhetoric in education debates, more than two decades after the publication of *A Nation at Risk*. The power of the rhetoric reflects the earlier transformation in the expectations of schools that vocational education provoked, the creation of a national debate over education, and the political flexibility of economic rhetoric. As explained earlier in this chapter, *A Nation at Risk* was not the first argument that schooling is connected to the economy. Proponents of vocational education had made that argument decades earlier, and it remained available well after the early twentieth century. *A Nation at Risk* echoed that earlier rhetoric rather than creating an entirely new argument.

While treading the same ground as vocational-education rhetoric, the new economic-purpose rhetoric also walked on ground that was at a different level, in national politics. Despite the national orientation of the rhetoric of Thomas Jefferson, Benjamin Rush, Noah Webster, and others, the most important education decisions were still taken at the local or state level for the nineteenth century and much of the twentieth. (See chapter 1 for a longer discussion of local control and its meaning.) The growth in state-level funding after World War II provoked more focus at the state level (Resnick, 1980), leading to a spate of politicians in the 1980s claiming to be an "education governor" and significant activities by the bipartisan National Governors Association motivated by economic concerns (Vinovskis, 1999). As Spring (1989) notes, national policy affected education in a fundamental way after World War II. From draft deferments to desegregation, the federal government was deeply involved in local educational matters in a way that was unprecedented. The rhetoric of educational politics also became firmly nationalized. National politicians talked about various crises in schooling and youth, from classroom space to crime comics, from desegregation to dropouts. Even those who came into office promising to dismantle the federal Department of Education were drawn into supporting greater federal involvement by *A Nation at Risk*, issued in President Ronald Reagan's first term by the commission his Secretary of Education appointed in 1981 (Bell, 1988). George H. W. Bush was the first major presidential candidate to promise to be an "education president" (George Bush for President, 1988), and both Bill Clinton and George W. Bush followed suit. Improving economic productivity was the most widely-discussed purpose of schooling while debate became irrevocably nationalized, and that combination helped support the continuing prominence of an economic rationale for reform.

Finally, the economic rationale is politically flexible. Both Democrats and Republicans have claimed to support school reform for economic purposes. In his campaigns and during his presidency, Bill Clinton repeatedly talked about education as critical "investments in our future" (Smith & Scoll, 1995) as in his first State of the Union address:

> Perhaps the most fundamental change the new direction I propose offers is its focus on the future and its investment which I seek in our children.... We have to ask more in our schools of our students, our teachers, our principals, our parents. Yes, we must give them the resources they need to meet high standards, but we must also use the authority and the influence and the funding of the Education Department to promote strategies that really work in learning. Money alone is not enough. We have to do what really works to increase learning in our schools. (Clinton, 1993, ¶¶ 29, 31)

His successor, President George W. Bush, also used the economic rhetoric in his first State of the Union address:

The quality of our public schools directly affects us all as parents, as students, and as citizens. Yet too many children in America are segregated by low expectations, illiteracy, and self-doubt. In a constantly changing world that is demanding increasingly complex skills from its workforce, children are literally being left behind. (Bush, 2001, p. ii)

The last four presidents have linked schooling to the economy and school reform to that economic purpose. The rhetorical uses of the economy in education politics fits into a national history and a more recent national debate that has consistently added to the list of what schools are responsible for.

The scope of schools' responsibilities has consistently increased in our history in part because the experience of the people has become increasingly centered around schooling. One hundred years ago, formal schooling was one of many ways that a child spent time. Far more 17-year-olds worked than studied in high schools. Even for younger children, attendance was sparse compared to the present. (That some children are regularly truant in today's schools is an exception that proves the rule; a century ago, attendance was less regular for most students.) Today, by contrast, children's and parents' lives in the United States revolve around the school schedule. Schooling has become an institution that dominates time and consciousness, affecting our assumptions about what is important. One response to such dominating organizations is to target those key institutions for inspection, concern, and responsibility for solving broader problems. Thus, voters are willing to credit politicians with concern about schools, legitimating expectations that no school reform effort could meet.

The scope of schools' responsibilities has also increased because we think of schooling as part of citizenship. As Katznelson and Weir (1985) explain, that link between schooling and citizenship may have been discussed in abstract by Jefferson, but it became a political reality in the first half of the nineteenth century, even if full citizenship was only defined by white male voting rights at the time. While European notions of social citizenship have historically included employment, retirement, and health care, education has historically been the bedrock of the American welfare state (Cohen, 2005; Hochschild & Scovronick, 2003). Public schools have responded to this political linkage by actively defending its legitimacy and authority, whether in expanding vocational education or in fighting Depression-Era federal programs (Krug, 1972). At one point, Cremin (1965) called this popularization of education the "genius" of American education.

And yet there are some clear costs of this political linkage. Some costs are most visible within schools. Cuban (1996) described the public school's tendency to add modules onto an existing structure as the dominant path of incremental change. As Powell, Farrar, and Cohen (1985) noted, this twentieth-century tendency for schools to add curriculum pieces to what already existed led to shopping-mall-like high schools with the educational equivalents of boutique shops but without a clear focus. But there have also been political costs: The political battles over education have led to greater and greater responsibilities for public schools. Cremin (1990) acknowledged the tensions that popular education brought. The political ties between education and citizenship have brought enormous power, including the first break in segregation, but they have also brought unwieldy political obligations for schools. Today, they form a set of expectations that schools can never meet.

FROM EXPECTATIONS OF SCHOOLS TO EXPECTATIONS OF STUDENTS

Thus far, the discussion of expectations has focused on what critics of schooling in the U.S. expected from *schools* in different times. This history puts the economic rationale for school reform in a broader historical context, but it does not explain the argument for testing that is linked to curriculum standards. Within a decade, specific goals followed the crisis-oriented rhetoric of *A Nation at Risk*, but that sequence was not inevitable. For many, that push for standards appears to be part of the same reform flow that started with *A Nation at Risk*. I am not as much a believer in inevitability as other observers. As the last chapter indicates, I am skeptical that the current state of testing provides clear indications of what students know and can do in comparison to any formal curriculum guidelines. There are other reasons to be skeptical of formal curriculum as a set of expectations for students. As Calhoun (1973) and Dreeben (1968) have suggested, focusing on expectations for students can displace responsibility for failure away from schools and the broader society. For the most part, however, jaded observers have not written education policy over the past 20 years. The recent history of curriculum policy has been full of hope that writing clear expectations for how students perform would lead to better tests and better teaching and students' learning more.

Before we look at contemporary curriculum policy and goal-setting, we can look at both the historical and international context for current curriculum and performance goals. Historically, there have been efforts to craft clear performance goals and use them as a lever to change schooling, if not at the scale or breadth we see currently in the United States. In the nineteenth century, common-school reformers such as Henry Barnard hoped that entrance exams to high schools would push grammar schools to improve, even though few students would ever attend high schools (Reese, 1995). Major reports in 1892 and 1918 tried to set national standards for what was important in high school; even if they were not government reports, the reports argued for national expectations (Angus & Mirel, 1999; Herbst, 1996; Krug, 1964; Reese, 1995).[2] The notion of describing what students should be able to do has also existed for decades. Teachers and administrators have been exposed to and expected to know how to craft learning objectives, identifying what students should be able to demonstrate as a result of learning the formal curriculum (e.g., Popham, 1972).[3] The federal government has also been involved in curriculum development, both indirectly through support of certain areas such as the National Vocational Education Act (1917) or directly through sponsorship of science curriculum development via the National Science Foundation in the 1950s (Kliebard, 1987; Rudolph, 2002; Spring, 1989).

As Kliebard (1987) has noted, parents, teachers, school officials, and school critics have often fought for multiple curriculum goals. In the early twentieth century, he identified four dominant themes—social efficiency, social change, developmentalism, and humanism. Kliebard's evidence is from local debates, and recent events suggest that standards at the local and state level would be prone to such conflict. Over the past decade, Ohio's and Kansas's state school boards have each made national news by controversies over the place of evolution in science standards (Blumenthal, 2006; Lafferty, 2005). Former U.S. Assistant Secretary of Education Diane Ravitch (2006b) suggested that national standards would be different:

> If we were to find the right means to develop national standards, either through the federal government (NAEP) or through private organizations like the College Board, I can promise you that the debate over evolution would disappear.... These are issues that arise as the district is local or even on a state level, but never on a national level. The very act of making the discussion national will elevate it. (¶ 44)

Like other advocates of a national curriculum framework, Ravitch argues that there could be a consensus about at least some core expectations. But political conflicts over the history and English standards in the mid-1990s suggests otherwise (e.g., Nash, Crabtree, & Dunn, 1997). There is a history of formal curriculum standards, and that history is a record of conflict.

A careful look at international curriculum frameworks also reveals that some of the central assumptions of standards advocates are misplaced. At a forum on measures of child well-being, Ravitch said, "most of the other nations have a national curriculum and we don't" (Brookings Institution, 2006, p. 52). Like other advocates of national curriculum standards, Ravitch (2006a) identifies some individual countries by name when looking for models for a national curriculum: England, France, and Japan. One could expand the list: New Zealand, Ireland, Korea, the Netherlands, Singapore, Sweden, South Africa, and the former Soviet Union all have or had centralized curriculum control. But not all industrialized countries have a national curriculum framework: Spain and Hungary have a common core, but regions have the authority to adjust the core curriculum or add to it. Italy's and Argentina's curriculum planning has become *less* centralized in the past decade. Australia, Canada, Germany, and Switzerland have federal systems, like that in the United States, where there is no central curriculum authority (Chisholm, 2005; Gvirtz & Beech, 2004; Jansen, 1999; O'Donnell, 2001). Even among countries with a centralized curriculum, the focus varies widely (Holmes & McLean, 1992). The United States is not out of step with the world, because there is no international consensus on the appropriate control of curriculum and expectations (or standards), let alone the content.

THE NATIONAL GOALS

The preceding section has but the barest sketch of historical and comparative perspectives, but they are important to understanding the development of official national goals for education in the late 1980s and 1990s. The creation of goals was new as a political process, if not particularly unusual in its elements. Even considered politically, it was not the first effort to create education goals at the national level (Vinovskis, 1999). On the other hand, it continued the political discussion of education at the national level and provided a vehicle for the translation of state-level accountability policies into a national policy in 2002.

The 1989 Education Summit and the National Education Goals

In the late 1980s and 1990s, both the first President Bush and President Bill Clinton and also the nation's governors turned an earlier, vague national rhetoric of education reform into a set of outcome-oriented goals. At a 1989 summit of President Bush and the governors in Charlottesville, Virginia, the participants committed themselves to agreeing on a short list of goals for the nation's schools, which became a set of six and later eight goals for education (Executive Office of the President, 1990; National Education Goals Panel, n.d.):

1. By the year 2000, all children will start school ready to learn.
2. By the year 2000, the high school graduation rate will increase to at least 90%.
3. By the year 2000, all students will leave Grades 4, 8, and 12 having demonstrated competency over challenging subject matter including English, mathematics, science, foreign languages, civics and government, economics, arts, history, and geography, and every school in America will ensure that all students learn to use their minds well, so they may be prepared for responsible citizenship, further learning, and productive employment in our Nation's modern economy.
4. By the year 2000, the Nation's teaching force will have access to programs for the continued improvement of their professional skills and the opportunity to acquire the knowledge and skills needed to instruct and prepare all American students for the next century.
5. By the year 2000, United States students will be the first in the world in mathematics and science achievement.
6. By the year 2000, every adult American will be literate and will possess the knowledge and skills necessary to compete in a global economy and exercise the rights and responsibilities of citizenship.
7. By the year 2000, every school in the United States will be free of drugs, violence and the unauthorized presence of firearms and alcohol and will offer a disciplined environment conducive to learning.
8. By the year 2000, every school will promote partnerships that will increase parental involvement and participation in promoting the social, emotional, and academic growth of children.

The 1989 summit came from the administrative and political needs of both the governors and the first President Bush. As explained earlier, almost all governors had become "education governors" in the 1980s, and they wanted their commitments and state needs acknowledged. At the same time, the first President Bush was elected with a solid majority of popular votes but faced a solidly Democratic majority in both houses of Congress. An education-oriented summit with governors could thus bypass the president's political opponents in Congress. Over the winter of 1988 and the first part of 1989, Bush's staff negotiated with the National Governors Association over the existence, structure, and outcomes of the summit. The cochairs of a key National Governors Association meeting in mid-September 1989, Republican South Carolina Governor Carroll

Campbell and Democratic Arkansas Governor Bill Clinton were both from the South, and the Southern Regional Education Board had just issued a set of goals for Southern education in 1988 (Edmonds, 2000). As Vinovskis (1999) documents, there were several possible directions for the end result of the summit that key White House staff members and the states discussed, including a focus on existing federal programs. In the end, the governors convinced White House staff members to have a list of national goals that were not tied to federal programs or legislation. The result was a list of goals very similar to the Southern Regional Education Board goals in format and language. The national education goals that followed the 1989 education summit certainly refocused media attention and political discussion on education, and it had three significant legacies: promoting a new "standards movement," creating a rhetorical and political basis for federal accountability legislation, and not being met.

Intended and Unintended Consequence of National Goals

What was new in the late 1980s and early 1990s were two ideas that were more political than educational, more effectively promoted than they were innovative. One idea *not* tied to the national education goals was the argument that if tests included more complex tasks than regurgitation on multiple-choice tests, then tests could be a legitimate target of instruction (e.g., Resnick & Resnick, 1992). Today, we talk about this concept as aligning tests with standards—in the language of curriculum, to make equal all different levels of curriculum from formal to tested and experienced (Goodlad, Klein, & Tye, 1979)—but the core argument in the early 1990s was the conceptual complexity of tests, a set of implicit standards that a test required from students. As is common with education jargon, the term *standards movement* overestimates the conceptual contributions of discussions about standards in the 1980s and 1990s.[4]

The second standards idea was that curriculum expectations should exist at the state level, politically supported and serving as the base for accountability. The development of such standards operated at multiple levels of government, was incomplete, and had mixed results. The first Bush administration supported the creation of voluntary standards through contracts such as the national history standards supported by the National Endowment for the Humanities, then headed by Lynne Cheney. But the national standards projects were controversial (Harnischfeger, 1995). In the mid-1990s, the history standards project collapsed as a model for state curricula when Lynne Cheney publicly attacked the standards, distorting the document that the National Center for History in the Schools produced (Council for Basic Education, 1996; Nash, Crabtree, & Dunn, 1997).[5] The standards written by national groups were entirely voluntary, and many states ignored the documents sponsored by the federal government. But standards creation also existed at the state level; most states claimed to be developing curriculum standards in the early 1990s (Pechman & LaGuarda, 1993). The quality of these early standards documents were inconsistent. Sometimes these state-level standards included checklists of compartmentalized factoids, such as Virginia's Standards of Learning in history, where among other expectations for fourth graders, the state insisted that

> The student will trace the history of Virginia in the 20th century, with emphasis on ... the accomplishments of prominent Virginians, including Woodrow Wilson, Harry F. Byrd, Sr., L. Douglas Wilder, and Arthur Ashe. (Virginia Board of Education, 1995, p. 13)

The standards document does have considerable language about larger historical concepts, but also odd requirements such as the one above. One might suppose that the board was balancing the historical racism of Wilson and Byrd with the fame of contemporary African American Virginians (and the Virginia standards became criticized for ethnocentrism, as Douglass, 2000, explains). More fundamentally, the almost absurd level of detail sprinkled in the standards illustrates that the standards comprised a laundry list rather than a clear set of priorities for teaching. Other sets of standards were conceptual in nature, if sometimes vague, such as Florida's Sunshine State Standards (Florida Department of Education, n.d.b; also see American Federation of Teachers, 1996, 2000). But they existed, which they had never before as a putatively coherent curriculum across all subject areas.

The legacy of a foundation for federal laws was not what the governors attending the 1989 summit intended. The governors were very clear in the presummit discussions that the goals were national, not federal—a set of objectives that primarily states would be responding to, not an agenda for federal legislation or control of schools (Vinovskis, 1999). Yet the summit and the goals became the foundation of President Clinton's first-term education initiative, Goals 2000, which in turn preceded the No Child Left Behind Act. (The No Child Left Behind was a reauthorization, or legislative renewal, of another major presidential education initiative, the Elementary and Secondary Education Act of 1965.)

The third legacy is one of unmet goals. "By the year 2000," each of the eight goals asserted, the nation would have kindergartners ready to learn, 90% graduation, "first in the world" achievement in science and math, a literate adult population, safe and drug-free schools, superb professional development for teachers, and committed parental involvement in schools. Overall, of the 28 key indicators chosen by the National Education Goals Panel, 16 showed either no improvement or declines by 2000. The most concrete goal, 90% graduation, was within striking distance in 1990 but eluded the country's collective grasp: 86% of 18-24 year olds had high school diplomas or alternative credentials in 1990, while 85% had credentials in 1998 (National Education Goals Panel, 1999). But the general conclusion of the 1999 report of the National Education Goals Panel entirely eschewed outcomes:

> We believe that the National Education Goals have moved America forward and, on balance, encouraged greater progress in education. We are clearer about what appropriate Goals are and how to measure progress toward them at the national and state levels. There is no doubt that the National Education Goals have encouraged a broad spectrum of educators, parents, students, business and community leaders, policymakers, and the public to work toward their attainment. Reporting progress toward the Goals has provided valuable information to states and inspired them to reach higher. Can we do better? Of course we can. But we are convinced that our gains have been greater because we have had National Education Goals to guide our efforts. Ten years of progress have shown us that the Goals are working. (p .6)

The singular discussion of process above seems to contradict the whole notion of evaluating policy using concrete outcomes. One should keep in mind the fact that the deadline itself was primarily an instrument of political rhetoric, in the eyes of its creators a useful goad for change. The focus on process in the report is a pedestrian rather than a weighty irony, in this instance. Still, the deadline reflects what the rest of the world often sees as prototypically optimistic boasting of the United States. Such optimism has some side effects, as Potter (1954) described almost half a century ago: a penchant for hype and disappointment.

The failure to meet the national education goals was the result of a common dynamic in school reform. The problem with the national education goals was not that they set virtually unreachable goals—one could conceive of them as "stretch" goals intended to motivate—but that they were one of a long line of impossible expectations for schools, here translated into specific outcomes. To the extent that we keep expecting schools to solve all our social problems, we are overestimating their power. Certainly no one could argue with "world-class" achievement for any child. But are there any world-class standards for family subsistence? The rhetoric of school reform is not merely a shadow-game. It has political power because it resonates at some level with parents' and other citizens' experiences. Parents may not know much about the debates over globalization, but most want their children to be able to get and keep jobs as adults, and they may well perceive the quality of an education or at least an educational credential as important to that goal. Some of those parents and their neighbors purchased their homes in part on the reputation of local schools. In addition, parents do not have the luxury of waiting five to ten years for deeper school reform to help their children. In the life of a child and family, a year is a very long time.

Rhetorically Clear, Obscure in Operation

The national education goals are perhaps the paradigmatic example of educational goals that appear straightforward at first glance but are hard to gauge. What does it mean for a 5-year-old child to be "ready to learn" (goal 1)? What is "competency over challenging subject matter" (goal 3)? A simple term such as "literacy" (goal 6) is highly contingent on context; historically, *literacy* is a flexible concept (e.g., Graff, 1979). Even the single goal that was quantified as 90% graduation implies that there was an agreed-upon definition of a graduation rate in 1989. There was no such consensus at the time, and there still is not (see Hauser, 1997, for some of the conceptual and empirical issues involved). Yet the goals statements served a clear political and rhetorical purpose—to focus on outcomes, even if they were not clearly measurable. In that, the goals succeeded wildly. By that standard, No Child Left Behind's two goals of having 100% of children be deemed proficient in math and reading (and eventually science) by 2014 and 100% of all teachers be "highly qualified" by 2006 are similarly clear in rhetoric if difficult to pin down concretely. How to define proficiency is left to the states, as is teacher qualifications. The process of defining those quantities is inevitably political.

POLITICALLY ACCEPTABLE LIMITS TO FAILURE

The definitions of academic proficiency and teacher qualifications are inherently political because someone will fail. How many and who fail have political consequences. This section explores three examples of such resistance. In one case described here, Arizona, political pressures built to delay a graduation test after parents discovered that the majority of students in the first cohort facing the exams would fail. When the consequences are tangible, some level of failure creates political resistance. In some cases, however, failure does not provide political pressure that changes policies. Even though both student graduation and teacher competency exams have different passing rates by race and ethnicity, this differential impact has in general not caused enough political turmoil to force withdrawal of test requirements, though disparate impact *has* led to lawsuits. In contrast to the potential for political backlash from gradua-tion and teacher competency exams, the various labeling practices of the National Assessment of Education Progress (NAEP) has not led to politi-cal backlash, though the proportion who has met the Proficiency thresh-old (or not) has frequently been used in education debates (most recently, to argue that the states' definitions of proficiency for the No Child Left Behind Act are generally low and self-serving). Because the definition of Proficiency for the NAEP has no real consequences for any state, the only ones who consistently object to their use are writers such as Bracey (2002), who has pointed out the flaws in the setting of the NAEP score thresholds for Basic, Proficiency, and Expertise. The threshold labels may have no basis in research, and they may be used to powerful effect rhetorically, but no one loses jobs or educational opportunities because of them. The tech-nical problems with NAEP threshold levels have not become a political problem because they do not currently have tangible consequences. What is a politically acceptable limit to failure will depend on the circumstances and context, but in general, the more concrete the consequence and the less insulated a policymaking body is, the lower the threshold for political problems from failure (see Ellwein & Glass, 1991; Ellwein, Glass, & Smith, 1988).

Arizona's Graduation Exams

In November 2000, the Arizona Department of Education backed off its stated policy to require passage of state tests before high school stu-dents could graduate (Kossan, 2000b). *Why* it did so is a classic case of politically unacceptable failure. Four years before, the state legislature had created the Arizona Instrument to Measure Standards (AIMS) and had given the state Board of Education the authority to withhold diplo-mas if students did not pass the tests. As in many other states, Arizona's Department of Education created a set of state standards and developed a test that consisted partly of questions from an established commercial test (the TerraNova) and partly of tests developed specifically for the state standards. The first administration of the AIMS test was in 1999, with the 2001 class the first cohort which needed to pass the test to graduate (*Espinoza v. Arizona Board of Education*, 2006). As reporters observed, the quick timeframe was guaranteed to cause problems (Kossan, 2000a). Not only were students from minority ethnic and racial groups more likely to fail the tests, but the general failure rate was extraordinarily high (Flan-nery, 2000; Kossan & González, 2000). In 2000, 87% of all Arizona 11th-grade students failed the math standards (Arizona Department of Education, 2002). Views of the public were very clear: The clear majority of those participating in public forums wanted the tests delayed (Koehler, 2001; Kossan & Flannery, 2001), and the state eventually delayed the graduation requirement until the 2006 graduating cohort (*Espinoza v. Arizona Board of Education*, 2006). In the intervening years, the state's curriculum standards changed, as did the test, and passing scores rose. Some interpreted the changes as a weakening of standards (e.g., Murray, 2005), but the alternative was not politically sustainable. In no state could a graduation requirement survive with any significant fraction being threatened with a withheld diploma, let alone 87% (also see Ellwein & Glass, 1989). In contrast to the general failure threatened in 2000, which included wealthy, disproportionately white suburbs such as Scottsdale, the disparate impact of graduation rates by race and ethnicity has led to only limited backlash, insufficient to stop the testing. Nationally, the disproportionate impact of graduation tests on students from racial and ethnic minorities led to lawsuits in Florida and in Texas, but courts decided that both states met legal requirements that the test have a valid purpose, be tied to the curriculum, and provide multiple opportunities for students to pass (*Debra P. v. Turlington*, 1983, 1984; *GI Forum v. Texas Education Agency*, 2000).

Teacher Proficiency Exams

In the late 1970s and early 1980s, the majority of states created requirements that those wanting to be teachers must pass exams before professional licensure (Haney, Madaus, & Kreitzer, 1987). The same general outcomes as graduation exit exams are also visible in teacher exams—high general passing rates, but with differences among racial and ethnic groups (Board on Testing and Assessment, 2000; Mitchell, Robinson, Plake, & Knowles, 2001). Many of the political dynamics in student graduation exams exist for teacher licensure tests, but with different key actors. In states with persistent teacher shortages, a high failure rate would cause serious administrative problems for local districts which needed teachers for every classroom. In those states, every failure meant that the district would be placing a temporarily-certified or substitute teacher in a classroom. There is no parallel requirement for there to be lawyers in front of every potential client, and state bar passing rates are generally lower than the teacher exam passing rates (Haney et al., 1987). As with student graduation exams, the differences in passing rates by race and ethnicity on teacher exams have also prompted lawsuits and concerns by administrators that such differences would make a diverse teaching force more difficult (Board on Testing and Assessment, 2000; Haney et al., 1987; Mitchell et al., 2001). A lawsuit is not the same as the political backlash such as that seen in Arizona in 2000 and 2001, nor the same organizational needs that create pressures for high *general* passing rates.[6]

Adequate Yearly Progress Standards and the Bush Brothers

In 2006, Florida Governor Jeb Bush criticized the federal Department of Education for the irrationality of standards in the No Child Left Behind Act. That summer, the state labeled more than 70% of public schools as A or B schools. By the guidelines the state had created in response to the federal No Child Left Behind Act, however, more than 70% of the schools were *also* labeled as not meeting the Adequate Yearly Progress (AYP) standards. When interviewed, Governor Bush said, "With all due respect to the federal system, our accountability system is really the better way to go" (Dillon, 2006, p. 1). Governor Bush's criticism made national news because the target was the federal government headed by his brother, but Florida is also the more extreme version of what most states face. Linn (2005) showed that the extent of the discrepancy between the Florida state labels and the AYP labels was unusual but that all states face similar discrepancies in judgment. Because the federal government set a goal of 100% proficiency by 2014 and requires that schools show progress toward 100% proficiency every year, no matter how a state defines proficiency, at some point almost every school would be judged as not meeting the AYP standard. Thus, given current law, in some year there will be a difference between the federal judgment that there is insufficient progress, on the one hand, and whatever label a separate state accountability system might generate.

Notably, Florida Governor Bush did *not* criticize the construction of the proficiency label by the National Assessment of Education Progress, even though the contrast between state and federal pictures of statewide student proficiency was just as severe using 2005 test achievement (see Table 4.1). The discrepancy between the state's labeling of individual schools based on the Florida accountability system and the federal accountability guidelines provoked the governor's criticism of AYP because they generated more publicity and because they had concrete consequences for school systems. In contrast to the NAEP results which state officials did not actively respond to, the state announced the Florida school labels and the AYP labels simultaneously. Those labels were attached to individual students, not the whole state population, and local reporters could easily identify individual schools that were given an A label by the state but a failure by the federal guidelines. In addition to the publicity that the school-level labels generated, the failure to meet AYP has concrete consequences. The No Child Left Behind Act requires that schools that do not meet AYP offer tutoring, let students transfer, and go through restructuring. The combination of publicity and concrete consequences turned the Florida AYP ratings into politically unacceptable failure and led Florida Governor Bush to criticize the mechanism in his brother's main education reform policy.

INCREMENTALISM'S PROMISE AND LIMITS

Given the political nature of setting goals—goals which often appear concrete but are difficult to judge in practice—one might ask whether alternatives might satisfy the political demands for accountability and yet have some research that supports their use. Glass (1978) suggested incremental improvements as an alternative to setting thresholds for graduation exams and other high-stakes purposes. Linn (2005) advocated incremental standards for student achievement when measured at the school level: annual improvements of 3% per year in the proportion of students meeting the median score during a benchmark year. Those are reasonable goals if the only purpose of accountability is to ensure that the next generation is smarter and maybe even wiser than the current crop of adults. However, the political pressures for accountability are not just about generational change. They are also about inequality, and the incremental standards commonly proposed do not address the achievement gap. Even though the goals established after the 1989 education summit and the goals in No Child Left Behind are equally vague in operation, they have more rhetorical weight. Moreover, incremental improvement does not help us understand what students are learning. The abstract concept of incremental improvements in achievement maintains distance between evidence of student achievement and our more mundane concepts of what we want students to be able to do.

**Table 4.1. Percentages of Students With
Achievement Labeled Proficient by Florida and
National Assessment of Education Progress (NAEP), 2005 Testing**

	Fourth Graders		*Eighth Graders*	
Subject	*State*	*NAEP*	*State*	*NAEP*
Math	64%	37%	60%	26%
Reading	71%	30%	44%	25%

Sources: Florida Department of Education (n.d.a), The Nation's Report Card (2006).

We can shift from incrementalism in broader accountability judgments to the individual mechanics of instructional decision making. From special education research comes an incremental approach that *does* address the achievement gap: the use of frequent formative assessment to guide instruction during a year. A substantial body of evidence suggests that when teachers respond to evidence of whether children's performance is improving by a reasonable amount by trying something new when a child does not improve, children with low achievement can close a large portion of the achievement gap within a classroom (Deno, 1985, 2003; Fuchs, 2004). The approach first used with students with disabilities in academic areas such as students labeled with specific learning disabilities is local, does not use tests for individual high-stakes purposes, has the strongest research support for formative measures are based on the broad curriculum rather than narrow sets of skills, and has rigorous research supporting its use. This research echoes research on formative uses of classroom assessment more broadly (Black & Wiliam, 1998).

One could design an accountability system based entirely on formative evaluation. A state could require that teachers collective formative data weekly (or twice a week for children who need extra monitoring) and make monthly instructional decisions based on the information. Teachers could be evaluated on their use of formative assessment—did they make instructional decisions based on the information, and did they follow through on the decisions? Such evaluation would be formative. In turn, administrators could be evaluated on their use of formative evaluation of teachers, who are supposed to be formatively evaluating student achievement. Any high-stakes decisions about teachers and administrators could be the endpoint of cumulative formative evaluation, based on whether the educator responded to the feedback her or his supervisor gave. Since the root of such a system would be based on solid research, there is at least some reason to believe it would have a greater effect on student achievement than the current systems of accountability.

Such a system would change the professional responsibilities of educators, shifting the emphasis away from knowing content and how to teach it and toward instructional adjustments based on assessment. This shift in professional responsibilities would encounter both political and organization resistance. Politically, defenders of high-stakes testing might well attack formative evaluation as lowering standards and without teeth. When compared to public education debates, formative evaluation does not set the type of goals that appear to raise expectations. Formative evaluation does not necessarily satisfy the political demands that push accountability.

Even if we could assume that formative evaluation would be acceptable politically, there are still organizational barriers to making the uses of formative evaluation a professional standard. According to researchers and teachers, teachers perceive that frequent assessment for formative purposes is a greater paperwork burden, and they would need greater assistance with the logistics of frequent assessment (e.g., Hasbrouck, Woldbeck, Ihnot, & Parker, 1999). Such concerns may mask a more fundamental basis for resistance: The culture of schools and the school year are at odds with formative evaluation. Teachers plan lessons and years by discrete units of time—a 2-week unit on addition with regrouping, a month on *Romeo and Juliet,* and so forth. The school year unfolds as a sequence of activities. Formative evaluation is a different way to organize a year, planning around instructional decisions instead of discrete chunks of time. At best, responses to formative evaluation would be a layer on top of existing curriculum. I have seen such an arrangement, and one that worked fairly well according to the teachers involved—but that success required university-based technical assistance and follow-up.

In addition, the past history of high-stakes testing creates two additional barriers to the effective use of formative evaluation. Those barriers come from those opposed to most standardized testing and also from educators who think they have accommodated testing appropriately. As described in chapter 2, thousands of parents and teachers possess lingering suspicions that any test with a quantifiable score threatens the integrity of education. In one recent attack on one type of kindergarten formative assessment, Goodman (2005) wrote that Dynamic Indicators of Basic Literacy Skills (DIBELS) "is a package of sub-tests designed to be administered in one minute each. Its basic premise is that it can reduce reading development to a series of tasks, each measurable in one minute" (p. 26). Regardless of the qualities of formative assessment, it would be subject to such skepticism.

Moreover, those who think they are accommodating high-stakes testing by teaching to the test and using test scores for crucial decisions about student opportunities and teachers would and can undermine formative evaluation. Goodman (2006) reports anecdotal evidence of teaching to the compartmentalized subtests of DIBELS and students' being retained based on DIBELS scores (both of which are actions of which DIBELS designers would disapprove). One state technical assistance center warns principals not to use DIBELS scores for retaining students or evaluating teachers (Florida Center for Reading Research, 2005). Some educators have socialized themselves too well and see every test as high-stakes and every test as something to be taught to. Formative evaluation can only work if students work hard on tests that have relatively low stakes. But test preparation is an endemic feature of schooling today. By itself, formative evaluation is unlikely to be a feasible replacement for high-stakes testing.

A BETTER FRAMEWORK

Deciding What is Important

We know that accountability has deep political roots, often for good reasons, but historians and other observers also know that our society has a hard time making distinctions between reasonable and unreasonable expectations of schools and students. Grandiose claims about "world-class standards" to the contrary, we need to be careful in crafting expectations that are both feasible and also satisfy the legitimate needs of accountability. We can begin with reasonable expectations of schools. Schools are not responsible for saving society in a broad sense, though their graduates can often use what they have learned to improve society when they are adults. But saving society is too broad a mission for any institution, and it gives the rest of society a free pass for too many issues. An economic recession? The schools are to blame! Poverty? Education can solve it! Crime and immorality? Teach character education! A failure of adults to appreciate history? Mesopotamian civilization in the first grade! Too many traffic accidents? Driver's education! Sometimes I wonder if schools will soon be commanded to solve the Crisis of Split-Ends with mandatory cosmetology classes.

I tend to come down on the side of schools' being responsible first for core academic skills and subjects. I am well aware of my biases: I attended school for 21 straight years, focusing as I advanced on academics and one of the most traditional subjects (history). I am well aware of the value of interdisciplinary studies, and in my mind, the term *core academic subjects* should be flexible in its boundaries. For example, history classes should address important questions that come from sociology, anthropology, and geography, among other fields. But there is an important reason for focusing on academics and not worrying at the moment about disciplinary boundaries and what counts as "core academics": In our society today, no institution other than schools is primarily responsible for students' learning academics. Those skills and that set of knowledge are important to being a responsible adult in almost any sense of the word. One need not ask schools to teach conformity to recognize the value of reading, of being able to judge the effects of a proposed zoning change or transportation policy, of understanding and evaluating fiscal and monetary policy, and of telling whether every proposal that comes down the pike is truly new or an echo from the past. Academics form the reasonable center of school expectations, at least for the foreseeable future.

Core academics do not constitute all of a school's roles and should not foreclose a broad education, as long as that broader education does not expect schools to solve all of society's ills and as long as that broader education does not interfere with academics. Significant non-academic activities in schools directly support academics—for example, addressing behavior problems, making sure students and especially young children have some physical activity during the school day, and student counseling. Others activities including art and music should be considered part of academics or a broader education. For a very small fraction of students with disabilities, an alternative curriculum is also necessary, with a more functional definition of academics. None of these facts should eliminate the centrality of academics to what we expect of schools.

If deciding on the focus on schools is contentious, so too the question of what reasonable expectations within academics would be. Part of the problem with setting expectations is the rhetorical nature of standard-setting today. Frequently, they are vapid, an itemized laundry list, or simply grandiose. The underlying political problem with standard setting is that for more than 20 years, we have operated as if schools are in crisis, our history of test-based accountability has marginalized other ways of thinking about schools, and the drafting of standards has proceeded as if there were a single crisis to be addressed by standards and a single approach to accountability. Our educational history has trapped us in assuming there must be one problem and one solution.

Stepping out of the Trap

In reality, there are three challenges facing public schooling in the United States, once we restrict schools' primary responsibility to academic matters. One challenge is to make sure that the next generation is smarter and wiser than we adults are. A second challenge is make sure that schools provide equal educational opportunities, including access to the best academic materials. The third challenge is to address true crises in education—the child who is struggling, the teacher who cannot keep a classroom orderly, a school that has lost its focus, or a local system that fails to support and expect much from its schools. While some aspects of these challenges overlap, they require fundamentally different approaches to accountability. The generational challenge requires that we expect today's children learn more than we did. The generational challenge requires accountability to keep a focus on what children should learn and how we can best teach *most* children. The equity challenge requires that we interrupt institutional structures and cultures that perpetuate low expectations and unequal access to educational opportunities. The equity challenge requires accountability to check insular institutions and cultures.

These first two challenges are clearly tied to the historically optimistic culture of the United States (Potter, 1954) and to the roots of education as a right of citizenship (Katznelson & Weir, 1985). Our society is fundamentally optimistic, and expecting that our children would know more than we would, would attain higher degrees than we did, fits in with our hopes that our children's lives will be better than ours. This hope does not make long-term improvement easy. As Hofstadter (1963) and Sizer (1992) have noted, there are deep anti-intellectual roots in our history and culture. We may be optimistic, but we may not connect our hope to the academic mission of schools. This society-wide inconsistency requires some hard choices about whether football is more important than physics, whether working a fast-food joint at night is more important than homework, whether we truly want to focus on academics. Political rhetoric about *world-class standards* does not eliminate our cultural inconsistency. Only hard talk about trade-offs will.

If we are optimistic as a society, we also hew to an ethic of equality, at least in theory. *Brown* and other post-World War II court decisions settled the fundamental question of whether our law would allow brutal second-class citizenship. Fortunately, most citizens now agree that our society should be fundamentally egalitarian. That consensus is most evident in education. Despite all its flaws, the distribution of educational resources is *more* equal than the distribution of income, wealth, health care, and housing. But the consensus in favor of equality is awkward. As discussed at the beginning of this chapter, many middle-class and wealthy parents would *not* accept a complete closing of the achievement gap, even though they want the benefits of schooling to be spread more equally than they are today. Rhetoric about *closing the achievement gap* will not change the tension between belief in equality and belief in protecting and advancing your own children's interests.

Only the last of these challenges deserves the term *crisis* —idiosyncratic crises of the child, classroom, school, and system. We cannot treat the generational challenge as a crisis, because it cannot be solved quickly. We cannot treat the equity challenge as a crisis, because it will take persistence to address inequalities that are deeply rooted in our society and institutions. While true educational crises are deeply related to inequalities, appearing disproportionately in contexts with unequal resources and expectations, we can and should treat them in a special way. True educational crises need to be addressed immediately. Unfortunately, no one has discovered a perfect approach to addressing educational crises. But among the requirements is focus. Labeling *all* schools as in crisis distracts us from the real problems in schools. Among all the discussion of reasonable and unreasonable expectations, the inevitable consequence of No

Child Left Behind is the uniform treatment of all problems as crises, distracting us from what should be a focus on true educational crises.

Setting Important and Reasonable Goals

Once we can identify the problems of education as separate entities, we should also identify different and complementary approaches to setting goals that are feasible and address the legitimate needs for accountability. The generational challenge is probably the easiest to address, and we can do it inductively. Gathering data about what today's students and adults know and can do is regularly done—with the National Assessment of Educational Progress (NAEP) and the National Assessment of Adult Literacy (NAAL)—although in the composite method described and criticized in chapter 3. Gathering data about what student and adult performance in more concrete tasks is no more complicated. We need not have data with the same psychometric properties as NAEP and NAAL scores to have a sense of what today's population is capable of. We should start our discussions of what we can expect from the next generation with that concrete information.

Such a discussion should be open and frank. This discussion should *not* be hidden in some federal agency or quasi-governmental body; they should not take place in the committee meetings of professional disciplinary associations; nor should they be obscured in administrative hearings that are nominally open to the public but generally controlled by a coalition of interest groups. I fully expect an open discussion about our generational challenge to be messy and full of disagreement. This is democracy in action! In truth, we should be having a regular debate over precisely these long-term curriculum issues. Will educators be confused by the multiple perspectives? Most teachers will tell you they are well aware of conflicting signals from the public. At least with an open debate, teachers will be aware of the range of expectations, regardless of what formal curricular structures exist.

The challenge to equality requires a different approach from the general curricular goals. We have a body of law describing the general requirements of equality. What we need is a way of putting a mirror in front of the behavior of school systems and of investigating and publicizing problems. Essentially, making states and local school systems more accountable for equal educational opportunities and for student outcomes requires some independent process to hold administrators and politicians responsible. This responsibility should extend beyond the boundaries of schooling—poverty is responsible for much of the achievement gap—but should not excuse schools from their central responsibilities. Given our country's history of inequality and the distrust many African-American and Latino residents feel toward school systems, that process must extend beyond test scores and must be independent of school systems. An appropriate mechanism would be the use of grand juries to examine the equality of educational opportunity in school systems and states. Grand juries that investigate civic affairs have subpoena authority, can call experts to testify, and are separate from the political structures of schools. Having a regular system of empaneling grand juries to investigate educational opportunities at the regional and state level would provide that independent voice which we need to address systematic educational inequalities.

Finally, our set of expectations should identify which children, classrooms, schools, and local systems are truly in crisis. While the solutions for educational crises are outside the scope of this chapter, a reasonable set of expectations should define what constitutes a crisis and how quickly the next level of supervision must respond. Because any attempt to solve a crisis requires investment of time and resources, such identification must be targeted. It is useless to identify 70% of schools as in crisis, as happened with Florida schools' AYP judgments in 2006. Essentially, we need an educational triage system. Creating such a system requires open discussion of what constitutes a crisis at each level, what evidence is relevant, whether intervention or "watchful waiting" is the default response to evidence (and for how long waiting is appropriate), and the maximum proportion of situations at any level that can be declared in crisis.

Many readers will note at this point that this last section is procedural rather than substantive. I have described *how* we should set general curricular standards, *how* we investigate and publicize inequality, and *how* we should define an educational crisis, but not *what* definitions of standards, inequality, or crisis are appropriate. That vagueness is deliberate. Because the fundamental questions of educational expectations are political, they must be decided politically. For those who are skeptical of educational politics, one lesson from the first chapter and this fourth chapter should be persuasive: Whatever standards exist must be defensible politically. Fundamentally, the political concerns of all adults in our society will determine the standards that teachers and children must meet. Only through an explicitly political process can we craft challenging and reasonable curricular expectations, identify serious inequalities, and decide what is a true educational crisis.

NOTES

1.   It should be no surprise that policymakers (mostly men) assumed that men were going to be the key technicians in the Cold War. The National Man-

power Council (1957) did issue a report, *Womanpower*, which was one of the few documents acknowledging the potential role of women.

2. The fact that the Committee of Ten report advocated an academic curriculum while the *Cardinal Principles of Secondary Education* argued for a largely non-academic curriculum does not eliminate the fact that each set of authors was trying to influence behavior across the country.

3. Such behavioral objectives have often set low expectations, but the formal language and central concept have existed for years.

4. For the flaws in assuming coherence in a "first wave" and "second wave" of post-*A Nation at Risk* reforms, see Center for Policy Research in Education (1989).

5. As the Council for Basic Education report indicated, the standards document was weak in several areas, but not with the ideological bias that Cheney and others claimed.

6. There are spot shortages in specific areas of law, notably with public defender officers (e.g., Amador, 2006; Hibbitts, 2006; Saltzman, 2004). The inconsistency in treatment of teacher exams may lead one to question whether the tensions between qualifications and needing warm bodies in classrooms implies a parallel with public-defender systems.

CHAPTER 5

CONSEQUENTIAL THINKING

The consequences of testing matter as much as the expectations we hold. Having concrete consequences is what makes an accountability have high stakes for educators and schools.[1] In many states—Florida and North Carolina among them (see chapter 3)—the department of education will use test scores to provide either cash rewards or public recognition, hoping that the opportunity to earn some form of distinction will motivate teachers. But policies responding to schools or systems in trouble have been less stable. Over the past decade and more, states have tried different approaches, from pressuring local districts to intervene with schools identified as failing to prepackaged curriculum or having the state department of education assume responsibility for administration of a school or district. At the federal level, the No Child Left Behind Act has a rigid sequence of consequences for schools repeatedly labeled as failing to meet their states' Adequate Yearly Progress (AYP) standards. For schools with concentrated poverty receiving federal funding, the consequences proceed from giving parents the choice to attend other schools that meet AYP to providing tutoring, a range of restructuring options (replacing some staff, mandating a new curriculum, appointing an outside consultant to help manage the school, extending the school day or year, or unspecified internal restructuring), and a range of "major" restructuring options (replacing most staff, turning the school management over to an outside com-

Accountability Frankenstein: Understanding and Taming the Monster, pp. 123–149
Copyright © 2007 by Information Age Publishing
All rights of reproduction in any form reserved.

pany, reopening the school as a public charter school, or unspecified major restructuring).

Under the No Child Left Behind Act, each additional year not meeting the AYP standards triggers a new set of actions. A cascade of cumulative consequences exists when a system labels failure. However, for rewards (such as Florida's and North Carolina's cash awards), state accountability systems typically have annual cycles. This asymmetry is important in understanding the structure of high-stakes accountability. In most high-stakes systems, recognition of a school's achievement is fleeting while the stigma of failure is a persistent threat. While most proponents of high-stakes accountability emphasize the motivation that a reward structure can create, the structure of accountability systems commonly emphasizes the threat tied to failure. This threat can be either tangible with the threat of firing teachers and staff or intangible—the scarlet-letter effect that many researchers identify as the motivating factor in such systems (e.g., Figlio & Rouse, 2006). (The term comes from Nathaniel Hawthorne's nineteenth century novel *The Scarlet Letter*, where Hester Prynne must wear a scarlet "A" on her clothing as punishment for adultery.)

This chapter provides historical and psychological perspectives on the argument that we must motivate teachers and other educators with either performance pay or harsh "no excuses" consequences tied to accountability policies.[2] The first section of the chapter focuses on the fundamental theory of action behind high-stakes consequences. It summarizes the research on the effects of high-stakes accountability, a literature which suggests limited effectiveness of incentives and consequences. It investigates the grand assumption behind high-stakes consequences, the idea that one can calibrate measures of student performance with a system of incentives that improves teacher effectiveness.

The second section uses the history of business and schooling to assess common assumptions about standardization in large organizations. Accountability policies are partly based on the notion that one can borrow a business model of organizational control to apply in schools. That assumption is not accurate if one examines the history of large businesses in the United States. It also assumes that schools have *not* standardized any large part of their operations, and that assumption is also false.

The third section provides historical perspective on the argument that some people are focused on children's interests while others are focused on adults' interests. We can see the conceptual problems with this claim more easily if we look at another period's reformers and *their* attempts to define what children's interests are … and how those claims were intimately tied to their own self-images, if not self-interest. This section describes the history of child-saving rhetoric and the Progressive-Era claim that contemporary reforms would "take the politics out of education." This section also makes distinctions among the different types of interests adults have, from material interests to our identities and how ideas about children and school reform are as much tied to our identities as to material interests. Accountability systems are often attempting to reinforce and use the material-interest perspective of adults even while their defenders warn us about the material interests of teachers. A healthier perspective would acknowledge that adults have multiple interests. The chapter ends with a discussion of complementary systems of motivation and support.

RESULTS AND MOTIVATION

Evidence on the Effects of High-Stakes Accountability

The bottom-line question on high-stakes consequences for many is whether it improves student performance as measured by test scores. There are many ways in which test scores are inadequate to measure all of the effects of a particular type of education policy. However, given the centrality of student achievement to the advocates of high-stakes accountability, the effect on test scores constitute a consistency check—that is, whether the policy in question addresses the concern of greatest relevance to its proponents. There are several difficulties with finding appropriate evidence to answer this question at the local or state level, leading Hamilton and Strecher (2002) to write, "Test-based accountability remains controversial because there is inadequate evidence to make clear judgments about its effectiveness in raising test scores and achieving its other goals" (p. 122).[3]

Consider a school system that raised consequences for teachers and school administrators. Since school systems typically adopt key education policies entirely or not at all, comparing systems with and without high-stakes policies is difficult. Commonly, advocates look at before-and-after comparisons. But such before-and-after comparisons may confuse any changes attributable to high-stakes consequences with general changes in achievement which would have happened in any case. A more appropriate approach is comparative: What happens with achievement in a high-stakes school district when compared to school systems that have not raised stakes? Smith and Mickelson (2000) demonstrated that after Charlotte-Mecklenburg, North Carolina, created test-based consequences for school in the 1990s, improvement in scores on state achievement tests was similar to the improvement in educational achievement in the state as a whole. Charlotte's students improved no more than students in the same period in other major urban areas in the state. Jacob (2005) found evidence of effects from Chicago's high-stakes system established in 1996-97. When only compared to performance on the test used locally for high-stakes purposes, Chicago's third, sixth, and eighth grade student performance looks like it improved dramatically after the establishment of test-based accountability. When compared to other Midwestern cities' student performance on their own tests, standardized within each test and adjusted for trends, Chicago's students also appeared to improve after the establishment of high stakes.

In the case of Jacob's (2005) analysis, an additional difficulty is the choice of measure. The measure that shows the greatest evidence of improvement is the measure that mattered most in the high-stakes test: the Iowa Test of Basic Skills. Since the 1980s, researchers have been aware of a common pattern in test regimes: Test scores rise after tests are put in place (e.g., Cannell, 1989). As Nichols and Berliner (2007) have argued, narrowing the curriculum, test preparation, and other strategic responses to the high-stakes test eliminate the independence and trustworthiness of such tests. For that reason, researchers generally acknowledge that one must avoid evidence gathered from the high-stakes test or check it against independent, lower-stakes tests that cover a broader range of material. When Jacob (2005) compared Chicago's student gains to other Illinois cities on the statewide test whose results were not part of the city's accountability system, Chicago's gains disappear for all students except eighth graders.

This caution is especially important when looking at state test results after the signing of the No Child Left Behind Act. States have shown rising student test scores on state tests, a test which some interpret as evidence of the law's success. But because of the cascade of consequences that follow failure on Adequate Yearly Progress criteria, the state tests cannot be used as an independent check on the policies tied to the same tests. Thus, researchers must look instead at student performance on the low-stakes National Assessment of Education Progress (NAEP), which gathers evidence of student achievement in each state as well as the entire country from a sample of students. When the 2005 NAEP test results were released in October 2005, most observers concluded that the scores showed no evidence of dramatic improvements as a result of No Child Left Behind (e.g., Chaddock, 2005; Romano, 2005a). More sophisticated analysis has not changed that initial impression. Fuller, Gesicki, Kang, and Wright (2006) and Lee (2006) compared trends on state-level NAEP results in the few years before No Child Left Behind with state NAEP trends after the passage of the new law and concluded that there was no general improvement in trends in fourth or eighth grade reading or math scores that could be attributed to NAEP and no decline in any achievement gap, perhaps with the sole exception of the White-Hispanic gap in eighth grade math in one analysis (Lee, 2006). There is scant evidence that No Child Left Behind has changed what its proponents think is measurable and important.

The third difficulty with researching the effectiveness of high-stakes accountability is the fact that carrot-and-stick systems commonly appear in combination with other policies as larger packages. Kentucky's and Texas's accountability systems in the 1980s appeared with substantial changes in school funding policies; should we attribute changes to the accountability systems or better school funding? In Florida, the 1999 accountability reforms signed by former Governor Jeb Bush included an expansion of state testing, the labeling of individual schools with letter grades, public- and private-choice programs tied to the letter-grade labels, monetary rewards for schools based on the letter-grade labels, and a variety of instructional support programs focused on elementary grades. When one looks at the mixed record of Florida school achievement since 1999 (e.g., Chatterji, 2004), can one attribute the fourth-grade gains on NAEP tests to the accountability system, to the instructional supports, or to preexisting policies such as an early-childhood intervention program started in the 1990s?[4]

To avoid the problems with such confounding factors, several researchers in the past decade have looked to state NAEP scores as a source of comparative data (Amrein & Berliner, 2002; Amrein-Beardsley & Berliner, 2003; Braun, 2004; Carnoy & Loeb, 2002; Grissmer, Flanagan, Kawata, & Williamson, 2000; Hanushek & Raymond, 2005, 2006; Klein, Hamilton, McCaffrey, & Stecher, 2000; Marchant, Paulson, & Shunk, 2006; Nichols, Glass, & Berliner, 2006; Rosenshine, 2003). Researchers have hoped to combine judgments of how high the stakes are within a state with NAEP scores as an outcome variable. One methodological problem with this research is the definition of accountability. Is it the publication of test scores, as Hanushek and Raymond (2006) use in one analysis, or does accountability require attaching some consequences to test scores, as they use in another analysis? Should one add accountability for students to the accountability for teachers and administrators? A conceptual definition of accountability becomes much more difficult to use when quantifying it.

A second methodological problem is handling historical changes in accountability systems. In most states, the stakes attached to tests have changed several times in the past 20 years. With current policy, one can look at both policies and perceptions of various stakeholders. But with rapid changes in policies, capturing the past pressures associated with accountability is tricky. In many cases, the written policies may not capture the informal and systematic accountability pressures or evasions that lie beyond the written word. Interviewing policymakers and key educators may not be sufficient to capture those changes because policymakers and administrators change frequently, and when policies and practices may change every few years, the memory of educators may not be accurate in pinning a particular level of pressure to single years. If one can surmount those difficulties, then one must also decide if one should look for immediate improvement or changes after a certain lag.

The most sophisticated published effort to capture state-level accountability changes gave paid raters a combination of written policies and journalistic accounts as a documentary base, and the researchers then combined raters' comparative judgments to place state policies on a comparative scale of accountability pressures (Nichols, Glass, & Berliner, 2006). Another, individual independent rater whose judgments correlated most highly with those combination ratings then was asked to rate changes in accountability policies over time.[5] The analysis of state NAEP results coming from this study show no gains in high-stakes states and years except for some moderate improvements in fourth-grade math. Other analyses overlap with this general result (Amrein & Berliner, 2002; Amrein-Beardsley & Berliner, 2003; Marchant, Paulson, & Shunk, 2006).

Other researchers report positive effects of high-stakes accountability on NAEP math scores (Braun, 2004; Carnoy & Loeb, 2002; Hanushek & Raymond, 2005).[6] Carnoy and Loeb's analysis is sensitive to the measures of accountability pressures; using their own measure, Nichols, Glass, and Berliner (2006) replicated the Carnoy and Loeb analyses and found no statistically-significant relationship between high-stakes testing and NAEP math achievement. Braun's (2004) analysis was in response to Amrein and Berliner (2002) and found in comparative analysis that looking at changes in the same grade level (fourth grade to fourth grade math scores) gave high-stakes states an advantage but looking at changes in test scores for a cohort (fourth graders to eighth graders 4 years later) gave low-stakes states a slight advantage.

Braun's (2004) analysis highlights a third methodological problem—questions about how to handle the NAEP test scores aggregated at the state level. The National Assessment of Educational Progress samples students in each state, and there is no follow-up with individual students from assessment to assessment. Should one look at changes in achievement within a single grade across time, across grades in a single administration, or within cohorts across time? The approach of Marchant et al. (2006) is probably best, looking at single cross-sections, changes in a single grade from assessment to assessment, and quasi-cohort measures from fourth grade to eighth grade 4 years later. The implicit reasoning of multiple approaches is that if multiple "slices" of NAEP lead to similar results, then those different slices provide confirming evidence for a conclusion.

None of those approaches has the advantages of a longitudinal sampling design, but NAEP does not afford that luxury.

Those conclusions are mixed at best for the advocates of high-stakes testing. The only area in which several researchers with different perspectives agree on the general conclusions is in math, where there is evidence of a small positive benefit for high-stakes regimes (e.g., Hanushek & Raymond, 2006; Marchant, Paulson, & Shunk, 2006; Nichols, Glass, & Berliner, 2006). There is no consensus evidence of a benefit in other areas, and the interpretation of the mild effects in math vary, from Hanushek and Raymond's (2002) claim that the evidence clearly supports high-stakes accountability to Nichols et al.'s claim that elementary math shows some evidence of effects because drilling discrete math facts for elementary tests is more likely to show results on tests.

The results may change as researchers begin to use individual-level data that are now available (Dorn, 2006). In addition, there will always be the design and interpretation difficulties with such interstate comparisons. But the evidence gathered thus far provides no clear-cut confirmation that accountability works in the way its advocates hoped, to increase student achievement on measures that the proponents of accountability think are important. The lack of clear evidence of benefits to high-stakes accountability may be interpreted in several ways. One possibility is that there are not sufficiently-sensitive independent measures to identify the benefits or to sort the effects of accountability systems from other policy changes. A second possibility is that accountability does not sufficient high-stakes yet, and pressure needs to be raised further (Hess, 2006). The third possibility is that high-stakes accountability has failed to accomplish the task which its proponents see as the *most* important outcome. Given the intrusive nature of high-stakes accountability systems and the documentation of serious side effects—part of what Nichols and Berliner (2007) call collateral damage—one should treat the lack of clear, consensual evidence in support of test-based accountability's benefits as a reason to look skeptically at the fundamental assumptions proponents make about attaching consequences to test-score statistics. Maybe test-based accountability fails to provide clear benefits because the assumptions about adult motivations are wrong.

Checking the High-Stakes Theory of Action

Few people have written carefully about the constellation of consequences and the assumptions behind it. In essence, the theory of action behind high-stakes consequences is that both rewards and punishments can motivate teachers and administrators as well as students and that one can calibrate the incentives to create the right environment for reform. Some advocates of high-stakes accountability have focused on the performance pay for teachers and resources flowing to schools meeting certain targets while others have focused on the punishments—loss of prestige, autonomy, resources, and jobs. In reality, any state that has a reward structure also has a punishment system, because No Child Left Behind mandates the cascading punishments. Thus, states can have a carrot-and-stick approach (rewards and punishments) or a stick-only approach (punishments only). Understanding that combination is important, because each research study is generally focused on one side only.

The empirical research supporting sticks as primary motivators is weak. Concrete punishments and school probations have little evidence of being a panacea for long-term problems in schools. Henrich Mintrop (2004) is one of several researchers who have found that putting schools on probation (identifying them as failures and putting them through some mandated remedial steps) has had inconsistent results, with wide variations in how teachers and administrators responded to probation (also see Burns, 2003; Debray, Parson, & Avila, 2003; Tracey, 2005; Wong & Shen, 2001; Ziebarth, 2002; but note Phenix, Siegel, Zaltsman, & Fruchter, 2005, as a counterexample in New York City). This inconsistency is important; in almost any state, one could point to individual schools that improved after threats of being labeled as failing. Such anecdotal evidence does not demonstrate that such a system will be effective for all or even a majority of schools.

For the loss of prestige, or stigma—a scarlet-letter effect—some supporting evidence exists, at least using a state's internal testing program. In many states, after the department of education identifies schools as particularly weak, the test scores of some proportion of those schools improve in the following years. In Florida, former Education Commissioner Frank Brogan created a list of several dozen "critically low-performing" schools in the mid-1990s. Within a few years, all of the schools had climbed off that last, meeting the criteria he had established (Figlio & Rouse, 2006). Experience in other states is similar. *Why* such "walls of shame" work at least nominally is not clear. It is possible that identifying relatively few schools in a public way motivates local districts to provide resources. It is possible that the criteria for leaving a list is easy to satisfy. It is possible that schools under such public pressure engage in inappropriate teaching to the test (e.g., Nichols & Berliner, 2007). Because the literature on public shaming is usually in the context of assessing more tangible consequences, there is little close examination of the scarlet-letter effect.

For using carrots—incentive pay structures—the evidence is stronger (e.g., Odden & Kelley, 2002; Stronge, Gareis, & Little, 2006). When structured as group incentives—such as a lump sum for a school divided among faculty and other staff, as part of a high-stakes accountability system—there is at least some evidence that the incentives can lead to higher achievement. This evidence is neither a consensus nor the result of strong research designs. The studies conducted in the United States tend to be based on local initiatives, leading to problems with identifying comparison groups, and they are often part of larger packages involving multiple policy changes, making the isolation of effects difficult (Harvey-Beavis, 2003). In addition, I am concerned about the temptation for distorting the curriculum (Nichols & Berliner, 2007).

Furthermore, advocates for various forms of performance pay are avoiding the conceptual difficulties by asserting that a range of motivation models all suggest the power of group incentives. Odden and Kelly (2002) write,

> Rather than contradicting one another, the various theories [of motivation] are best understood as approaching the issue of motivation from different angles and, combined, offer a more comprehensive understanding of how and why workers are motivated to higher performance, and the context in which various compensation programs work. (p. 70)

I suspect that the defenders of the different models would disagree with the implication that one can ignore their differences! More pragmatically, it is questionable whether combining the models of motivation in an abstract sense would lead us to better guidelines when borrowed as ad-hoc rationalizations. In some cases, as with Heneman (1998), that borrowing leads to omissions of important parts of the literature:

> Moreover, borrowing from goal-setting theory, characteristics of the student achievement goals may help shape expectancy perceptions in terms of intensity, focus, and persistence. In particular, goals that are perceived as meaningful, clear, specific, and challenging will foster high expectancy perceptions by teachers. (p. 45)

Heneman is omitting important studies which suggest that such broad assertions about the power of setting goals do not hold for complex tasks (e.g., Chesney & Locke, 1991, Durham, Knight, & Locke, 1997; Seijts & Latham, 2001, 2005; Winters & Latham, 1996; Wood, Mento, & Locke, 1987). Teaching is a complex job with multiple skills, and the same studies hint that setting goals for learning skills or strategies might be more powerful than any student performance goal-setting one might establish. I emphasize that there is too little research in this area, and one should be hesitant to make sweeping policy decisions based on the lack of research. But this research on motivation and teacher performance pay is far from the world of policymakers who establish high-stakes accountability policies.

MOTIVATIONS AND THE CULTURE OF SCHOOLING

What matters to politicians and other policymakers is the thumbnail sense that schools should "run like businesses," including tying pay to performance, a rhetoric of hard-headed business management. Since the early 1980s, there has been a recurring argument that schools should be much more like businesses in several ways (Berliner & Biddle, 1995; Tyack & Cuban, 1995). Schools should reward teachers by higher salaries for better skills or higher student test scores, as businesses reward better workers with higher salaries and benefits. Former Florida Governor Jeb Bush (n.d.) justified the use of high-stakes consequences by reference to private industry: "The private sector has long used incentives to improve performance. It works! The public sector however sometimes confuses uniformity with fairness. The true measure of fairness is when compensation matches the quality of work." According to the advocates of business-like incentives, schools should have to face competition as businesses do, to force improvements in teaching and to reduce costs for the same services (e.g., Chubb & Moe, 1990; Friedman, 1962).

The philosophical response of many educators is to say that schools should not be like businesses. Students are not raw materials but individuals (e.g., Cuban, 2004a).The goal of schools is not to produce computer components but to help thinking human beings become citizens. Moreover, as Meier (1999-2000) writes, standards must be on a human scale, with children seeing close adults' modeling and debating expectations: "[W]e need standards held by real people who matter in the lives of our young. School, family, and community must forge their own, in dialogue with and in response to the larger world of which they are a part" (¶ 47). Moreover, to reduce teachers to automatons in the service of schools is to eliminate their role as the largest group of professional intellectuals in society. Michael Apple (1988) has written eloquently about the policies that look deliberately for cowed, unthinking teachers in the service of standardization. What he calls "intensification" of professional lives

> acts to destroy the sociability of non-manual workers. Leisure and self-direction tend to be lost. Community tends to be redefined around the needs of the labor process. And, since both time and interaction are at a premium, the risk of isolation grows.... [A] number of these aspects of intensification are increasingly found in teaching, especially in those schools which are dominated by behaviorally prespecified curricula, repeated testing, and strict and reductive accountability systems. (pp. 42-43)

On a principled basis, then, many educators and social critics oppose the intrusion of market incentives in schools.

While I am sympathetic with these arguments, the focus on what *should be* has largely overshadowed questions of *what is* and *what could be*. Are businesses truly competitive and standardized? Are schools truly the shoddy, slipshod organizations that the broadcast media portray? In short, the question of whether Ford Elementary could be like Ford Motor Company is as important as whether it should be. The assumption in the schools-should-be-more-like-business argument is that schools and companies took very different paths over the past 150 years. There are then two historical issues to explore. One is the history of standardization in for-profit companies. The second is the history of standardization in education.

Standardization in Business

Even the largest businesses can only standardize some processes. Many parts of businesses certainly are standardized, and most people are familiar with the standardized products of companies. Manufacturers can measure and then standardize the materials they work with, the processes for turning raw materials into products, and the expectations for or quality assurance of the finished goods. They can also standardize the distribution process and prices, even complex systems of discounts. Companies that provide services can also standardize some processes and the types of services provided and the prices. All publicly-owned companies also have standardized ways of reporting costs and revenues—or at least until Enron and Worldcom we generally assumed they were both standardized and accurate—and governments require standardized reporting of revenues and profits for tax purposes as well as for wages and benefits provided for employees.

From a business owner's or a manager's perspective, standardization controls what a company does and what happens to a company. For example, a computer-chip manufacturer needs to know that the chips it produces perform to written specifications so the companies who buy that chip will be satisfied with its performance—because that company, in turn, needs to make computers, copy machines, or bread machines reliable enough for someone to buy them. The most obvious problem with trying to control what happens to a company is that managers and business owners of a company that produces things cannot control who buys products, how much, or at what price. To some extent, they also are at the mercy of the markets for raw materials and labor.

Within companies, though, there are also many parts of a business that remain nonstandardized. The key nonstandardized parts of businesses include how individual managers and other employees relate to each other, understand the priorities of the company, and understand their own roles. The common term today for this collection of relationships and understandings is corporate culture, and the conventional wisdom is that one cannot standardize corporate culture. The big news question when very different companies merge is whether a suits-and-tie culture will mesh well with the so-called jeans culture of the other company. If corporate culture were easily standardized, Scott Adams' *Dilbert* cartoon would not be as widely popular as it is, with its depictions of irrational managers such as the pointy-haired boss who sets impossible and meaningless goals and dysfunctional "cubicle residents" such as Wally, the employee who never does any work (e.g., Adams, 1996). The popularity of books on corporate culture testifies to the fact that culture is an intractably messy part of private businesses. I will return to this matter of workplace culture in a few pages, because it is crucial to understanding why cookie-cutter business models generally do not work in education.

Even if one focuses on the parts of businesses that are standardized, the extent to which there is standardization in businesses is the result of over two centuries of effort to change behavior and expectations in work. Sometimes, business owners have been the ones wanting standardization. In the nineteenth century, factory owners struggled for decades to get employees to come to work for set hours. The tendency of laborers to set their own hours or take off a "blue Monday" after a weekend of partying continued long after owners would have liked a standardized work schedule (Brody, 1989; Gutman, 1977). On the other hand, workers have also pushed for standardization in some ways. Unions argued for a 40-hour work week, regulations to improve the safety on jobs, and restrictions on child labor (e.g., Licht, 1989).

The effort to standardize one piece of business has on occasion had a domino effect. The story of standardizing consumer products is one such example. When Eli Whitney originally proposed the production of guns with interchangeable parts, no one could produce them yet. Even when companies made parts that were supposedly interchangeable, they still needed skilled "fitters" to put together the pieces together, because the pieces were not precisely identical. Thus, one part of the story is the long effort to standardize parts, which required much more time than Eli Whitney had anticipated. But then, once companies could make bicycles, guns, stoves, and other material goods in large quantities, relatively cheaply, they faced another problem. They needed to sell them! Companies then began to develop marketing efforts and distribution networks. In doing so, such companies created one type of "vertical integration" of industry, the attempt to control more than one step of the path from raw material to market (Hounshell, 1985).

Alfred Chandler tells the story of the other half of vertical integration, the way companies grew to manage the acquisition of raw materials in the late nineteenth century. The development of monopolies and so-called trusts was the attempt to control various markets—what Chandler called the very "visible hand" of companies attempting to determine their own future. They purchased other companies, the rights to various raw goods, and the transportation and other systems necessary to create an *internal* system of production. The acquisition of that power required internal organization. Companies attempted to standardize internal communications and the flow of information. They invented red tape—to manage information rather than to stifle it—and as a result they shifted the process of writing from handwritten pieces of paper to typed memoranda and reports that could be read more easily. Thus, the creation of huge monopolies in the nineteenth century was concurrent with the creation of a market for typewriters. At the same time, companies shifted clerical work from a skilled job reserved for men to a supposedly semiskilled job for women (Chandler, 1980; Davies, 1982).

The most "rigorous" attempt to standardize workers' movements also turned out to be the most obvious failure. Frederick Taylor published his first and most famous book on time-and-motion studies in 1911, claiming that businesses could become more efficient merely by studying worker movements and teaching employees to eliminate the unnecessary motions. Raymond Callahan (1962) has noted that many educators took up Taylor's claim as a rallying cry for administrative "efficiency" in education (also see the discussion in chapter 2 and Berman, 1983; Rees, 2001). The truth is somewhat duller: Taylor's claims about improvement in efficiency were exaggerated, and many businesses as well as workers resisted his analysis of workers as automotons. More successful attempts to "reengineer" businesses required considerably better understandings of what happened on a shop floor or in an office. Edward Deming, the "total-quality" guru whose writings are now well-known among some educators, was popular in Japan because he understood that shaming individual workers was not only humiliating but violated cultural taboos in Japan. Thus, his efforts were devoted to *creative* efforts to reduce errors and variations in physical products.

In addition, all of the preceding history is from documents from large businesses. Small businesses are much less standardized in either what they do or how businesses treat employees. Nonetheless, one would be making a fair comparison between public schools and large businesses because public schools are typically parts of larger systems. The larger picture here is that standardization has been a long-term, very messy affair involving wholesale changes in organizational structures, the relationship of workers to each other, and negotiations and conflict among various parties. There has rarely been a "quick fix" in private companies. Perhaps we recognize this fact of life better after the dot-bomb crash and the exposure of supposed corporate turnover expert "Chainsaw Al" Dunlap as an opportunistic fraud (Danner, 2002). But the metaphor of schools-as-businesses has been a persistent idea in educational history (e.g., Dorn & Johanningmeier, 1999; Tyack & Cuban, 1995), and one can be sure that, every decade or two, someone will claim that businesses can effectively standardize operations much more quickly than schools can ... or than what the history of work shows.

Standardization in Schools

Private businesses are less standardized than the rhetoric of efficiency might lead one to believe; what about schools? Maybe public schools have standardized *some* parts of education, and maybe we should compare the types of standardization that exist in public schools with the standardization that exists in private business. Public schools cannot standardize the students who enter the door, even through rigid, extensive tracking. But public schools have standardized more parts of education than one might assume. Most school systems have standardized the core academic curriculum in three ways: through the broad sets of expectations that one might call either a curriculum framework or a set of standards; through the purchasing of a common set of instructional materials, most commonly textbooks; and through assessment that has become more and more standardized over the past century. Public schools also have standardized pay schedules, accounting procedures, retirement plans, and hiring and promotion practices.

What remains nonstandardized is important: day-to-day instructional practices. In some cases, schools have tried to standardize instruction, either by mandating a rigorous schedule or pacing calendar for "coverage" of the curriculum or by mandating a particular method for teaching reading, math, or other subjects. Some educational researchers have advocated such standardization, arguing that teaching is too inconsistent otherwise. But while scripts exist for some instructional programs, the larger constraints on teaching are the political and social pressures on schools to teach a certain type of material. Larry Cuban (1993) argued that the late 1960s and early 1970s movements for "open classrooms" and self-directed learning were not adopted widely and largely disappeared within a decade, in some measure because a "back to basics" effort by social conservatives in the mid- to late-1970s criticized efforts by schools to escape a structured curriculum. In theory, instructional techniques are not tied to the curriculum. For example, one could teach Latin or ancient Greek in an open classroom or with individualized contracts instead of class lectures. However, the pressures on schools to focus on an academic curriculum in the late 1970s and since created less *internal* support for innovative instruction. As Cuban noted, individual teachers can still decide to try new methods on their own initiative, but pressures buffet them constantly. The theoretical freedom to teach independently exists within a set of constraints.

THE RHETORIC OF "CHILDREN'S INTERESTS"

When teachers and others point out that the run-schools-like-a-business rhetoric is unlikely to help schools, the response often claims that teachers and their unions are selfish. A case in point is education reporter Joe Williams, who is an advocate of performance pay for teachers. In 2005, Williams published *Cheating our Kids: How Politics and Greed Ruin Education*. From his work on newspapers in Milwaukee and New York City, Williams fashioned an argument about whose interests come first in schools:

> [O]ur once-heralded system of education ... has been captured by groups—
> teachers and other employees, politicians, philanthropists, higher educa-
> tion institutions, vendors, consultants, et cetera—whose interests and egos
> are protected and advanced through competent and powerful organiza-
> tions, including unions, lobbying firms, and even the major political parties
> themselves. (p. 3)

To Williams, the choice is between a system serving adult interests and a system serving children's interests. His attack on school union contracts is typical of the book's tone:

> [T]he contracts [unions] have successfully negotiated with management
> over the years ... put the needs of children after the wants of adults. Teach-
> ers who are assigned to schools based on seniority, not on their fit with the
> school; custodians who earn more than principals but who don't paint above
> ten feet high (a different union handles anything above ten feet); teachers
> who don't have to do lunchroom duty. (p. 86)

Williams claims that a cartel of adult interest groups have captured the public school system, making the system serve their adult material interests. To Williams, good teachers are held hostage to a dysfunctional system, and bad educators are tolerated, even protected.[7] The solution? Parents need to fight back: "Parents are the only special interest within the system capable of truly making the needs of their children their primary motivation" (Williams, 2005, p. 211). Joe Williams is not the first critic of teachers and teachers unions to make this argument. Myron Lieberman, who used to be a union activist, is harsher. In his 2000 book, *The Teacher Unions: How They Sabotage Educational Reform and Why*, Lieberman says that the NEA and the AFT misrepresent themselves and how they spend money and largely block any reform of schools. The conventional criticism of teachers is often that they are undereducated, lazy, and protected by union and bureaucracy rules. They are selfish, in other words. Williams' argument is the softer version, but the general claim is that opponents of accountability put adults' and especially teachers' interests over children's interests.

For both Williams, a supporter of charter schools and performance pay, both as market mechanisms in education, and also Lieberman, who favors considerable privatization of education, the irony of this perspective is that they have simultaneously attacked teachers unions for protecting the material interests of teachers and argued in favor of policies that would only work if teachers are motivated by their material interest. Often, the same people who want teachers to stop defending their material self-interest through unions want to motivate teachers through their material self-interest. The inconsistency illustrates the distrust of teachers' perspectives embodied in high-stakes accountability. There is a deeper problem with the arguments by Williams, Lieberman, and other advocates of market mechanisms and monetization to motivate teachers and administrators. The rhetorical ploy, "We are motivated by the children's interests, and our opponents are motivated by their material self-interest," ignores the fact that all motivations in education policymaking are adult ones. The values and assumptions of education politics are all *adult* values, and we make decisions on behalf of children because we presumably know their needs better than they do. (Accountability systems would be very different if student perceptions were guiding education policy.) But this era is not the first in which some reform advocates argued that they were on the side of the child and their opponents were not. This section explores the late nineteenth and early twentieth century child-saving movement and broader arguments about children's interests.

Child-Saving

In the second half of the nineteenth and in the early twentieth century, middle-class reformers changed the broader meaning and value of childhood. Sociologist Viviana Zelizer (1985) traced the changes in the legal valuation of children as an indicator of this cultural shift. In the nineteenth century, the wrongful death of one's child was frequently compensated based on expected future earnings, but today grieving parents of children wrongfully killed are compensated for pain and suffering. In the nineteenth century, adults who adopted children often expected them to work, so adopting children was sometimes a strategy to gain labor for the household. But today, parents have paid thousands of dollars to adopt children with no expectation of gaining from their labor. In the eyes of the law and much of the country, children shifted from having a concrete value as workers to being priceless, valued for their being children. The advocates of such changes often said that they were working in the interests of children, and the *child-saving movement* was a common term used by advocates to discuss their actions. The child-saving movement is a good historical case to examine motivations on the parts of reformers and other historical actors.

Child-saving efforts in the second half of the nineteenth century and early twentieth century included a broad range of activities, from the playground movement to the creation of kindergartens, from the struggle to restrict child labor to attempts to wrest children from poor families. In general, advocates in all of these efforts assumed that they knew what the interests of children were, that the benefits of their efforts were self-evident, and that the political battles they were engaged in were moral struggles. New York charity reformer Charles Loring Brace was the most visible child-saving figure in the nineteenth century, and he disdained the views of many poor parents. In his 1872 book *The Dangerous Classes of New York and Twenty Years among Them,* he described one New York City neighborhood:

> A certain block, called "Misery Row," in Tenth Avenue, was the main seedbed of crime and poverty in the quarter, and was also invariably a "fevernest." Here the poor obtained wretched rooms at a comparatively low rent; these they sub-let, and thus, in little, crowded, close tenements, were herded men, women and children of all ages. The parents were invariably given to hard drinking, and the children were sent out to beg or to steal. Besides them, other children, who were orphans, or who had run away from drunkards' homes, or had been working on the canal-boats that discharged on the docks near by, drifted into the quarter, as if attracted by the atmosphere of crime and laziness that prevailed in the neighborhood. (p. 317)

Together with child-saving organizations—the Charity Organization Society in New York and various Societies for the Prevention of Cruelty to Children—Brace was convinced not only that thousands of children lived in pitiful circumstances but that reformers could do better. To that end, child savers sought the approval of local courts to remove children from parents perceived as abusive or neglecting. Between the mid-nineteenth century and the Great Depression, Brace and his successors organized what could best be described as the outsourcing of childrearing away from New York and other eastern cities, with "orphan trains" shipping hundreds of thousands of children westward to adults who were willing to adopt children (Holt, 1994). Others were placed in a burgeoning industry of orphanages (Hacsi, 1998). Only a portion of these "orphans" had lost both parents. Others were truly abandoned or had been taken from their families by the courts for various reasons.

As Sherri Broder (2002) documents, the picture was more complex than what Brace and his colleagues described. The Pennsylvania Society to Prevent Cruelty to Children (SPCC) sought to reduce what they identified as the moral indignities of poverty: abandonment, destitution, and the temptation to put young children to work in factories or in the city's prostitution trade. Philadelphia's child-savers wanted working-class women to sue their wayward spouses for child support, and they turned to the courts in attempts to take custody of some children, to have delinquents (commonly girls or young women) directed into charity-run services, and to crack down on prostitution and other vice crimes. Male labor leaders had similar concerns, but from a very different perspective; labor leaders wanted a crackdown on child labor earlier than middle-class Progressive reformers in Philadelphia did. And the perspectives of white and African American working-class women often diverged from those of both the male labor leaders and the middle-class child savers. To the mothers in working-class communities, the patronizing intrusion of the SPCC was probably best captured by the group's ironic nickname, "The Cruelty."

The child-savers occasionally had allies for their campaigns—labor unions when attacking child labor and schools when pushing kindergartens—but what was unique about their efforts was a particular moralizing focus. The problem with poverty was not just the material conditions of children but the vices that poverty led to and in turn was reinforced by. Thus, child-savers in Philadelphia focused on prostitution and other vice trades (Broder, 2002). They were not the only group in society with a focus on morals—many working-class families often had a similar perspective on morality—but child-savers had the resources to shape public policy that assumed a linkage between poverty and immorality. In an era of increasing industrialization and urbanization, reformers were critical in shaping the definition of a newly-emerging middle class. The existence of this middle-class perspective did not mean that poor children went unabused—of course many children lived in abusive circumstances in the late nineteenth and early twentieth centuries—but that the child-savers tended to assume that their insular perspective was the primary one that mattered.

School attendance and child labor was one case where the perspectives of middle-class reformers differed from those of many working-class families. As Tyack (1974) pointed out, many working-class children in the late nineteenth and early twentieth century attended school inconsistently. They explained to those who asked that schools were crowded and boring and that their families needed them to work. Miriam Cohen (1993) noted that the first generation of teenage girls of Italian-American immigrants in early 20th century New York City were far less likely to attend school than their own children in the 1930s. For their families, there was an immediate opportunity cost of sending their teenagers to school: The teens would not be working. Poor and working-class families often struggled to make ends meet, and the most frequent strategies available to poor urban families—taking in boarders, having the mother work, or sending older children to work—all had real consequences: overcrowding, not having an adult watch the younger children, and child labor.

The ideals of middle-class reformers could not remove the painful choices of poor families, and what child savers thought was in the children's best interest was not always a viable option from poor parents' perspectives. To poor parents, it was sometimes in the best interest of their children to have enough family income, and they saw child labor as a viable option. I do not raise the history of the child saving movement to argue in favor of child labor—in this, I agree with the reformers and labor leaders at the time. Rather, I see a crucial difference between identifying *one* definition of a child's self-interest and assuming that one's adult definition of a child's interest is the only plausible one. Child savers defined children's interests from their perspectives, both as adults and in a certain social-class position. Today, we can see the middle-class perspective of the progressive reformers and understand that their definition of children's best interest depended on social class.

Adults and the Interests of Children

If child savers came to their movement from their own experiences, we come to a debate about high-stakes testing from our own experiences. That accountability debate is also one inevitably rooted in adult perspectives. As parents and as adult citizens more broadly, we have opinions based in our sense of what children should know as well as from memories of our own school experiences. We might believe that we know better than children, but confidence in our greater wisdom should be tempered by the fact that we do not face the same stakes that children have. We just have to make decisions about their fate. Each generation is an experiment. Adults often assume that our decisions are correct because we cannot go back and make different ones. But adults cannot escape from the responsibility to make decisions on behalf of children. Parents have power and authority over their children, and adults in society more broadly have power over children. That power is not absolute—children and especially adolescents have their own perspectives and historically have made their own lives within the boundaries that adults try to set (Graff, 1995). But adults have the greater power, and to pretend otherwise is misleading for children and perhaps delusional on the part of adults.

My own sense is that a proper education challenges and engages children without abdicating adult responsibilities. Being an adult does not require ignoring children's perspectives and interests, and there are many reasonable balance points between structure and freedom. But there have also been times and places where adults have fantasized about leaving the most important choices to children. A long history of educational thought from Rousseau (1762) to the present includes the assumption that education should rely on the good nature of the child and a corresponding argument that the best education is child-centered. As an historian, I am cautious about attributing any truth to the claim that children ever *have* made all of the choices in their lives. As Cuban (1993) explained, teachers have commonly created hybrid arrangements that provide considerable structure but also provide some choices for students.

Beyond the hybridized arrangements of many classrooms, I am skeptical of claims that any education is unstructured. A child does not choose the circumstances of her or his birth, and many advocates of de-schooling or un-schooling (terms chosen by those who advocate little or no structure in education) obscure the important ways in which their support and interaction with children inevitably create structure. What is easier to document are the many cases when some adults have *claimed* that they were not coercing children's behavior. One example of such a claim is an argument by contrast: middle-class white parents who decry the physical discipline that working-class parents impose on their own children. As Delpit (1995) points out, we should be skeptical that middle-class parents are truly less coercive. What *may* be true is that they may couch coercion in softer terms. Telling a child, "Which toy would you like in your bath tonight?" is no less coercive than "Get in the tub." At some age, children catch on to the trick. Or, to take an example from my own adolescence, when my mother asked me after dinner, "Would you like to take out the garbage?" there was only one acceptable answer.

When educators *have* made claims about the need to respond to children's interests, such claims have obscured the adult assumptions behind the argument. Boyd Bode pointed this fact out in his 1938 criticism of the extremes of progressivism, *Progressive Education at the Crossroads*. Rousseau's program for an education left to the whim of individual nature was as absolutist as a rigid curriculum based on ancient texts; Rousseau's argument "comes close to saying that we should not educate at all," Bode wrote (1938/1971, p. 38). And the Progressive-era advocates of a child-centered education had retained that germ of absolutism:

> The faith of progressive education in the individual, and in the power of intelligence to create new standards and ideals in terms of human values and in accordance with changing conditions, entitles it to consideration as expressive of the spirit of democracy. As against this, however, stands the fact that it has never completely emancipated itself from the individualism and absolutism of Rousseau. Instead of turning to the ideal of democracy for guidance, it has all too often turned to the individual. It has nurtured the pathetic hope that it could find out how to educate by relying on such notions as interests, needs, growth, and freedom. (Bode, 1938/1971, pp. 39-40)

Adults had to make a choice about what was important in education, Boyd argued. To pretend otherwise was delusion.

Today, those who write and talk about high-stakes accountability as if they had a monopoly on understanding children's best interests are at best misguided and at worst manipulative. Not only do we all have material interests, but we also have more complex motivations rooted in our sense of identity and position in the world. Teachers and test makers both want to make money. But as important as those material interests might be, teachers and test makers have also invested time and energy in careers, jobs and goals that they think are socially useful. Their sense of children's best interests will inevitably be connected to those jobs—and those views will not be monolithic within those broad categories of *teacher* and *test publisher employee*. Creating a false dichotomy between *those who are idealistic* and *those who are materialistic* may feed the underlying stories that the fiercest advocates and opponents of high-stakes testing tell, but that dichotomy is wrong. To some degree we are all captives of our own experiences and positions in society. Because of that fact, identifying others in a debate as having solely material interests is misleading. And because of that fact, we must acknowledge our adult responsibilities to make decisions about education and not rely on the rhetoric of "children's interests."

MOTIVATION AND SUPPORT

To summarize the chapter's argument, we can say a few things about high-stakes accountability and the arguments for consequences. Research evidence does not currently support the claims of its advocates that high-stakes accountability improves student achievement. The theory of action behind the argument for consequences assumes ideas about motivation that are not supported by research or experience. The business-metaphor argument that businesses create material incentives and run operations in a very concrete style is based on a false understanding of the history of standardization in businesses and schools and ignores the importance of work culture. The psychological model of high-stakes accountability rooted in fear and material interest has little foundation. In addition, as mentioned briefly at the beginning of the chapter, the evidence suggesting some power in group pay incentives is isolated from the combination of consequences that currently exists: either threats only or the possibility of rewards along with threats. As explained earlier, under the No Child Left Behind Act, the threats are persistent while most state rewards for school-level performance are fleeting. Finally, the rhetoric in favor of high-stakes consequences is sometimes supported by false claims about the lofty idealism of its proponents and the baseness of opponents, rhetoric that falls in a longer historical pattern of claiming that reform is "in the children's interests." Such claims ignore the very adult way we construct and should take responsibility for public policy.

A more sensible accountability policy must reflect two facts about motivation, facts that reflect our complex human nature. The first fact is that human beings have more than one source of self-interest.[8] Material self-interest certainly exists; I would not deny some pleasure with every raise, or at least thinking about where to distribute the money! On the other hand, money is only one facet of my self-interest. Each of us has invested time and energy in our current jobs and daily routines, and our identity is shaped by those commitments. Our ideas about democracy and equal opportunity are also tied up with a sense of self—many ordinary white Americans who supported the civil rights movement in the 1960s did so because they did not want to live in a country where Alabama police would turn fire hoses on African American children. Human decency is often connected to our sense of self, and in some ways, it is a fundamentally selfish interest to want to live in a country one is proud of. Ultimately, our ideas of what and how children should learn is intimately interwoven with those commitments and our sense of self. In that regard, high-stakes accountability may do inestimable damage to teachers' ability to work within their chosen professional identities (e.g., Booher-Jennings, 2005). Despite the fact that teachers spend years investing in their personal notions of education, few politicians or other policymakers acknowledge this intangible identity or think about how to use it.

The second fact of human nature is that urging administrators, teachers, and students to reach a prescribed goal is useless without providing support (Darling-Hammond, 2004; Hamilton & Strecher, 2002). There are two areas of psychology research that provide a warning about making demands that appear unreachable. Expectancy theory argues that motivation depends at least partly on the expectation that one can accomplish the goals, something that is tied to teachers' perception of reasonableness (e.g., Johnson, 1986). Research on goal-setting as motivation provides evidence that difficult goals on complex tasks are less effective at motivation than focusing on strategy acquisition tied to those complex, high-level goals: "[W]hen primarily learning rather than motivation is required to master a task, setting an outcome goal can have a detrimental effect on performance" (Seijts & Latham, 2001, p. 292). These caveats do not forever preclude tying accountability to pay. Teacher surveys conducted by Marsden and Belfield (2006) indicate that several years of experience with performance pay in England since 2000 has reduced teachers' and school principals' skepticism about the fairness of the process. However, the system in England is very different from the type of high-stakes consequences in American accountability: Objectives for performance pay are negotiated individually between teachers and their immediate supervisors, and the vast majority of teachers reported that they could influence the objectives and that teachers were "in a position to achieve [the] objectives" (Marsden & Belfield, 2006, p. 15). For teachers to believe that they are *in a position to achieve objectives* requires more than the possibility of earning more pay or threats to one's job. It requires both a perception that the goal is achievable (expectancy) and the skills to do the job.[9]

It is in the area of motivation—the consequences attached to testing—that the advocates of high-stakes accountability most fail to pay attention to hard data. There is slim evidence that the current pattern of asymmetrical consequences will effectively motivate teachers. Often, advocates of high-stakes accountability use the rhetoric of science—the term "scientifically-based" appears 119 times in No Child Left Behind. Why do the advocates of high-stakes accountability ignore the research on the mismatch between their theory of action and the real motivations of teachers and others who work in schools? With a few exceptions, most high-stakes accountability advocates are probably unaware of the research on motivation or are disinclined to believe research that is contrary to the ideas they find self-evident. However, the stubbornness that is useful politically is not useful when crafting policy. The inconsistency between the rhetoric of evidence-based actions and today's accountability systems is a reflection of the deeply political roots of accountability. We have always treated children as guinea pigs, because school reform is always rooted in adults' ideas and interests and reform is experimental by its very nature. Yet the advocates of high-stakes accountability have not closely examined the assumptions behind the system of consequences or treated their ideas as experimental, subject to invalidation. After all, if there is no reason to believe that high-stakes consequences for test results will improve education, how else can we keep schools accountable?

NOTES

1. This book does not directly address systems that have high stakes for students, such as withholding standard diplomas for low test scores.
2. The chapter focuses on North America, omitting the history of performance-pay attempts in other education systems, such as Payment by Results introduced in the 1860s in England (Lowe, 1994).
3. Hamilton and Strecher assume that the lack of clear evidence about achievement test scores is the primary reason for the controversy.
4. Haney (2006) argues that increasing third-grade retention since 2002 pollutes Florida's fourth-grade NAEP scores.
5. The independent ratings across time were not the direct result of the more sophisticated procedure; this weakens the conclusions to some extent.
6. Other work whose are omitted here focus on student consequences rather than school consequences (e.g., Bishop, 2005).
7. Williams's claims about teacher transfers and seniority is not consistent with evidence from federal surveys (Nelson, 2006).
8. I have avoided the terms *extrinsic* and *intrinsic* in discussing motivation because it seems a false dichotomy from a social-science perspective.
9. Contrary to some beliefs, teachers union locals will negotiate performance pay provisions of collective bargaining agreements when they have significant input in the shape of programs and perceive it to be in the best interests of their members; Denver's ProComp plan was devised in close coordination between the administration and the Denver teachers union.

CHAPTER 6

A BETTER WAY

Fear not that I shall be the instrument of future mischief. My work is nearly complete. Neither yours nor any man's death is needed to consummate the series of my being, and accomplish that which must be done; but it requires my own.

—Frankenstein's Creature, describing his intent to kill himself
(Shelley, 1818/1869, p. 176)

Two poor choices are generally described by proponents of high-stakes accountability: maintaining high-stakes testing or eliminating accountability entirely. Neither is appropriate, and neither is necessary. Before I describe alternatives to high-stakes accountability, a brief summary of the arguments thus far is in order. The first chapter explained how accountability has deep political roots in the healthy skepticism of public agencies, in human capital rhetoric, and in the modern civil-rights movement. The common experiences of most adults in the U.S. provide both a clear set of expectations for what the academic curriculum should be and also a political basis for the use of testing for high-stakes purposes, both for students and for holding schools accountable. Relying on standardized tests to judge schools has several costs: Testing requires time to administer the tests and encourages the use of time to prepare for them (beyond ordinary instruction). Testing also encourages the narrowing of the curriculum to tested subjects. Test-based accountability tempts us to judge the value of all policies by test scores and only test scores.

Accountability Frankenstein: Understanding and Taming the Monster, pp. 147–172
Copyright © 2007 by Information Age Publishing
All rights of reproduction in any form reserved.

147

The second chapter explored the trust that most accountability policies require from the techniques of testing. Our trust in testing comes in part from the cooptation of testing as an administrative tool, the rise of professional expertise in psychology as well as in administration, a folk version of positivism, and the political utility of replacing judgment with statistical autopilots. But high-stakes testing is not inevitable in a political sense. The social status of expertise, the existence of alternatives to high-stakes testing, and the administrative feasibility of such alternatives are important political factors in shaping accountability policies.

The third chapter explained the fragility of accountability systems. The mechanics of testing place several layers of abstraction between student performance and our ordinary expectations of what students should be able to do. The composite nature of test scores, the circumscribed nature of tests, the focus on comparisons, and the demand for consistency all weaken the conclusions we can draw from test scores, even as they solidify the test characteristics in a more narrow sense. The recent enthusiasm for measuring achievement growth illustrates the ability of testing mechanics to obscure the central political questions involved in accountability. *How much growth?* is not just a technical question. Its answer depends on our political expectations of schools and the extent to which the U.S. public truly wants equality.

The fourth chapter focused on the fundamentally political question of what we expect from schools and students. While most reform talk today conflates the two, the chapter separates them into the demands historically laid on schools, on the one hand, and the debates over curricular expectations and goals for students, on the other hand. The multiple, almost impossible set of burdens on schools—what Cuban (1990) called the consequence of schools' being "legatee institutions"—makes it harder to distinguish between reasonable and unreasonable expectations. That is true both of the broader purpose of schooling and also concrete expectations of students. The recent era of school reform has seen statements that rhetorically focus on outcomes, whether the national goals for 2000 established after the 1989 education summit or the 100% teacher-quality and student-proficiency mandates of the No Child Left Behind Act. Both initiatives continue the impossible demands of education politics, now in expected outcomes for students as well as for schools. Incrementalism in judging schools and replacing summative judgments with a standard in formative evaluation are neither politically feasible by themselves nor easy to implement.

The fifth chapter explores the implicit theory of action behind high-stakes accountability: Can one calibrate rewards and punishments tied to student test scores in a way that will motivate better teaching? The evidence on the results of high-stakes accountability is weak at best, perhaps because high-stakes accountability's implicit assumptions about human nature are inconsistent with what we know about motivation. The asymmetrical construction of high-stakes consequences is a choice to motivate teachers and administrators mostly with fear and a little bit with the possibility of monetary rewards. Such an asymmetry is unlikely to motivate dramatic improvement, and various rhetorical claims about defending children's interests and borrowing from business management are inconsistent with the history of public policy and of businesses.

BASIC PRINCIPLES

This chapter is about potential solutions, alternatives to high-stakes accountability. We can begin with what we know about the political and human realities of accountability:

- Accountability has deep roots, and we should not attempt to undermine legitimate efforts to equalize education. On the other hand, the importance of holding schools accountable does not mean that high-stakes testing is the inevitable form of that accountability, and high-stakes testing has real costs and "collateral damage" (Berliner & Nichols, 2007).

- As a society, we distrust schools but trust test scores. The obscurity and abstraction of most practical decisions about high-stakes testing is in conflict with the transparency that accountability demands while it eases political discomfort with tackling serious conflicts about the purposes of schooling. A better accountability system requires that we face the political nature of decisions about test use.

- Because we have historically expected more than schools can deliver, we need to narrow our expectations to what is reasonable to expect from schools and then distinguish among generational challenges, equity concerns, and management crises.

- We must acknowledge the multiple ways in which adults craft their priorities for children, how their identities are intertwined with their notions of justice, and the ways in which a high but vague goal can undermine motivation.

From this list, we can identify the criteria for a better accountability system.

Public policy must hold schools accountable to satisfy the legitimate public need for transparency and public responsibility. The political roots of accountability are deep and sensible. We *should* hold school systems accountable for how they spend public money and manage schools. We *should* hold schools accountable for providing equal educational opportunities. We *should* hold schools accountable for pushing students to learn and do more than their parents did in school. To hold schools accountable is consistent with holding students accountable for their own efforts and with giving teachers the authority they need. But students are not entirely responsible for their learning, and no public official or professional has the right to unlimited discretion.

Our expectations of schools and students must be reasonable and debated openly. In the past 20 years, the construction of standards at the state or national level have tried to answer one overarching question: *Ideally,* what should schoolchildren learn and know? *Ideally,* maybe high school graduates should know the constitution by heart, read some of the Federalist Papers and most of Shakespeare's plays, construct geometry proofs and wooden chairs, converse intelligently in English and one other language, evaluate arguments over how the Civil War started and the Cold War ended, understand how taxes and viruses work, and differentiate political positions and polynomials. But few adults are this accomplished! I have no special expertise in setting standards, but neither do any of the groups that have tried to set them in the past, and they are usually crafted in isolation from what young (or older!) adults have learned. That isolation is unnecessary and unwise. The result of such standard-setting is either a set of vague standards or expectations divorced from the realities of the generational challenge.

To make sure that this generation of children grows up smarter and maybe even wiser than their parents, we all need to know what the parents have learned. Frequently, after reports from the National Assessment of Educational Progress, the National Assessment of Adult Literacy, or other surveys of what high school seniors and young adults know, public commentary is about how stupid we are or are becoming (e.g., Romano, 2005b).[1] Instead, this information should be used to identify a key benchmark: what do young adults know today? Such a benchmark should not be an excuse to set low expectations, but we need to have a public debate about what we expect students to learn and what improvement in those standards over one or two decades is reasonable. Idealism in standard setting is no substitute for a messy but necessary debate.

Accountability policy must separate the generational, equity, and management challenges and treat them differently. Currently, all educational problems are treated as crises, and that common treatment is destructive. When the state of learning in every classroom is treated as a crisis, then we cannot target intervention. When all standards are identified as low, then we cannot trust our fellow citizens to debate expectations in an honest way. This crisis mentality is perhaps a result of the need to frame issues as crises to gain attention—to construct an issue as a social problem—but the crisis mentality is a poor way to hunt for solutions.

The generational challenge is the easiest to meet, because the solution is incremental and long term. In reality, the United States has historically prospered with a school system that has had low academic expectations for virtually everyone. For years, pundits have claimed that the new service economy in the 1980s, now the information economy, would require higher achievement. In doing so, such pundits have ignored the role of corporate practices, government monetary and fiscal policies, and trade policies in the United States and elsewhere (e.g., Berliner & Biddle, 1995). While the skills that children learn in school do translate in many cases into economic productivity, there is no clear link between academic performance standards and economic outputs (e.g., Levin, 1998). Realism about the connection between schooling and the economy is not a barrier to better schooling, however. Since parents would like their children to accomplish more than they did, I suspect most parents and our fellow citizens would support long-term, incremental changes in academic expectations.

The equity challenge is harder to meet. While educational inequality is less severe than inequality in the labor market, in wealth, in health care, and in housing, it still violates our commitment as a nation to equal educational opportunity (see Katznelson & Weir, 1985). Some part of the gap is attributable to factors outside school (Rothstein, 2004), but that fact does not excuse schools for providing unequal opportunities. In some cases, the achievement gap among students of different backgrounds and opportunities are a matter of inadequate technical skill among teachers, or sometimes explicit prejudice can be identified. However, most causes of educational inequality are structural, requiring constant political arguments to remove and block. Barriers include the conflicting purposes of schooling (e.g., Hochschild & Scovronick, 2003; Labaree, 1997) and the tendency of those with resources to hoard opportunities (Tilly, 1998). A technocratic accountability standard is no substitute for the political arguments necessary to address inequality.

Addressing the real crises of individual students, teachers, schools, and systems is the hardest challenge to meet. Tools exist to meet the challenges of many individual students in crisis, but few such tools exist at other levels. As described in chapter 5, the attempts to put individual schools in probationary status or for a state to take over a school or district have generally failed. The one notable exception is a New York City administrative unit called the Chancellor's District. In the mid-1990s, former Chancellor Rudy Crew created the Chancellor's District to take some of the schools identified by the state as under-performing and intervene in a focused effort. The Chancellor's District included some centralization of control and also capacity-building efforts. After several years, the schools in the Chancellor's District outperformed other city schools labeled under-performing by the state, schools that did not have the resources and supervision that Chancellor's District schools had (Phenix, Siegel, Zaltsman, & Fruchter, 2005). I highlight Crew's efforts not because they are stellar but because success in addressing organizational crises is rare. Despite the acceleration of punitive consequences in high-stakes accountability systems, there is scant research on tools to address legitimate crises in schooling. Because the identification of failure is integral to the No Child Left Behind Act, most states and local districts have had most of their efforts absorbed by general compliance, with few resources left to address the true education crises.

Accountability systems must be transparent and understandable to educators, to parents, and to the general public. An accountability system must be as transparent as the student achievement it is supposed to measure and respond to. At a minimum, the construction of tests and test statistics must be open. In all probability, the composite scales that are constructed to compare students must be sacrificed so that open discussions of concrete measures of achievement are possible. There already are limits on statistical sophistication, but they are rooted in administrative feasibility more than in making democratic debate possible; as explained in chapter 3, few states use the most advanced statistical tools in their growth models, and state accountability systems are often jerry-built affairs. Yet despite these flaws, politicians and millions of fellow citizens assume that an accountability policy can rely on autopilot mechanisms and test-score statistics.

The consequences attached to accountability must take advantage of the multiple interests and motivations of administrators and teachers. Sarason (1993) argued that burnout exists among elementary and secondary teachers in part because the institution is identified publicly as being *for children*. As explained in chapter 5, such a representation is false—we manage public schools for adult reasons. Because we are reluctant to face that fact, the public treatment of teachers is contradictory, simultaneously respecting their efforts and denigrating their skills, giving them responsibilities over dozens of children and then micromanaging them, insisting that their job is service-oriented and then creating accountability systems that rely on their material self-interest for motivation. Our current accountability system has an asymmetrical set of mechanisms to motivate teachers and administrators, an asymmetry that leans toward fear. Commonly, accountability policy is constructed without input from teachers, an additional factor that is a barrier to buy-in. Motivation can and should be more sophisticated.

The consequences attached to accountability must support administrators' and teachers' skills. Both common sense and research suggest that we guarantee failure if we assign teachers a task they perceive to be impossible. Two natural responses are to leave teaching and to comply superficially—teaching to the test—and we have seen too much of both responses in the last decade (Berliner & Nichols, 2007; McNeil, 2000). Put bluntly, most accountability systems in the United States treat teachers' and administrators' motivation as the primary requirement for higher educational achievement. Most advocates and opponents of high-stakes accountability acknowledge the importance of teacher quality (e.g., Darling-Hammond, 1993, 2000, 2004). However, linking accountability to developing teachers' and administrators' skills is done crudely in many policies or not at all. For example, the No Child Left Behind Act required that 100% of teachers be "highly qualified" by 2006—a utopian expectation and one met only by paper compliance and fudging the criteria for what *highly qualified* means (Education Trust, 2003)—but has no explicit provision to support teachers' and administrators' skills when schools are in crisis.

Accountability policy must acknowledge the potential for harmful consequences and actively include structures to dampen or ameliorate such consequences. With the publication of the Center for Education Policy (2006) report documenting the narrowing of the curriculum in response to No Child Left Behind, and with Berliner and Nichols's (2007) study of the harmful side-effects of high-stakes accountability in the classroom, one might expect an open debate about teaching to the test and the narrowing of the curriculum, but I am not hopeful. Linda McNeil's (2000) book on the classroom consequences of high-stakes accountability in Texas was largely ignored in the debate before the passage of the No Child Left Behind Act. And most responses to concerns about teaching to the test are to diminish its prevalence, to claim that it is somehow good, or that administrators and not high-stakes accountability comprise the culprit (e.g., Mathews, 2006a). Such responses are counterproductive and border on the edge of intellectual dishonesty; why would one *not* be concerned about and want to reduce the potential side-effects of what one advocates?

HOW IT MIGHT LOOK

The seven criteria listed above are general guidelines, not specific policy recommendations. There are many ways to implement them. The following set of 15 options should be considered as a sample of what is available and still different from today's high-stakes accountability policies.

General Expectations

Arguing from Large-Scale Data Collection

At the state or national level, an assessment of a sample of graduating seniors and other young adults would provide concrete evidence of what young adults currently know. That data could serve as a basis for discussion of what we should expect in the future. As explained earlier, the danger is to dismiss the current performance of young adults as pathological, instead of seeing it as a legitimate benchmark and a point from which we can judge what is both challenging and feasible.

Arguing from Portfolios

When Deborah Meier (1995) was the director of the small Central Park East Secondary School, the school would conduct an annual evaluation of the curriculum by inviting community members to join the teachers to review the portfolios of that year's graduates, each of whom had to complete a 14-subject portfolio for graduation. The quality of work in those portfolios became the basis for an annual discussion of whether the school was setting the right expectations for students as well as whether students were meeting those expectations. Using portfolios would be easiest at the local level, for individual schools and small districts, but surveys of such work would be possible if more expensive for larger districts and states.

One Challenge Every Decade

Based on either the formal curriculum or the performance of young adults in a state or the country, one could add a single reasonable challenge every ten years in a set area of the curriculum. Suppose that one would choose the challenge in middle-school social studies that students in middle school should start to use historical documents in explaining events. Reading, evaluating, and using so-called primary documents is a challenging set of skills, but it is one that I think is feasible. (I expect some teachers and others would argue that with me, and that expected disagreement is why these debates should be open!) Setting that goal would then require long-term plans for how we get middle-school students to the point where they could read and use primary documents. There is the professional-development side: Teacher education would have to require the use of historical documents, a step which might pressure university history departments to require primary sources in the standard survey, and there would be mid-career professional development about primary documents. There is also the prerequisite skills necessary that would logically change reading instruction in younger grades, asking elementary teachers to begin using short historical documents as reading material and as part of social-studies instruction. Even choosing *one* challenge in a content area has long-term cascading consequences and would be a healthy challenge for any system.

Gathering Information

Site Visits

Rhode Island's School Accountability for Learning and Teaching (or SALT) has a rotating set of site visits to schools in the state. A team of educators who have been oriented to site visits together spends several days in a school, looking not only at a paper self-study by the school staff but also visiting classes, listening to lessons, talking with teachers and students, and probably visiting the cafeteria at times. Modeled after the old English school inspection system (e.g., Wilson, 1997), the site visits are more intensive than secondary-school accreditation, and they result in a formal report back to the school and the community on the strengths and weaknesses of a school. Kentucky has used site visits to recommend changes but not to make public judgments as part of the state's accountability system.

Sampling of Items Across Students

Currently, most state assessments require individual student scores, with three-digit scores and implied differences in the single digits. Such a patina of precision is misleading, given both measurement error of all assessment and the arbitrary nature of any item specification. The National Assessment of Education Progress (NAEP) works differently, involving only a sample of students and, for each student taking the assessments, giving only a limited number of questions from a broad range of areas. One does not have individual-level scores from NAEP, but in return, NAEP can gather information about several domains and have accurate estimates of average student performance.[2] Kentucky has operated a similar system for several years (Kentucky Department of Education, 2006). One could construct a hybrid test structure which included a list of core items for all students and a range of supplementary items sampled from a broader pool, so that there could be much greater accuracy for a school or school district on a range of more specific domains. Such a structure could theoretically tell us how well 9-year-olds know single-digit multiplication (or other specific skills), information that annual tests typically do not provide.

Locally-Crafted Assessment

Currently, Nebraska is unique in having a state assessment system that is not a state assessment system: it leaves the decision about the nature of assessment to local school districts, and many of the tests are designed and constructed by teachers. At first refused approval by the U.S. Department of Education in the summer of 2006, Nebraska's Education Commissioner Douglas Christensen appealed and argued for the legitimacy of the policy that was focused on local decision-making (Nebraska Department of Education, 2006). In September 2006, the U.S. Department of Education gave tentative approval to Nebraska's system (Johnson, 2006), retreating from its hard-line position. Locally-constructed assessments can be sensitive to local conditions, and there is also the potential for a hybrid system with some state tests balanced with local assessment.

Assessment for Formative Evaluation

In evaluation, Michael Scriven (1967) described the difference between decision-making that made final judgments (summative evaluation) and decision-making that was feedback for changing course in a classroom or program (formative evaluation). As described in chapter 4, there is a solid research base for short frequent assessments tied to instructional decision making, or formative evaluation (also called curriculum-based measurement or progress monitoring). Shifting to formative evaluation would change the nature of information gathered about students: It would be more frequent than performance on a single annual test, and it would be more useful for teachers. As explained in chapter 4, an accountability system is unlikely to survive if based entirely on formative evaluation, but it is a sensible option as part of a broader reform of accountability.

Public Release of Test Items

Currently, Texas releases all items for its annual tests, and New York state law has long required that college admissions test publishers release items after each test. This openness is part of the transparency that rarely exists today in accountability. The release of test items does not fundamentally change the nature of a high-stakes system, but it is a prerequisite for a democratic debate of accountability that does not have to rely on secrecy.

Surveys of Teachers, Parents, and Students

Currently, the full extent of test preparation is unknown, though anecdotal reports are widespread (Nichols & Berliner, 2007). One tool to monitor the taught curriculum would be annual surveys of teachers, parents, and students organized by the state or a district and that include items to gauge the extent of potential side effects of any accountability system. Kentucky surveys students at the time of testing, and the results are part of each school's report.

Use of Data

Test Scores as Screening Devices

Currently, most accountability systems use test scores as a final judgment of a school's performance. One alternative would be to use test scores as screening to prompt a site visit or other close examination. While site visits are not inordinately expensive (a few thousand dollars per visit, according to state department staff in Rhode Island), the professional development required for site-visit teams and the scheduling involved limits the frequency of site visits to once or twice a decade, if one distributes site visits evenly across all schools. A state could use site visits in two ways: as an occasional but powerful outside check of a single school's work culture and as a follow-up for a state's student assessment system. If an accountability system guaranteed that punitive consequences would only follow a site visit, then a testing system would become a screening instrument rather than the final judgment, and the personal visiting of classrooms by trained teams of observers would be the critical linchpin in a reformed accountability system.

Site visits are also important to solving the problem of low student performance at the local level. Most intervention programs impose a one-size-fits-all solution on schools—often requiring a choice from a menu of particular programs that are curriculum- or management-focused—plans which may or may not address the needs of a particular school. While individual packages may show evidence of success in a particular dimension (such as reading performance), such programs may not address other issues in a school. Schools are unique, and a formulaic approach to intervention thus far has shown little evidence of success.

Reverse Triage

If a state or district is to treat a school in trouble as a crisis to be addressed urgently, then one must face the limits of a system's capacity for intervention: Not every school can be treated as if it is in crisis.[3] For practical reasons, any state or district must limit the identification of schools in crisis to those that can be targeted for intensive intervention. Such intervention could be at least as intensive as what happened in the Chancellor's District during Rudy Crew's tenure in New York City. But for such intervention to have enough resources and focus, the targeted group must be limited. In the same way that most teachers can only target a few students for intensive efforts, a principal can only focus on rescuing a few teachers whose careers are in serious trouble, and a school district or state can only intervene directly in a few schools (see Fuchs & Fuchs, 1995, for one system perspective).

Grand Jury Investigations

Given the country's history of racial inequality and the distrust many residents feel toward local school systems, any reformed accountability process must be independent of school systems. Those who advocate high-stakes accountability for civil-rights reasons have a point: Without an independent check, many school districts *will* treat some groups unequally. An appropriate mechanism for such a concern would be the use of grand juries to assess the degree of equal educational opportunities in school systems. California's grand juries investigate the effectiveness of local governments, and many states used to give grand juries similar authority (Jameson, 2000). Granting authority to a grand jury to investigate local government would not be the first expansion of grand-jury authority in many states (for example, see Florida Statutes 905.31-905.40). A grand jury has subpoena power and can go beyond test scores to investigate local conditions and report plausible solutions. Such an investigation could be a periodic requirement in any state, rotating the burden and opportunity for investigation every few years. A report by an independent authority such as a grand jury would carry significant weight in most local political environments.

Solving Problems

Investments in Systems Approaches to Schools in Crisis

While high-stakes accountability systems claim to be systematic approaches, broad changes in educational systems do not always lead to changes in the culture of individual schools or systems—and it is that change in culture that is essential to deeper commitments to student performance (e.g., Fullan, 1995, 2002; Fullan, Miles, & Taylor, 1980). With the emphasis on punitive consequences—the asymmetrical consequences described in chapter 5—teachers and administrators are in a structural position of being scapegoats, with the assumption that they have a deficit of skills or motivation. That position often excludes a systematic approach, something that is not helped by an emphasis on consistency when viewed at the top of a system by policymakers, not by those in schools (Fullan, 1996). Because schools are a site of work culture, problems are commonly a school-level issue, not an individual-level one. The frequent imposition of whole-school programs *over* the existing work culture does not guarantee a change in the work culture of a school. Nor does a partial or substantial change in personnel. Until there is considerably more research, I suspect that programmatic approaches to schools in crisis will work in only a haphazard sense, and for that reason there will need to be considerable investment in individual schools in crisis to address work culture issues.

Personnel Shuffles That Provide Developmental Leave Time

There *are* decision points in any system when a structure is not working or someone does not work well in a particular role. Most school accountability systems treat reorganizations in a way that destroys the professional dignity of administrators and teachers, with short notice for reassignments or terminations with no chance for rehabilitation. Such a system has the stench of an abattoir and is corrosive to morale in other schools, even where teachers are untouched by a reorganization. Reorganizations and reassignments could be handled in a way that preserves dignity for educators; Fliegel (1993) described such efforts in Spanish Harlem's secondary school choice program in the 1980s. Most school systems have a substantial investment in the expertise of individual teachers and administrators. To fire an educator without attempting to rescue a career is poor resource management as well as inhumane. In addition to treating educators moved out of positions humanely and sensitively, a school system would do well to negotiate with teachers unions explicit plans to provide developmental leave, perhaps 6-8 weeks of paid education and professional development, including time in a classroom with feedback.

Group Incentives for Sharing Resources and Expertise

Commonly, high-stakes accountability systems with group incentives provide bonus money to teachers and staff at schools with evidence of high academic performance (see Odden & Kelley, 2002, for more on group incentives). Such incentives focus entirely on material self-interest and create tension with the frequently-expressed ethic of public purpose, shared interests with other schools, and a concern over the equity of such rewards. Instead, group incentives could involve opportunities for sharing resources and perspectives with other school. Paying for substitutes to cover classes is as much of a concrete benefit as a bonus, and it would provide schools with a flexible tool to share the expertise and experience of their staff. In some states, schools have options on how to spend the reward cash, but the common pattern has been for one-time bonuses. States could encourage sharing expertise by providing a formula that provides more money when part of it is used for substitute pay or other techniques to share expertise.

The 15 ideas described above address specific needs for an accountability system that addresses the three challenges we face in schools— making sure our children are smarter and wiser than we are, addressing the inequalities in education, and solving specific crises. These activities would not corrode the morale of those in schools and instead is consistent with our expectations of an accountability system that is as democratic and transparent as we expect our society to be. I expect that readers can develop other specific options. Implementing these ideas would make school accountability policies more sane and sustainable in the long term. Even with the existence of alternatives to high-stakes accountability, our society faces three fundamental problems in crafting a reformed accountability system. We still face the problem of using expertise in a democratic context, the problem of multiple purposes for accountability, and the problem of test preparation as a widespread behavior that is a substitute for instruction. No one should pretend that reform of accountability would eliminate the use of expertly-constructed tests—nor do I think that the elimination of tests should be a high priority. However, we must change our perspective on tests and the role of testing expertise. We have inherited a world where test scores are more important than human judgment, instead of test scores' being used to aid debate and judgment. That world is not the fault of psychometricians—though there are many who will gladly take jobs at test publishers to produce and analyze high-stakes tests, there many others who will acknowledge the limitations of such tests and analyses. The decision to rely on test scores and autopilot mechanisms is a political one and can only be remedied by a political decision to move away from such autopilot policies. The fault lies in ourselves, not in the bar charts. The next two sections discuss the multiple purposes of accountability and test preparation.

THE PROBLEM OF MULTIPLE PURPOSES

One problem of creating a sane accountability system is sorting out the multiple purposes of accountability in a political system. We hear the word *accountability* and assume it means one thing (whether we like that meaning or not). We know that the historical roots of high-stakes accountability include the business metaphor of efficiency, an assumed political quid pro quo for greater resources from central governments, and a civil-rights rationale. But the rhetorical debates today do not acknowledge such subtlety. Often, the assumed axioms underlying policies silence other relevant concerns (Fine, 1991). Despite more than 20 years of debate about the statistical performance of students in the United States and the proper direction for school reform, remarkably few voices in public have questioned the primary assumptions behind the move toward accountability (early exceptions include Martin, Overholt, & Urban, 1976). This silencing shows what we are avoiding when we speak glibly of a political consensus around school accountability. While we are agreeing to high-stakes testing, what uncomfortable issues are we not discussing? The broad political legacy of statistical accountability systems is the narrowing of legitimate topics for public debate. We do not often discuss the purpose of accountability or who will be making the key decisions to keep schools accountable.

Accountability for What Purposes?

The dominant discussion of accountability leaves vague the goal of accountability mechanisms. The improvement of schools is an insufficient goal because accountability is fundamentally a political and not a technical process. This book has described the political roots of accountability, acknowledging the multiple origins, but I have not yet addressed the goals that others currently see. Accountability has multiple meanings, in both a general sense and also the current sense in education of statistical judgment (Darling-Hammond & Ascher, 1991). The apparent consensus for accountability hides the differences (and the conflicts) among the following meanings of statistical systems.

Judging Public Schools as Institutions

One may use test score statistics to judge schools as a set of institutions. Judging the worth of schools in general by test scores is one of the most widely used tools in school politics. The annual release of average SAT scores in the late 1970s prepared the ground politically for the claim of declining school effectiveness made by the National Commission on Educational Excellence (1983). One political legacy of judging public schooling by test scores is the assumption that schooling is a monolithic entity that fails or succeeds as a single body. What this myth of a monolithic system hides is wide variations in schooling, especially between poor and wealthy schools—the differences among the challenges our schools face. Another political legacy is that citizens may face difficulty reconciling popular conceptions of failing schools with information gathered in other ways. Polls consistently show that parents' perceptions of their local schools are more positive than their perceptions of schooling nationwide (e.g., Rose & Gallup, 2005, 2006). In addition, private interests may subvert policies based on the gross judgment of schools. For example, some wealthy parents in one Michigan district deliberately pulled their children out of high-stakes standardized testing when they perceived that it might hurt their children (Johnston, 1997). They may well have been willing to have high-stakes testing for "other people's children" (to borrow from Lisa Delpit's 1995 book title) but not theirs. This consequence is the educational equivalent of urban development NIMBY (Not in My Back Yard) syndrome.

Judging Teachers and Other Educators

One may also justify accountability as a way to raise or clarify expectations and goals for teachers and administrators. An explicit part of accountability systems in the last few years has been the evaluation of teachers, principals, and other administrators. For example, the Tennessee Value-Added Assessment System, passed in 1992, originally mandated statistical measures of student gain as part of personnel evaluation (Educational Improvement Act, 1992). An earlier variant of judging teachers, schools, and school systems by comparative statistics was the U.S. Department of Education's "Wall Chart" instituted by Terrence Bell as an attempt to spur reform (Ginsburg, Noell, & Plisko, 1988). This use of accountability, focusing on teachers and administrators, is the one most criticized as encouraging teaching to the test and "gaming" test results. The political legacy may be even more harmful: By setting up a system based on the distrust of teachers, we make alternative ways of judging teachers and schools more difficult.

Judging Students

In many states and school systems, standardized tests have high stakes not only for educators but also for individuals students, as scores can be among the criteria for entrance to academic programs, grade promotion, or other real rewards and punishments in schooling. The use of tests to sort students U.S. began with monitorial schools in the early nineteenth century and admissions tests to early public high schools (Beadie, 2004; Kaestle, 1973; Labaree, 1988; Reese, 1995). More recently, the use of so-called minimum competency tests emerged in the late 1970s as a response to allegedly lowered standards of public schools (Resnick, 1980). The rationale of using tests to make students accountable is that, having test scores as a clear goal, students and schools would meet the expectations. One potential legacy of such high stakes, however, is the rhetorical scapegoating of students. Calhoun (1973) describes one purpose of testing in schools as displacing blame for ineffective teaching onto students. If a student fails a test, one may reason, the failure is the student's intelligence and lack of diligence. That consequence is already evident in many states with high-stakes testing. In Tennessee, the teachers union pressed to exempt scores of students with disabilities from teacher value-added statistics ("Sanders model to measure 'value added,' " 1991). One might presume that children with disabilities are those on whom we should most focus attention in evaluating teaching effectiveness. Yet the union argued that teachers asked for the exclusion of scores because including such scores would be unfair to teachers. The displacement of blame for failed schooling onto students is a legacy of testing that existed well before high-stakes standardized testing, but accountability systems may exacerbate such tendencies (e.g., Booher-Jennings, 2005).

Judging Public Policy

One might use standardized test scores (like other information) to evaluate public policies. Begun in 1969, the National Assessment of Educational Progress is theoretically a means for using non-high-stakes testing to evaluate public school policy with objective data. NAEP data is at the heart of debate about school and student performance.

Building Organizations

In a broad sense, standardized testing supports the determination or control of curriculum content at the state and national levels. Some such as Ravitch (1995) explicitly advocate curriculum content standards and see teaching to the test as valid with appropriate testing and content. However, one consequence of statistical accountability is the creation of new public and private organizations producing educational statistics. Publicly, states now have accountability or evaluation offices whose job is to provide the technical expertise in analyzing test data, and the federal government has the National Center on Educational Statistics, which contracts out NAEP as well as compiling and disseminating a wide variety of educational statistics. Private organizations supported by testing are the companies that write and sell tests or contract with agencies for the creation of specific tests. With each public release of test score statistics, popular news sources, politicians, administrators, and the public rely more on relatively anonymous technocrats to explain what is happening in schools. Other new professions this century, such as nuclear science, have also staked their claim to expertise on political factors (Balogh, 1991a). The fact that this reliance on statisticians stems from political pressure for reform usually escapes notice (Turner, 2003).

Marketing

Schools occasionally use student statistics as part of public marketing strategies, either to attract students who have choices as in selective colleges or to bolster public support. One of the largest metropolitan school systems in the country produced a pamphlet in the late 1990s boldly titled, "Our Students' Test Scores Reflect Academic Achievement" (Hillsborough County Public Schools, 1997). While one paragraph cautions that test scores are not the sole basis for evaluating students or schools, the rest of the pamphlet trumpets above-average achievement. The use of accountability data for marketing is an open secret among administrators.

As Dennie Wolf said in the John Merrow documentary *Testing ... Testing ... Testing* (1997), "Districts sell real estate based on test scores." Figlio and Lucas's (2004) study documenting a link between Florida's judgment of schools and real estate values should be no surprise. With the decline of administrative authority described elsewhere in this article, superintendents have considerable interest in boasting about their systems using any tools at their command.

These varied purposes of accountability are not necessarily congruent. The use of test scores to bash public schools is not compatible with a nuanced debate over public policy, and students and teachers may have conflicts of interest when tests have high stakes for both. In addition to inconsistent purposes, the aims of accountability do not easily include other issues relevant to education: equity, the direction of curriculum, or the purposes of education more broadly in a changing world (Darling-Hammond, 1992). One dominant assumption of accountability systems is that the goals of education are agreed upon and we need only establish a system to measure whether schools and students meet those goals. The creation of high-stakes accountability systems may have frozen the assumption of a single purpose of statistical accountability into a framework for the politically accepted discussion in education for years hence.

Who Keeps Schools Accountable?

A second assumption rarely examined is that central bureaucracies and popular news media are the logical, natural places for holding schools accountable for performance. In most school testing regimes, central offices at the state or local level are responsible for the general logistics of testing and compiling results. Results at some level are then available to administrators, public boards of education, and media organizations. In many states and regions, newspapers publish test score statistics, often ranking schools or systems based on the scores. As described earlier in this chapter, Nebraska's system of local assessment is a unique response to the No Child Left Behind. Who is not among the key organizers of and direct targets of test score dissemination is as important as who is.

Judges and Advocates Monitoring School System Compliance in Discrimination Cases

Judges and advocates overseeing compliance with nondiscrimination orders such as desegregation generally have not been intended users of "accountability" information. Despite promises by school systems to pay closer attention to achievement in desegregation cases, local systems have a very spotty record in demonstrating success after the end of desegregation orders. Orfield, Eaton, and the Harvard Project on School Desegregation (1996) has compiled evidence that, in several of the major cases the past two decades, school districts released from desegregation monitoring by the courts not only experienced resegregation but growing achievement gaps between white and minority students (also see Borman et al., 2004). The new accountability system does not appear geared to keep systems accountable in this respect. Many advocates appointed to monitoring and advisory commissions have reported to Orfield and his associates that local systems have either denied information such as disaggregated test scores outright or made the gathering of data extremely difficult. In addition, the Supreme Court decision in *Missouri v. Jenkins* (1995) declared that district court judges should consider test scores as marginally important (at most) as a measure of compliance with racial equity requirements. The only major case where a court has continued to monitor standardized test scores as part of a major equity lawsuit has been in New Jersey, where the state's supreme court continued to criticize inequalities between the education offered children in the wealthiest and poorest systems of the state (*Abbott v. Burke*, 1997). In that case, the court broadened its focus from just monetary support of schools to include measurable outcomes. The New Jersey Supreme Court has been a lonely exception to the general rule, especially in the federal judiciary: To the courts, accountability does not appear to require even reasonably equitable outcomes.

Parents and the General Public

Parents receive test scores of their children, but rarely do they or the general public have direct access to test score results or their limitations. Popular news sources mediate the transmission of information, often deleting information critical to understanding the limits of such data or transforming the statistics in ways either incomprehensible to readers or to create invalid statistical comparisons. The reporting of high-stakes test data by Nashville metropolitan newspapers form a case in point. Beginning in 1993, the state of Tennessee reported test results of schools and districts using a complex statistical system called the Tennessee Value Added Assessment System. The state's newspapers quickly rushed to print school-by-school scores including rankings, even where schools many rankings apart had negligible differences in scores (in other words, when the rankings were unjustified by the statistics). For example, in 1996 the *Nashville Tennessean* transformed the value-added scores into percentile ranking, even though the technical documentation for value-added scores would not support such an interpretation (Bock & Wolfe, 1996; Klausnitzer, 1996; Tennessee Department of Education, 1996). Why did the *Tennessean* transform value-added scores that were the result of a prior statistical manipulation, and why did the paper then rank schools? One reporter explained:

> We chose to report in percentile ranks because it helps people see how their school stacks up against the rest of the state, and because this information is not available anywhere else. It was calculated by *The Tennessean*... [because] we wanted to offer something unique. We also wanted to answer our readers' number one question about the test scores: How does my child's school compare to the other schools? (L. Green, personal correspondence, December 5, 1996)

In addition, the newspaper reported percentile rankings by 10ths (for example, 50.1 instead of 50th percentile). The same reporter acknowledged that the newspaper staff did not consciously justify that apparent precision:

> There's really no need to report these numbers down to the tenth of a percentile. However, the programming for the site was written last year ... so the computer automatically included the decimal place, and we didn't think it was necessary to take it off.

In this case, a metropolitan newspaper's desire to have "something unique" conflicted with its readership's interest in having clearly understandable information to interpret independently or information with a justifiable level of detail. Even if one assumes that the value-added scores are comprehensible, transforming those into percentile rankings was neither valid nor necessary for rankings (itself a method of reporting scores which the state's external evaluators recommended against). In no case did the newspaper note what the evaluators clearly stated, that school scores were unstable and could not be relied on for clear distinctions in performance (Bock & Wolfe, 1996). The dissemination of information through two intermediaries (the state government and news sources) in essence created one dominant way to analyze scores in the metropolitan Nashville area: how did schools "stack up" in competition with each other? The false precision in percentile rankings suggested that readers could rely on the numbers as rigorous, objective facts. The accuracy of newspaper reporting is also questionable; the *Tennessean* had to reprint its comparative tables in 1994 because of acknowledged gross errors in reporting ("How Midstate Schools Stack Up," 1994a, 1994b). While comparisons among schools may be appropriate in some ways, the presentation of school scores suggested a certainty which was incompatible either with the statistical calculations or the mediation of state agencies and newspapers in transmitting test scores.

Moreover, the dissemination and discussion of today's school account-ability systems strip parents and the general public of control and owner-ship of information. In the case of Nashville, a reporter reduced parental evaluation of schools to examining rankings in a table, akin to sports league rankings (see Goldstein & Spiegelhalter, 1996). One might con-trast the typical method of disseminating accountability statistics with two alternative local methods of accountability: the "visiting committee" of town elders in the eighteenth and early nineteenth-century district schools, on the one hand, and the calculation of dropout statistics by a Hispanic activist organization in Chicago in the 1980s, on the other. In many district schools, a small committee of citizens held the power of hir-ing and firing over schoolteachers and could visit the school at any time (e.g., Jeffries, Armitage, Collson, Forsyth, & Lyman, 1737/1973). Accountability in district schools was a rough-and-tumble affair, often unfair to teachers, but local citizens could form judgments in a simple way: watching classrooms. Independent gathering of data today is also possible. In the 1980s, Aspira, Inc., a Hispanic activist organization, sus-pected that official dropout statistics from the Chicago public schools were inaccurate or fraudulent and conducted its own research. Activists then used the independent statistics to help prod Chicago toward urban school reform (Hess, 1991; Kyle & Kantowicz, 1991). In both cases, indi-viduals at the local level produced and acted on their own judgments of schools. Reliance on centrally-calculated statistics in accountability sys-tems often overrides local, independent judgment of schools.

The fundamental issue of control is directly connected to the purposes of accountability: Individuals in different roles would ask different ques-tions of accountability mechanisms. Politicians might ask whether schools "measure up" to some standard such as a national norm. Business leaders might ask about workplace-related skills and behavior. College faculty would want students to have some intellectual foundation. Parents might ask whether their children are getting enough individual attention. Who should be asking the hard questions about schools? Because of pressures within government, doubts about its utility and cost, and disagreements about what it should measure, the U.S. Department of Education-col-lected Common Core of Data for many years gathered relatively innocu-ous information in a history Janet Weiss and Judith Gruber (1987) described as "managed irrelevance." Of all the information used by the National Commission on Excellence in Education (1983) to lambaste the condition of schools, none came from the official federal education data-base (Weiss & Gruber, 1987). What we face is not an explicit consensus but a hidden one, never debated clearly, founded on the spread of stan-dardized test scores. Statistical accountability systems suggest an objectiv-ity and universality of coverage which is impossible. As Sizer (1995) noted with regard to the debate about educational standards, "The word system has come up again; ... Essentially, it implies a technocratic approach" (p. 34). We should not evade the political question of the purposes of schools through the production of statistics. The current penchant for statistical accountability systems diverts resources to a mechanism that hinders discussing the nuts and bolts of schooling. We hide behind the apparently objective notion of an accountability system.

THE PROBLEM OF TEST PREPARATION

The last problem discussed in this chapter and probably the most difficult to address is the practice of test preparation, defined operationally as superficial techniques designed primarily to raise test scores and not as substantively educational in themselves (Nichols & Berliner, 2007). Test preparation can include activities in the classroom such as drills focused on specific questions known or anticipated to be on a high-stakes test, the redesign of classroom activities around the formats of tests such as teachers' asking questions or requiring responses in the format of the high-stakes tests, or activity outside the classroom such as all-school assemblies before high-stakes tests or even changing school breakfast and lunch programs (Smith, 1991a). Test preparation can be short-term, such as the changes in school meals analyzed by Figlio and Winicki (2005), and it can be long-term, such as when classroom routines change to suit the vagaries of specific tests.

In discussing test preparation, one must separate out the responses to tests that are instructionally valid, responses that are neutral, and responses that are inimical to either short- or long-term goals in schooling. When my children complain about "FCAT prep," as they call it, I probe further. Some responses to high-stakes accountability will be reasonable. When my children's fourth-grade teachers spent class time on writing and giving detailed feedback on a variety of forms of writing, they were responding to Florida's fourth-grade writing test in a way that was educationally sound. While there are a range of opinions on the writing test, few would question the legitimacy of providing more opportunities for writing practice with feedback. Some responses to high-stakes accountability are neutral in the way they affect the routines of teachers and students. Calling an assignment "test prep" is a labeling exercise and does not by itself change the routines in classrooms.[4] I know no studies of this relabeling practice, but my anecdotal observation is that it is often in response to parents' or principals' wanting to know if a teacher is preparing students for a test—and teachers often oblige the request by labeling what they already do as test preparation. But in addition to the responses to high-stakes testing that improve instruction or are neutral, there is also significant evidence of test preparation that has no discernible long-term value, no matter what one's interest in accountability (Nichols & Berliner, 2007). I have seen my children come home with commercial test-preparation booklets, materials geared entirely to the format of a test and a subset of skills the booklet's authors is guessing is important to success. Some minimize the extent and effect of test preparation in a high-stakes environment. I challenge such critics to find a single local public high school in Florida where 9th and 10th grade students spend more time studying Shakespeare's plays than they spend in superficial test-preparation activities.[5]

The critical question for those concerned about test preparation is whether this pattern is reversible. Some critics of high-stakes testing would point to the asymmetrical structure of accountability. If test preparation is just a response to the pressures of accountability, then reversing the trend toward greater test consequences would also reverse the incentives for test preparation. I am firmly convinced that the current high-stakes environment encourages superficial test preparation and that reducing the asymmetrical pressures of accountability is a necessary step to reversing test preparation.

However, I am not convinced that eliminating high-stakes accountability would eliminate test preparation. The asymmetrical pressures tied to accountability comprise only part of the picture. As explained in chapter 3, test preparation has existed for some time, most visibly in connection with admissions tests to colleges and graduate and professional schools. A recognizable part of any bookstore is the section on test preparation for the SAT, ACT, LSAT, MCAT, GRE, GED, TOEFL, AP exams, and a variety of professional licensure exams. There are now parallel versions for state K-12 tests, but they are the newcomers in the test-prep genre. Companies such as Princeton Review and Kaplan also earn millions of dollars annually through test-preparation workshops. Test preparation is a part of modern culture in the United States, and eliminating the most damaging aspects of high-stakes accountability would not eliminate the culture of test preparation.

Historian and sociologist David Labaree (1988, 1997) would say that the culture of test preparation comes from the private uses of public schooling. Parents see part of the job of schooling to prepare their children for success in life. That private goal of parents parallels but is not identical to the human capital argument that investing in education makes people more productive and is socially useful. The benefits of education may include the knowledge, schools, and habits one learns in school, but to parents and students the paper credential of a degree is crucial. A degree has both use and exchange value, in Labaree's terms:

You not only learn while earning a degree, but you can also use a degree to exchange for a job or further education, which in turn provides another degree that can be exchanged for a job. For millions, the purpose of education is reduced to earning a degree or succeeding in school without really learning, as Labaree put it. With this instrumentalist view of education, test preparation is a positive good, as it achieves an aim with significant payoff or at least avoidance of pain. The superficiality of test preparation demonstrates the extent to which the private mobility goals of education have displaced other goals.

The failures of formative evaluation techniques are closely related to the spread of a test preparation culture. When the immediate consequence of an exam drives the prospective response of test preparation, attempts to use tests as feedback to reshape instruction will face an uphill battle. Superficiality has trumped feedback, something clearly evident in the anecdotal reports of principals wanting to use early-childhood phonemic-awareness assessments to retain children and evaluate teachers, as well as anecdotal reports of teachers trying to "teach to the test" by drilling young children on nonsense syllables (Goodman, 2006). In the long run, the best chance to drive superficial test preparation out of schools is to champion formative evaluation. Similarly, those who advocate formative evaluation must acknowledge that a work culture that values test preparation is the greatest barrier to the spread and use of formative evaluation. Driving test preparation out through the spread of formative evaluation is probably the greatest challenge to those who think we have built an accountability Frankenstein monster. It is a greater generational challenge than changing the curriculum.

No one should expect the immediate shrinking of high-stakes accountability. The political dynamics continue to encourage two-dimensional perspectives on accountability, whether it is Education Secretary Margaret Spellings's insistence that No Child Left Behind is "99.9% pure" (Romano, 2006) or the calls by some opponents for Congress to refuse to reauthorize the No Child Left Behind Act (Kovacs, 2006). I suspect that many fellow critics of high-stakes accountability will call this book tepid, insufficient, and a watered-down thesis. I also suspect that defenders of high-stakes accountability will also use the term *watered-down*, though in their case to refer to my expectations of schools. Accusations will immediately claim that any set of alternatives whether proposed by me or others is lowering standards, abandoning the concept of equal educational opportunity, or wanting to "go back to the bad old days."

Pragmatically, some parts of an alternative accountability system would likely be implemented incrementally and in several cases already has. Nebraska has local assessment; Rhode Island has site visits; Texas releases test items publicly. Some state may survey stakeholders to monitor the taught curriculum and the extent of superficial test preparation. Piecemeal reform can be valuable victories at the local level but frequently take years to spread, if they ever do. But they nonetheless can work using the policy feedback described in chapter 1. As more people have experience with better accountability systems, the political chances of accountability reform are greater. The piecemeal amelioration of high-stakes accountability will not change the damaging effects of the No Child Left Behind Act overnight, but it can set the stage for broader changes.

Moreover, I hope that along with Sharon Nichols and David Berliner's (2007) *Collateral Damage*, this book establishes useful perspectives on accountability for its most vigorous defenders, its harshest critics, and those of us who are somewhere in the middle. If you thought high-stakes accountability was necessary and appropriate before reading the book, I have tried to make you uncomfortable with the consequences. If you signed the Kovacs (2006) petition or otherwise thought that accountability has no place in schooling, I have written some of this book to make you rethink your opposition to accountability. And if you are like me and think accountability is necessary but out of hand, this book was mainly written for you, to show where our accountability Frankenstein monster came from and how we can tame it and force it to do some useful work.

Remember, that I am thy creature: I ought to be thy Adam; but I am rather the fallen angel, whom thou drivest from joy for no misdeed. Every where I see bliss, from which I alone am irrevocably excluded. I was benevolent and good; misery made me a fiend. Make me happy, and I shall again be virtuous.

—Frankenstein's Creature (Shelley, 1818/1869, p. 78)

NOTES

1. As Somerby (2006) notes, Romano and many of her informants ignore confounding factors behind the drop in the proportion of college graduates identified as proficient in various categories of literacy: The increase in the number of college graduates, in the number of college graduates for whom English is a second language, and the changing age structure all may be contributing factors.

2. Restricted-use data sets do allow researchers to pull from a distribution of scores, but that capacity to impute individual scores is different from the lay association of a score with a student's performance.

3. I start this discussion at the school level because the school campus is the most relevant unit for work culture.

4. I am agnostic on the potential for such relabeling to change the broader discussion of what is legitimate education; my argument elsewhere in this

section suggests that such relabeling is a consequence of existing incentives for test preparation, not a cause.

5. In the spring of 2006, I issued a public challenge looking for such schools. The only responses I received came from Massachusetts.

REFERENCES

Abbott v. Burke. (1997). 149 N.J. 145. Retrieved September 27, 1997, from http://www-camlaw.rutgers.edu/decisions/supreme/m-622-96.opn.html.

Abrams, L. M., Pedulla, J. J., & Madaus, G. F. (2003). Views from the classroom: Teachers' opinions of statewide testing programs *Theory into Practice, 42*(1), 18–29.

Adams, S. (1996). *The Dilbert principle: A cubicle's-eye view of bosses, meetings, management fads, & other workplace afflictions.* New York: HarperCollins.

Addams, J. (1910/1999). *Twenty years at Hull House.* New York: Signet Classics.

Amador, G. (2006, November 26). Public defenders office out of cash. *Miami Herald.* Retrieved November 27, 2006, from http://www.miami.com/mld/miamiherald/16099260.htm.

American Educational Research Association, American Psychological Association, and National Council on Measurement in Education. (1985). *Standards for educational and psychological testing.* Washington, DC: Author.

American Educational Research Association, American Psychological Association, and National Council on Measurement in Education. (1999). *Standards for educational and psychological testing.* Washington, DC: Author.

American Federation of Teachers. (1996). *Making standards matter.* Washington, DC: Author.

American Federation of Teachers. (2000). *Making standards matter.* Washington, DC: Author.

American Federation of Teachers. (2006). NCLB watch. *American Teacher,* Retrieved August 14, 2006, from http://www.aft.org/pubs-reports/american_teacher/feb06/nclb.htm.

Amrein, A. L. & Berliner, D. C. (2002). High-stakes testing, uncertainty, and student learning *Education Policy Analysis Archives, 10*(18). Retrieved October 30, 2006, from http://epaa.asu.edu/epaa/v10n18/.

Amrein-Beardsley, A., & Berliner, D. (2003). Re-analysis of NAEP math and reading scores in states with and without high-stakes tests: Response to Rosenshine. *Education Policy Analysis Archives, 11*(25). Retrieved October 30, 2006, from http://epaa.asu.edu/epaa/v11n25/.

Angus, D. & Mirel, J. (1999). *The failed promise of the American high school, 1890-1995.* New York: Teachers College Press.

Apple, M. W. (1988). *Teachers and texts: A political economy of class and gender relations in education.* New York: Routledge.

Apple, M. W. (1996). *Cultural politics and education.* New York: Teachers College Press.

Arenson, K. W. (2006, April 9). Class-action lawsuit to be filed over SAT scoring errors. *New York Times,* p. 33. Retrieved December 9, 2006, from http://www.nytimes.com/2006/04/09/us/09sat.html.

Arizona Department of Education. (2002). *Summary report for spring 2002 test administration for grades 3, 5, 8, and high school.* Phoenix: Author. Retrieved October 22, 2006, from http://www.ade.state.az.us/ResearchPolicy/AIMSResults/2002AIMSExecSum.pdf.

Aschbacher, P. R. (1991). Performance assessment: State activity, interest, and concerns. *Applied Measurement in Education, 4*(4), 275–288.

Ash, J. (2006, December 24). Bush built powerful legacy. *Florida Today.* Retrieved December 24, 2006, from htp://www.floridatoday.com/apps/pbcs.dll/article?AID=/20061224/NEWS01/612240335/1006.

Augenblick, J. G., Myers, J. L., & Anderson, A. B. (1997). Equity and adequacy in school funding. *The Future of Children, 7,* 63–78.

Axtell, J. (1974). *The school upon a hill: Education and society in colonial New England.* New York: W. W. Norton.

Ayres, L. P. (1918). History and present status of educational measurements. In G. W. Whipple (Ed.), *The measurement of educational products. The seventeenth yearbook of the National Society for the Study of Education* (Part II, pp. 9–15). Bloomington, IL: Public School Publishing.

Baker, F. (2001). *The basics of item response theory.* College Park, MD: ERIC Clearinghouse on Assessment and Evaluation. Retrieved August 14, 2006, from http://edres.org/irt/baker/

Baker, S. (1995). Testing equality: The National Teacher Examination and the NAACP's legal campaign to equalize teachers' salaries in the South, 1936–1963. *History of Education Quarterly, 35,* 49–64.

Ballou, D., Sanders, W., & Wright, P. (2004). Controlling for students background in value-added assessment of teachers. *Journal of Educational and Behavioral Statistics, 29*(1), 37–66.

Balogh, B. (1991a). *Chain reaction: Expert debate and public participation in American commercial nuclear power, 1945–1975.* New York: Cambridge University Press.

Balogh, B. (1991b). Reorganizing the organizational synthesis: Reconsidering modern American federal-professional relations. *Studies in American Political Development, 5*(1), 119–172.

Barnes, R. E., & Ginsburg, A. L. (1979). Relevance of the RMC models for Title I policy concerns. *Educational Evaluation and Policy Analysis, 1*(2), 7–14.

Beadie, N. (2004). Moral errors and strategic mistakes: Lessons from the history of student accountability. K. A. Sirotnik (Ed.), *Holding accountability account-*

able: What ought to matter in public education (pp. 35–50). New York: Teachers College Press.

Bell, T. H. (1988). *Thirteenth man: A Reagan cabinet memoir.* New York: Free Press.

Berk, R. A. (Ed.). (1982). *Handbook of methods for detecting test bias.* Baltimore, MD: Johns Hopkins University Press.

Berliner, D. C., & Biddle, B. J. (1995). *The manufactured crisis: Myths, fraud, and the attack on America's public schools.* Reading, MA: Addison-Wesley.

Berliner, D. C., & Nichols, S. L. (2007). *Collateral damage: How high-stakes testing corrupts America's schools.* Cambridge, MA: Harvard Education Press.

Berman, B. (1983). Business efficiency, American schooling and the public school superintendency: A reconsideration of the Callahan thesis. *History of Education Quarterly, 23,* 297–321.

Bestor, A. E. (1953). *Educational wastelands: The retreat from learning in our public schools.* Champaign, IL: University of Illinois Press.

Beveridge R., Ducharme J., Janes L., Beaulieu S., & Walter S. (1999). Reliability of the Canadian emergency department triage and acuity scale: Interrater agreement. *Annals of Emergency Medicine, 34*(2), 155–159.

Bielinski, J., Scott., J., Minnema, J., & Thurlow, M. (2000). *Test publishers' views on out-of-level testing.* Out-of-Level Testing Project Report 3. Minneapolis, MN: University of Minnesota, National Center on Educational Outcomes. Retrieved August 14, 2006, from http://education.umn.edu/NCEO/OnlinePubs/OOLT3.html.

Bishop, J. (2005). High school exit examinations: When do learning effects generalize? In J. L. Herman & E. H. Haertel (Eds.), *Uses and misuses of data for educational accountability and improvement. The 104th yearbooks of the National Society for the Study of Education* (Part II, pp. 260–288). Malden, MA: Blackwell Publishing.

Black, P., & Wiliam, D. (1998). Assessment and classroom learning. *Assessment in Education: Principles, Policy and Practice, 5*(1), 7-73.

Blanton, C. K. (2004). *The strange career of bilingual education in Texas, 1836–1981.* College Station, TX: Texas A&M University Press.

Bledstein, B. (1976). *The culture of professionalism: The middle class and the development of higher education in America.* New York: Norton.

Block, J. H. (1978). Standards and criteria: A response. *Journal of Educational Measurement, 15*(4), 291–295.

Blount, J. M. (1998). *Destined to rule the school: Women and the superintendency, 1873–1995.* Albany, NY: State University of New York Press.

Blumenthal, R. (2006, August 1). In Kansas, evolution's backers are mounting a counterattack. *New York Times,* p. A1.

Board on Testing and Assessment. (2000). *Tests and teaching quality: Interim report.* Washington, DC: National Research Council. Retrieved October 23, 2006, from http://fermat.nap.edu/books/0309069467/html/.

Bock, R. D., & Wolfe, R. (1996). *Audit and review of the Tennessee Value-Added Assessment System (TVAAS): Final report.* Nashville: Tennessee Comptroller of the Treasury.

Bode, B. H. (1938/1971). *Progressive education at the crossroads.* New York: Arno Press.

Bond, H. M. (1924). Intelligence tests and propaganda. *The Crisis, 28,* 64.

Booher-Jennings, J. (2005). Below the bubble: "Educational triage" and the Texas accountability system. *American Educational Research Journal, 42*(2), 231–268.

Borman, K., Eitle, T. M., Michael, D., Eitle, D. J., Lee, R., Johnson, L., et al. (2004). Accountability in a postdesegregation era: The continuing significance of racial segregation in Florida's schools. *American Educational Research Journal 41,* 605–631.

Bourne, W. O. (1870). *History of the public school society.* New York: William Wood.

Brace, C. L. (1872). *The dangerous classes of New York and twenty years among them.* New York: Wynkoop and Hallenbeck.

Bracey, G. W. (1995). *Final exam: A study of the perpetual scrutiny of American education.* Bloomington, IN: Technos Press.

Bracey, G. W. (2002). The 12th Bracey report on the condition of public education. *Phi Delta Kappan, 84*(2), 135–150.

Bracey, G. W. (2004, Fall). The perfect law. *Dissent,* pp. 62–66. Retrieved June 12, 2006, from http://www.dissentmagazine.org/article/?article=318.

Brady, M. (2000, May). The standards juggernaut. *Phi Delta Kappan, 81*(9), 648–651.

Brandt, A. M. (1987). *No magic bullet: A social history of venereal disease in the United States since 1880* (expanded ed.). New York: Oxford University Press.

Braun, H. (2004, January). Reconsidering the impact of high-stakes testing. *Education Policy Analysis Archives, 12*(1). Retrieved October 30, 2006, from http://epaa.asu.edu/epaa/v12n1/.

Brint, S. (1994). *In an age of experts: The changing roles of professionals in politics and public life.* Princeton, NJ: Princeton University Press.

Broder, S. (2002). *Tramps, unfit mothers, and neglected children: Negotiating the family in nineteenth-century Philadelphia.* Philadelphia: University of Pennsylvania Press.

Brody, D. (1989). Time and work during early American industrialism. *Labor History, 30,* 5–47.

Brookings Institution. (2006). *Measuring child well-being: The education flatline?* Center on Children and Families briefing. Washington, DC: Author. Retrieved October 24, 2006, from http://www.brookings.edu/comm/events/20060328.pdf.

Brown v. Board of Education, 347 U.S. 483 (1954).

Brownson, O. (1839, October). Article I—Second annual report of the Board of Education. *Boston Quarterly Review,* pp. 393–434.

Bryk, A. S., & Raudenbush, S. W. (1992). *Hierarchical linear models: Applications and data analysis methods.* Newbury Park, CA: Sage.

Buder, L. (1971, March 19). Clark assails education board on an outside testing contract. *New York Times,* p. 25.

Burke, A. (2006, August 6). No mas. Message posted to the ARN-L electronic mailing list. Retrieved August 7, 2006, from http://interversity.org/lists/arn-l/archives/Aug2006_date/msg00023.html.

Burns, P. (2003). Regime theory, state government, and a takeover of urban education. *Journal of Urban Affairs, 25*(3), 285–303.

Bush v. Holmes, Fla. SC04-2323 (2006). Retrieved December 28, 2006, from http://www.floridasupremecourt.org/decisions/2006/sc04-2323.pdf.

Bush, G. W. (2001). *No child left behind*. Washington, DC: White House. Retrieved October 21, 2006, from http://www.ed.gov/nclb/overview/intro/presidentplan/proposal.pdf.

Bush, J. (n.d.). *Plan for education*. Tallahassee, FL: Florida Office of the Governor. Retrieved September 25, 2002, from http://www.myflorida.com/myflorida/government/governorinitiatives/aplusplan/planEducation.html.

Calhoun, D. H. (1973). *The intelligence of a people*. Princeton, NJ: Princeton University Press.

Callahan, R. E. (1962). *Education and the cult of efficiency: A study of the social forces that have shaped the administration of the public schools*. Chicago: University of Chicago Press.

Callender, J. (2004). Value-added student assessment. *Journal of Educational and Behavioral Statistics, 29*(1), 5.

Campbell, N. M. (2002, July 29). Area schools to receive cash bonuses. *San Gabriel Valley Tribune* Retrieved December 30, 2006, from the LexisNexis Academic database.

Cannell, J. J. (1989). *How public educators cheat on standardized achievement tests: The "Lake Wobegon" report*. Albuquerque, NM: Friends for Education. (ERIC Reproduction Document Service No. ED 314 454).

Carnoy, M., & Loeb, S. (2002). Does external accountability affect student outcomes? A cross-state analysis. *Educational Evaluation and Policy Analysis, 24*(4), 305–331.

Carnoy, M., Jacobsen, R., Mishel, L., & Rothstein, R. (2005). *The charter-school dust-up*. Washington, DC: Economic Policy Institute. Retrieved June 10, 2006, from http://www.epinet.org/content.cfm/book_charter_school.

Centeno, M. A. (1993). The new leviathan: The dynamics and limits of technocracy. *Theory and Society, 22*(3), 307–335.

Center for Policy Research in Education. (1989). *State education reform in the 1980s. CPRE Policy Briefs*. RB-03-11/89. New Brunswick, NJ: Author. Retrieved October 21, 2006, from http://www.cpre.org/Publications/rb03.pdf.

Center on Education Policy. (2004). *Pay now or pay later: The hidden costs of high school exit exams*. Washington, DC: Author. Retrieved June 12, 2006, from http://www.cep-dc.org/pubs/hiddencost_may04/HiddenCostFinal.pdf.

Center on Education Policy. (2006). *From the capitol to the classroom: Year 4 of the No Child Left Behind Act*. Washington, DC: Author.

Chaddock, G. R. (2005, October 20). America's pupils progress in math, falter in reading. *Christian Science Monitor*. Retrieved December 20, 2006, from the LexisNexis Academic database.

Chandler, A. D. (1980). *The visible hand: The managerial revolution in American business*. New York: Belknap Press.

Chandler, M. (1999). *Secrets of the SAT* [Video]. Produced for *Frontline*. Documentary Web site at http://www.pbs.org/wgbh/pages/frontline/shows/sats/. Transcript of interview with Katzman retrieved July 20, 2006, from http://www.pbs.org/wgbh/pages/frontline/shows/sats/interviews/katzman.html.

Chatterji, M. (2004, April). *Good and bad news about Florida student achievement: Performance trends on multiple indicators since passage of the A+ legislation.* Educational Policy Studies Laboratory policy brief EPSL-0401-105-EPRU. Retrieved February 25, 2005, from http://www.asu.edu/educ/epsl/EPRU/epru_2004_Research_Writing.htm.

Chesney, A., & Locke, E. (1991). An examination of the relationship among goal difficulty, business strategies, and performance on a complex management simulation task. *Academy of Management Journal, 34,* 400–424.

Chisholm, L. (2005). The making of South Africa's *National Curriculum Statement. Journal of Curriculum Studies, 37*(2), 193–208.

Chubb, J. E., & Moe, T. M. (1990). *Politics, markets, and America's schools.* Washington, DC: Brookings Institution.

Citizens' Commission on Civil Rights. (2005). *Statement by Citizens' Commission on Civil Rights on NCLB "growth model" experiment* [Press release]. Washington, DC: Author. Retrieved August 15, 2006, from http://www.cccr.org/news/press.cfm?id=23.

Civil Rights Act, 42 U.S.C. § 1971 (1964).

Clinton, W. J. (1993, February 17). *Address before a joint session of Congress on the State of the Union* [Electronic version]. Retrieved October 21, 2006, from http://www.c-span.org/executive/transcript.asp?cat=current_eventyear=1993.

Cohen, M. (1993). *Workshop to office: Two generations of Italian women in New York City.* Ithaca, NY: Cornell University Press.

Cohen, M. (2005). Reconsidering schools and the American welfare state. *History of Education Quarterly, 45,* 511–537.

Cohen, S., (Ed.). (1973). *Education in the United States: A documentary history.* New York: Random House.

Coleman, J. S. (1966). *Equality of educational opportunity.* Washington, DC: Department of Health, Education, and Welfare.

Congressional Office of Technology Assessment. (1992). *Testing in American schools: Asking the right questions.* Washington, DC: U.S. Government Printing Office. Retrieved June 12, 2006, from http://www.wws.princeton.edu/cgi-bin/byteserv.prl/~ota/disk1/1992/9236/9236.PDF.

Cooperative Accountability Project. (1974). *Legislation by the states: Accountability and assessment in education, Report No. 2.* Colorado: Author.

Council for Basic Education. (1996). *History in the making: An independent review of the voluntary national history standards.* Washington, DC: Author.

Cravens, H. (1978). *The triumph of evolution: American scientists and the heredity-environment controversy, 1900–1941.* Philadelphia: University of Pennsylvania Press.

Cremin, L. A. (1957). *The republic and the school: Horace Mann on the education of free men.* New York: Teachers College Press.

Cremin, L. A. (1965). *The genius of American education.* New York: Vintage Books.

Cremin, L. A. (1990). *Popular education and its discontents.* New York: Harper & Row.

Cronbach, L. J., & Furby, L. (1970). How should we measure "change"—or should we? *Psychological Bulletin, 74,* 68–80.

Cross, C. T. (1979). Title I evaluation: A case study in Congressional frustration. *Educational Evaluation and Policy Analysis, 1*(2), 15–21.

Cuban, L. (1990). Reforming again, again, and again. *Educational Researcher, 19*(1), 3–13.

Cuban, L. (1993). *How teachers taught: Constancy and change in American classrooms, 1880–1990* (2nd ed.). New York: Teachers College Press.

Cuban, L. (1996). Myths about changing schools and the case of special education *Remedial and Special Education, 17*(2),75–82.

Cuban, L. (2004a). *The blackboard and the bottom line: Why schools can't be businesses.* Cambridge, MA: Harvard University Press.

Cuban, L. (2004b). Looking through the rearview mirror at school accountability. In K. A. Sirotnik (Ed.), *Holding accountability accountable: What ought to matter in public education* (pp. 18–34). New York: Teachers College Press.

Danner, P. (2002, September 5). Ex-Sunbeam chief Dunlap to pay $500,000 on SEC fraud charges. *Miami Herald.* Retrieved December 30, 2006, from Gala Group database.

Danziger, K. (1990). *Constructing the subject: Historical origins of psychological research.* New York: Cambridge University Press.

Darling-Hammond, L. (1992). Educational indicators and enlightened policy. *Educational Policy, 6,* 235–265.

Darling-Hammond, L. (1992–93). Creating standards of practice and delivery for learner-centered schools. *Stanford Law and Policy Review, 4,* 37–52.

Darling-Hammond, L. (1993). Reframing the school reform agenda. *Phi Delta Kappan, 74*(10), 752–761.

Darling-Hammond, L. (2000). Teacher quality and student achievement: A review of state policy evidence. *Education Policy Analysis Archives, 8*(1). Retrieved November 21, 2006, from http://epaa.asu.edu/epaa/v8n1/.

Darling-Hammond, L. (2004). Standards, accountability, and school reform. *Teachers College Record, 106*(6), 1047–1085.

Darling-Hammond, L., & Ascher, C. (1991). *Creating accountability in the big city school systems.* Urban Diversity Series No. 102. New York: National Center for Restructuring Education, Schools, and Teaching. (ERIC Reproduction Document Service No. ED 334 339).

Davies, M. (1982). *A woman's place is at the typewriter: Office work and office workers, 1870–1930.* Philadelphia: Temple University Press.

Davis, A. (1991). Upping the stakes: Using gain scores to judge local program effectiveness in chapter 1. *Educational Evaluation and Policy Analysis, 13*(4), 380–388.

Davis, O. L., Jr. (2005). Schooling in the service of the state: Great War foreshadowing of changed educational purpose. In L. M. Burbaw & S. L. Field (Eds.), *Explorations in curriculum history* (pp. 311–328). Greenwich, CT: Information Age.

Debating the success of charter schools. (2004, August 30). *Talk of the Nation.* Retrieved September 5, 2006, from http://www.npr.org/templates/story/story.php?storyId=3879237.

Debra P. v. Turlington, 564 F. Supp. 177, 186 (1983).

Debra P. v. Turlington, 730 F.2d 1405 (1984).

Debray, E., Parson, G., & Avila, S. (2003). Internal alignment and external pressure: High school responses in four state contexts. In M. Carnoy, R. Elmore, & L. S. Siskin (Eds.), *The new accountability: High schools and high stakes testing* (pp. 55–86). New York: RoutledgeFarmer.

Dee, T. S. (2003, Summer). Lessons from the "first wave" of accountability. *Education Next*. Retrieved August 14, 2006, from http://www.educationnext.org/unabridged/20033/index.html.

Delpit, L. (1995). *Other people's children: Cultural conflict in the classroom*. New York: New Press.

Deno, S. L. (1985). Curriculum-based measurement: The emerging alternative. *Exceptional Children, 52*(3), 219–232.

Deno, S. L. (2003). Developments in curriculum-based measurement. *Journal of Special Education, 37*(3), 184–192.

Dewey, J. (1916/2004). *Democracy and education*. Whitefish, MT: Kessinger.

Dewey, J. (1927). *The public and its problems*. New York: Henry Holt and Company.

Dillon, S. (2006, September 28). As 2 Bushes try to fix schools, the tools differ. *New York Times*. Retrieved December 9, 2006, from http://select.nytimes.com/gst/abstract.html?res=F60C13FC3D540C7B8EDDA00894DE404482.

Donovan, M. S., & Cross, C. T. (Eds.). (2002). *Minority students in special and gifted education*. Washington, DC: National Academies Press.

Dorn, S. (1996). *Creating the dropout: An institutional and social history of school failure*. Greenwood, CT: Praeger.

Dorn, S. (2002). Public-private symbiosis in Nashville special education. *History of Education Quarterly, 42*, 368–394.

Dorn, S. (2006). No more aggregate NAEP studies? [Editorial]. *Education Policy Analysis Archives, 14*(31). Retrieved November 22, 2006, from http://epaa.asu.edu/epaa/v14n31/.

Dorn, S., & Johanningmeier, E. V. (1999). Dropping out and the military metaphor. *History of Education Quarterly, 39*, 193–198.

Douglas, D. M. (1995). *Reading, writing & race: The desegregation of the Charlotte schools*. Chapel Hill: University of North Carolina Press.

Douglass, S. L. (2000). *Teaching about religion in national and state social studies standards*. Fountain Valley, CA, and Nashville, TN: Council on Islamic Education and the Freedom Forum. Retrieved October 21, 2006, from http://www.freedomforum.org/publications/first/teachingaboutreligion/teachingaboutreligionfullreport.pdf.

Draper, N. (2002, November 26). Test firm to pay $ 7 million for error. *Minneapolis Star Tribune*, p. 1A. Retrieved December 30, 2006, LexisNexis Academic database.

Dreeben, R. (1968) *On what is learned in school*. Reading, MA: Addison-Wesley.

Dunn, L. M. (1968). Special education for the mildly retarded: Is much of it justifiable? *Exceptional Children, 23*, 5–21.

Durham, C., Knight, D., & Locke, E. (1997). Effects of leader role, team-set goal difficulty, efficacy, and tactics on team effectiveness. *Organizational Behavior and Human Decision Processes, 72*, 203–231.

Dzuback, M. A. (2003). Gender and the politics of knowledge. *History of Education Quarterly, 43*(2), 171–195.

Dzur, A. W. (2003, April). *Professionals vs. democracy: the critique of technocratic expertise.* Paper presented for presentation at the annual meeting of the Midwestern Political Science Association, Chicago. Retrieved November 24, 2006, from http://mpsa.indiana.edu/conf2003papers/1032035123.pdf.

Edmonds, R. (2000). *A perspective—Educational goals and changes, 1988–2010.* Educational Benchmarks 2000 Series. Atlanta: Southern Regional Education Board (ERIC Reproduction Document Service No. ED 457 586). Retrieved October 21, 2006, from http://www.sreb.org/main/Benchmarks2000/APerspective.pdf.

Education of All Handicapped Americans Act, Pub. L. No. 94–142 (1975).

Education Trust. (2003). *Telling the whole truth (or not) about highly qualified teachers.* Washington, DC: Author. Retrieved December 28, 2006, from http://www2.edtrust.org/NR/rdonlyres/C638111D-04E3-4C0D-9F68-20E7009498A6/0/tellingthetruthteachers.pdf.

Education Trust. (2005, November 18). *Education Trust statement on U.S. Department of Education's announcement of a growth-model pilot program.* Retrieved August 16, 2006, from http://www2.edtrust.org/EdTrust/Press+Room/growthmodel.htm.

Educational Improvement Act. Tennesse Acts ch. 353. 1992.

Edwards, H. (2002, July 30). 347 L.A. schools earn major cash bonuses. *Los Angeles Daily News.* Retrieved December 30, 2006, from the LexisNexis Academic database.

Elementary and Secondary Education Act, Pub. L. No. 89-10 (1965).

Ellwein, M. C., & Glass, G. V. (1989). Ending social promotion in Waterford: Appearances and reality. In L. S. Shepard & M. L. Smith (Eds.), *Flunking grades: Research and policies on retention* (pp. 151–173). New York: Falmer Press.

Ellwein, M. C., & Glass, G. V. (1991). Testing for competence: Translating reform policy into practice. *Educational Policy, 5*(1), 64–78.

Ellwein, M. C., Glass, G. V., & Smith, M. L. (1988). Standards of competence: Propositions on the nature of testing reforms. *Educational Researcher, 17*(8), 4–9.

Emery, K., & Ohanian S. (2004). *Why is corporate America bashing our public schools?* New York: Heinemann.

Engelhart, M. D., & Thomas, M. (1966) Rice as the inventor of the comparative test. *Journal of Educational Measurement, 3*(2), 141–145.

Espinoza v. Arizona State Board of Education, Superior Court of Arizona, Maricopa County, Case CV2006005616 (2006). Order denying request for temporary restraining order. Retrieved October 22, 2006, from http://www.superiorcourt.maricopa.gov/publicInfo/rulings/rulingsReaditem.asp?autonumb=222.

Evans, J. H. (2006). Between technocracy and democratic legitimation: A proposed compromise position for common morality public bioethics. *Journal of Medicine and Philosophy, 31,* 213–234.

Executive Office of the President. (1990). *National goals for education.* Washington, DC: Author. (ERIC Reproduction Document Service No. ED 319 143).

Fass, P. S. (1980). The IQ: A cultural and historical framework. *American Journal of Education, 88*(4),431–458.

Figlio, D. N., & Getzler, L. S. (2002). *Accountability, ability and disability: Gaming the system.* NBER Working Paper 9307. Retrieved December 26, 2006, from http://bear.cba.ufl.edu/figlio/w9307.pdf.

Figlio, D. N., & Lucas, M. E. (2004). What's in a grade? School report cards and the housing market. *American Economic Review, 94*(3), 591–604.

Figlio, D. N., & Rouse, C. (2006). Do accountability and voucher threats improve low-performing schools? *Journal of Public Economics, 90*(1–2), 239–255.

Figlio, D. N., & Winicki, J. (2005). Food for thought: the effects of school accountability plans on school nutrition. *Journal of Public Economics, 89*(2–3), 381–394.

Filene, P. G. (1970). An obituary for "the Progressive movement." *American Quarterly, 22*(1), 20–34.

Fine, M. (1991). *Framing dropouts: Notes on the politics of an urban public high school.* Albany, NY: State University of New York Press.

Fineout, G. (2006, March 7). Politicians take aim at FCAT. *Miami Herald.* Retrieved December 30, 2006, from Lexis-Nexis Academic database.

Fischer, F. (1990). *Technocracy and the politics of expertise.* Newbury Park: Sage.

Fischer, F. (2003). *Reframing public policy: Discursive politics and deliberative practices.* Oxford, England: Oxford University Press.

Fisher, T. H. (1996). *A review and analysis of the Tennessee Value-Added Assessment System: Part II.* Nashville, TN: Tennessee Comptroller of the Treasury.

FitzGerald, F. (1980). *America revised: History schoolbooks in the twentieth century.* New York: Random House.

Flannery, P. (2000, October 8). AIMS: Story of missteps, false starts. *Arizona Republic.* Retrieved December 30, 2006, from the NewsBank database.

Flaugher, R. L. (1978). The many definitions of test bias. *American Psychologist, 33*(7), 671–679.

Fliegel, S. (1993). *Miracle in East Harlem: The fight for choice in public education.* New York: Times Books.

Florida Center for Reading Research. (2005). *Florida's Reading First assessment: Principal's guide.* Tallahassee, FL: Author. Retrieved October 23, 2006, from http://www.fcrr.org/assessment/pdf/principlesguide.pdf.

Florida Department of Education. (1999). *School accountability report guide June 1999.* Tallahassee, FL: Author. Retrieved August 14, 2006, from http://data.fldoe.org/school_grades/9899/guide99.asp.

Florida Department of Education. (2000). *2000 School accountability report guidesheet.* Tallahassee, FL: Author. Retrieved August 14, 2006, from http://www.firn.edu/doe/schoolgrades/guide00.htm.

Florida Department of Education. (2001). *2001 School accountability report guidesheet.* Tallahassee, FL: Author. Retrieved August 14, 2006, from http://www.firn.edu/doe/schoolgrades/guide01.htm.

Florida Department of Education. (2002a). *Grading Florida public schools 2001–2002.* Tallahassee, FL: Author. Retrieved August 14, 2006, from http://www.firn.edu/doe/schoolgrades/pdf/guide02.pdf.

Florida Department of Education. (2002b). *Science grade 10 test item and performance task specifications* [Draft]. Tallahassee, FL: Author. Retrieved December 24, 2006, from http://www.firn.edu/doe/sas/fcat/fcatis01.htm.

Florida Department of Education. (2006). *Grading Florida public schools.* Tallahassee, FL: Author. Retrieved July 30, 2006, from http:// schoolgrades.fldoe.org/pdf/0506/schlGrds_06_master_final_ADApdf.pdf.

Florida Department of Education. (n.d.a). *Assessment and school performance* [Web site]. Tallahassee, FL: Author. Retrieved October 23, 2006, from http:// firn.edu/doe/sas/fcat/fcinfopg.htm.

Florida Department of Education. (n.d.b). *Sunshine state standards.* Tallahassee, FL: Author. Retrieved October 21, 2006, from http://www.firn.edu/doe/menu/ sss.htm.

Florida School Recognition Program. (n.d.). *2006 general information* [Web site]. Retrieved July 30, 2006, from http://www.firn.edu/doe/evaluation/ geninfo.htm.

Fla. Statutes ch. 99–398.

Forum on Educational Accountability. (2006, January 2). *Joint statement on No Child Left Behind.* Retrieved August 14, 2006, from http://www.nsba.org/site/ doc.asp?TRACKID=&VID=2&CID=1611&DID=37578.

Franklin, V.P. (1991). Black social scientists and the mental-testing movement, 1920- 1940. In R. L. Jones (Ed.), *Black psychology* (3rd ed., pp. 207–224). New York: Harper & Row.

Frederiksen, N. (1994). *The influence of minimum competency tests on teaching and learning.* Princeton, NJ.: Educational Testing Service, Policy Information Center.

Friedman, M. (1955). The role of government in education. In R. A. Solo (Ed.), *Economics and the public interest* (pp. 123–144). New Brunswick, NJ. Rutgers University Press.

Friedman, M. (1962). *Capitalism and freedom.* Chicago: University of Chicago Press.

Friedson, E. (1984). Are professions necessary? In T. L. Haskell (Ed.), *The authority of experts* (pp. 3–27). Bloomington, ID.: Indiana University Press.

Fuchs, D., & Fuchs, L. S.. (1995). Special education can work. In J. M. Kauffman, J. W. Lloyd, D. P. Hallahan, & T. A. Astuto (Eds.), *Issues in educational placement: Students with emotional and behavioral disorders* (pp. 363–377). Hillsdale, NJ: Erlbaum.

Fuchs, L. S. (2004). The past, present, and future of curriculum-based measurement Research. *School Psychology Review, 33,* 188–192.

Fuchs, L. S., & Fuchs, D. (1993). Formative evaluation of academic progress: How much growth can we expect? *School Psychology Review, 22,* 27–48.

Fullan, M. (1995). The school as a learning organization: Distant dreams. *Theory into Practice, 34*(4), 230–235.

Fullan, M. (2002). *Change forces with a vengeance.* New York: Routledge.

Fullan, M. G. (1996). Turning systematic thinking on its head. *Phi Delta Kappan,77*(6), 420–423.

Fullan, M., Miles, M. B., & Taylor, G. (1980). Organization development in schools: The state of the art. *Review of Educational Research, 50,* 121–183.

Fuller, B., Gesicki, K., Kang, E., & Wright, J. (2006). *Is the No Child Left Behind Act working?* Berkeley, CA: Policy Analysis for California Education. Retrieved November 24, 2006, from http://pace.berkeley.edu/NCLB/ WP06-01_Web.pdf.

Furner, M. O. (1975). *Advocacy and objectivity: A crisis in the professionalization of American social science, 1865–1905.* Lexington, KY: University of Kentucky Press.

GI Forum v. Texas Education Agency, 87 F. Supp. 2d 667, 670 (W.D. Tex. 2000).

Galambos, L. (1970). The emerging organizational synthesis in modern American history. *Business History Review, 44,* 279–290.

Gedan, B. N. (2005, July 5). SALT gives Greenbush School a mixed review. *Providence Journal*, p. D1. Retrieved December 30, 2006, from the LexisNexis Academic database.

General Accounting Office. (2006). *No Child Left Behind Act: States face challenges measuring academic growth that education's initiatives may help address.* Report GAO-06-661. Washington, DC: Author. Retrieved August 16, 2006, from http://www.gao.gov/cgi-bin/getrpt?GAO-06-661.

George Bush for President. (1988). *The leader America needs for the future* [Campaign pamphlet]. Washington, DC: Author. Retrieved October 21, 2006, from http://www.4president.org/brochures/georgebush1988brochure.htm

Gillborn, D., & Youdell, D. (2000). *Rationing education: Policy, practice, reform, and equity.* Buckingham, England: Open University Press.

Ginsburg, A. L., Noell, J., & Plisko, V. W. (1988). Lessons from the wall chart. *Educational Evaluation and Policy Analysis, 10,* 1–12.

Glass, G. V (1978). Standards and criteria. *Journal of Educational Measurement, 15*(4), 237–261.

Glass, G. V. (1990). Using student test scores to evaluate teachers. In J. Millman & L. Darling-Hammond (Eds.), *The new handbook of teacher evaluation* (pp. 229–240). Newbury Park, CA: Sage.

Goldschmidt, P., Choi, K., & Martinez, F. (2003). *Using hierarchical growth models to monitor school performance over time: Comparing NCE to scale score results.* Los Angeles: National Center for Research on Evaluation, Standards, and Student Testing (CRESST). Retrieved December 22, 2006, from http://www.cse.ucla.edu/Reports/R618.pdf.

Goldstein, A. (2004, June 6). "Paige calls NEA a 'terrorist group,' " *Washington Post*, p. A19. Retrieved June 6, 2006, from http://www.washingtonpost.com/ac2/wp-dyn/A64712-2004Feb23.

Goldstein, H. (1997). Value added tables: the less-than-holy grail. *Managing Schools Today, 6,* 18–19.

Goldstein, H. (2003). Multilevel modelling of educational data. In D. Courgeau (Ed.), *Methodology and epistemology of multilevel analysis* (pp. 28–42). London: Kluwer.

Goldstein, H., & Spiegelhalter, D. J. (1996). League tables and their limitations: Statistical issues in comparisons of institutional performance. *Journal of the Royal Statistical Society, Series A, 159,* 384–443.

Goldstein, J., & Behuniak, P. (2005). Growth models in action: Selected case studies. *Practical Assessment Research & Evaluation, 10*(11). Retrieved August 16, 2006, from http://pareonline.net/getvn.asp?v=10&n=11.

Goodkin, S. (2005, December 27). Leave no gifted child behind. *Washington Post*, p. A5. Retrieved September 23, 2006, from http://www.washingtonpost.com/wp-dyn/content/article/2005/12/26/AR2005122600553.html .

Goodlad, J., Klein, F. M., & Tye, K. (1979). The domains of curriculum and their study. In J. Goodlad (Ed.), *Curriculum inquiry* (pp. 43–76). New York: McGraw-Hill.

Goodman, K. S. (2005). DIBELS: The perfect literacy test. *Language Magazine, 5*(1), 24–27.

Goodman, K. S. (Ed.). (2006). *Examining DIBELS: What it is and what it does.* Brandon, VT: Vermont Society for the Study of Education.

Gordon, D., Reich, M., & Edwards, R. (1982). *Segmented work, divided workers: The historical transformation of labor in the United States.* New York: Cambridge University Press.

Gordon, R. (2005, June 6). What Democrats need to say about education. *New Republic.* Retrieved September 5, 2006, from http://www.tnr.com/doc.mhtml?pt=aQv7Q66Pcy65XAVIyW2UIX%3D%3D.

Gould, S. J. (1996). *The mismeasure of man* (rev. ed.). New York: Norton.

Graff, H. J. (1979). *The literacy myth: Cultural integration and social structure in the nineteenth century.* New York: Academic Press.

Graff, H. J. (1995). *Conflicting paths: Growing up in America.* Cambridge, MA: Harvard University Press.

Grant, G. (1988). *The world we created at Hamilton High.* Cambridge, MA: Harvard University Press.

Greene, J. P., Winters, M. A., & Swanson, C. (2006, March 29). Missing the mark on graduation rates. *Education Week.* Retrieved June 26, 2006, from http://www.edweek.org/ew/articles/2006/03/29/29greene.h25.html.

Grissmer, D., Flanagan, A., Kawata, J., & Williamson, S. (2000). *Improving student achievement: What state NAEP test scores tell us.* Santa Monica, CA: RAND. Retrieved December 22, 2006, from http://www.rand.org/pubs/monograph_reports/MR924/.

Gudrais, E. (2004, February 3). SALT team report faults high school, facilities. *Providence Journal-Bulletin,* p. C1. Retrieved December 30, 2006, the from the LexisNexis Academic database.

Gutman, H. G. (1977). *Work, culture, and society in industrializing America: Essays in American working-class and social history.* New York: Random House.

Gvirtz, S., & Beech, J. (2004). From the intended to the implemented curriculum in Argentina: Regulation and practice. *Prospects, 34*(3), 371–382.

Hacsi, T. A. (1998). *Second home: Orphan asylums and poor families in America.* Cambridge, MA: Harvard University Press.

Hall, D. (2005, June). *Getting honest about grad rates: How states play the numbers and students lose.* Washington, DC: Education Trust. Retrieved June 26, 2006, from http://www2.edtrust.org/NR/rdonlyres/C5A6974D-6C04-4FB1-A9FC-05938CB0744D/0/GettingHonest.pdf.

Hambleton, R. K. (1978). On the use of cut-off scores with criterion referenced tests in instructional settings. *Journal of Educational Measurement, 15,* 277–290.

Hamilton, L. S., & Strecher, B. M. (2002). Improving test-based accountability. In L. S. Hamilton, B. M. Stecher, & S. P. Klein (Eds.), *Making sense of test-based accountability in education* (pp. 121–144). Santa Monica, CA: RAND.

Hampel, R. L. (1986). *The last little citadel: American high schools since 1940.* New York: Houghton Mifflin.

Haney, W. M. (2006, September). *Evidence on education under NCLB (and how Florida boosted NAEP scores and reduced the race gap)*. Boston National Board on Educational Testing and Public Policy. Paper presented at Hechinger Institute, Broad Seminar for K-12 Reporters, New York City. Retrieved December 29, 2006, from http://www.bc.edu/research/nbetpp/statements/nbr6.pdf.

Haney, W. M., Madaus, G., & Kreitzer, A. (1987). Charms talismanic: Testing teachers for the improvement of American education. *Review of Research in Education, 14*, 169–238.

Haney, W. M., Madaus, G., & Lyons, R. (1993). *The fractured marketplace for standardized testing*. Boston: Kluwer Academic.

Hanson, F. A. (1993). *Testing, testing: Social consequences of the examined life*. Berkeley, CA: University of California Press.

Hanushek, E. A., & Raymond, M. E. (2002). Sorting out accountability systems. In W. M. Evers & H. J. Walberg (Eds.), *School accountability* (pp. 75–104). Stanford: Hoover Institution Press.

Hanushek, E. A., & Raymond, M. E. (2005). Does school accountability lead to improved student performance? *Journal of Policy Analysis and Management, 24* (2), 297–327.

Hanushek, E. A., & Raymond, M. E. (2006). Early returns from school accountability. In P. E. Peterson (Ed.), *Generational change: Closing the test score gap* (pp. 143–166). Lanham, MD: Rowman & Littlefield.

Hardy, R. A. (1995). Examining the costs of performance assessment. *Applied Measurement in Education, 8*(2), 121–134.

Harnischfeger, A. (1995). Fad or reform? The standards movement in the United States. In W. Bos & R. H. Lehmann (Eds.), *Reflections on educational achievement: Papers in honour of T. Neville Postlethwaite* (pp. 107–118). Münster: Waxmann.

Harris Interactive. (2005). Firemen, doctors scientists, nurses and teachers top list as "most prestigious occupations" [Press release]. *Harris Poll, 69*. Retrieved July 19, 2006, from http://www.harrisinteractive.com/harris_poll/index.asp?PID=599.

Harrison, B., & Bluestone, B. (1988). *The great u-turn: Corporate restructuring and the polarizing of America*. New York: Basic Books

Harry, B. (1992). An ethnographic study of cross-cultural communication with Puerto Rican-American families in the special education system. *American Educational Research Journal, 29*(3), 471–494.

Harvey-Beavis, O. (2003, February). *Performance-based rewards for teachers: A literature review*. Paper prepared for the Third Workshop of Participating Countries on OECD's Activity Attracting, Developing and Retaining Effective Teachers, Athens, Greece. Retrieved November 19, 2006, from http://www.oecd.org/dataoecd/17/47/34077553.pdf.

Hasbrouck, J. E., Woldbeck, T., Ihnot, C., &. Parker, R. I. (1999). One teacher's use of curriculum-based measurement: A changed opinion. *Learning Disabilities Research and Practice, 14*(2), 118–126.

Hauser, R. M. (1997). Indicators of high school completion and dropout. In R. M. Hauser, B. V. Brown, & W. R. Prosser (Eds.), *Indicators of children's well-being* (pp. 152–184). New York: Russell Sage Foundation.

Haycock, K. (2006, July 27). *Statement before the House Committee on Education and the Workforce, "No Child Left Behind: Can growth models ensure improved education for all students."* Washington, DC: Education Trust. Retrieved August 16, 2006, from http://www.house.gov/ed_workforce/hearings/109th/fc/nclb072706/haycock.htm.

Heneman, H. G., III. (1998). Assessment of the motivational reactions of teachers to a school-based performance award program. *Journal of Personnel Evaluation in Education, 12*(1), 43–59.

Henriques, D. B. (2003, September 2). Rising demands for testing push limits of its accuracy. *New York Times*, p. 1. Retrieved December 30, 2006, from the LexisNexis Academic database.

Herbst, J. (1996). *The once and future school.* New York: Routledge

Hernandez, R. (1996, December 1). New curriculum from Albany: The Irish potato famine, or one view of it. *New York Times*, p. 52.

Herrington, C., & McDonald, V.-M. (2001). Accountability as a school reform strategy: A 30-year perspective on Florida. In C. Harrington & K. Kasten (Eds.), *Florida 2001: Educational policy alternatives* (pp. 7–34). Jacksonville: Florida Institute of Education.

Hess, F. M. (2006). *Tough love for schools: Essays on competition, accountability, and excellence.* Washington, DC: American Enterprise Institute Press.

Hess, F. M., & Finn, C. (2004, Fall). On leaving no child behind. *Public Interest*, pp. 35-56.

Hess, G. A. (1991). *School restructuring, Chicago style.* Newbury Park, CA: Corwin Press.

Heubert, J. P., & Hauser, R. M., (Eds.). (1999). *High stakes: Testing for tracking, promotion, and graduation.* Washington, DC: National Academy Press.

Hibbitts, B. (2006, July 29). New Orleans judge will start releasing prisoners if trials put off much longer. *Jurist*. Retrieved November 27, 2006, from http://jurist.law.pitt.edu/paperchase/2006/07/new-orleans-judge-will-start-releasing.php.

Hillsborough County Public Schools. (1997). *Our students' test scores reflect academic achievement* [Pamphlet]. Tampa, FL: Office of Communications and Governmental Relations.

Hobson v. Hansen, 269 F. Supp. 401 (D.D.C. 1967).

Hochschild, J., & Scovronick, N. (2003). *The American dream and the public schools.* New York: Oxford University Press.

Hofstadter, R. (1963). *Anti-intellectualism in American life.* New York: Knopf.

Holmes, B., & McLean, M., (Eds.). (1992). *The curriculum: A comparative perspective.* London: Routledge.

Holt, M. I. (1994). *The orphan trains: Placing out in America.* Lincoln: University of Nebraska Press.

Horn, J. (2005, August 8). Jeb Bush and "integrity that is unquestioned." *Schools Matter* [Blog]. Retrieved August 6, 2006, from http://schoolsmatter.blogspot.com/2005/08/jeb-bush-and-integrity-that-is.html.

Horn, J. (2006, August 5). The poor, the immigrants, and the testing sanity gap: When will decency demand no mas? *Schools Matter* [Blog]. Retrieved August 7,

2006, from http://schoolsmatter.blogspot.com/2006/08/
poor-immigrants-and-testing-sanity-gap.html.

Hounshell, D. A. (1985). *From the American system to mass production, 1800–1932: Development of manufacturing technology in the United States.* Baltimore: Johns Hopkins University Press.

House, E. R. (1975). The price of productivity: Who pays?" In W. J. Gephart (Ed.), *Accountability: A state, a process, or a product?* Bloomington, IN: Phi Delta Kappa.

How midstate schools stack up. (1994a, October 15). Nashville *Tennessean*, p. 4A.

How midstate schools stack up. (1994b, October 16). Nashville *Tennessean*, pp. 6A–7A.

Hox, J. J. (1995). *Applied multilevel analysis.* Amsterdam: TT-Publikaties. Retrieved August 14, 2006, from http://www.soziologie.uni-halle.de/langer/multilevel/books/hox95mla.pdf.

Hoxby, C. M. (2002). The costs of accountability. In W. M. Evers & H. J. Walberg (Eds.), *School accountability* (pp. 47–73). Stanford, CA: Hoover Institution Press.

Improving America's Schools Act of 1994. (1994). Pub. L. No. 103–382. Retrieved September 3, 2006, from http://www.ed.gov/legislation/ESEA/index.html.

Independent Review Panel. (2001). *Improving the odds: A report on Title I.* Washington, DC: Author. Retrieved September 3, 2006, from http://www.cep-dc.org/pubs/improvingoddsreporttitlei_irp/improvingoddsreporttitleipanel.pdf.

Individuals with Disabilities Education Act Amendments. (1997). Pub. L. No. 105–117.

Issel, W. H. (1978). The politics of public school reform in Pennsylvania, 1880–1911. *Pennsylvania Magazine of History and Biography, 102,* 59–92.

Jacob, B. A. (2005). Accountability, incentives, and behavior: The impact of high-stakes testing in the Chicago Public Schools. *Journal of Public Economics, 89,* 761–796.

Jameson, M. (2000). *The grand jury: An historical overview.* Cedar Ridge, CA: California Grand Jurors Association. Retrieved from http://www.nvo.com/cgja/nss-folder/briefhistoryofgrandjuries/Grdjry.rtf.

Jansen, J. D. (1999). The school curriculum since apartheid: Intersections of politics and policy in the South African transition. *Journal of Curriculum Studies, 31*(1), 57–67.

Jefferson, T. (1787/1954). *Notes on the state of Virginia.* New York: W. W. Norton & Company.

Jeffries, J., Armitage, J., Collson, D., Forsyth, A., & Lyman, C. (1737/1973). Inspection of the schools by the Boston school board. In S. Cohen (Ed.), *Education in the United States: A documentary history* (p. 407). New York: Random House.

Jennings, J. F. (1991). Chapter 1: A view from Congress. *Educational Evaluation and Policy Analysis, 13*(4), 335–338.

Johanningmeier, E. V. (2004). The transformation of Stuart Appleton Courtis: Test maker and progressive. *American Educational History Journal, 31*(2), 202–210.

Johnson, H. L. (2006, September 14). *Letter to Douglas D. Christensen.* Washington, DC: Department of Education. Retrieved November 22, 2006, from http://www.nde.state.ne.us/documents/06_ESEA_NCLB.pdf.

Johnson, J., Arumi, A. M., & Ott, A. (2006). *Reality-check public survey: Is support for standards and testing fading?* New York: Public Agenda. Retrieved November 27, 2006, from http://www.publicagenda.org/research/pdfs/rc0603.pdf.

Johnson, S. M. (1986). Incentives for teachers: What motivates, what matters? *Educational Administration Quarterly, 22*(3), 54–79.

Johnston, R. C. (1997, April 9). Just saying no [Electronic version]. *Education Week.* Retrieved September 27, 1997, from http://www.edweek.com.

Jonçich, G. (1968). *The sane positivist: A biography of Edward L. Thorndike.* Middletown, CT: Wesleyan University Press.

Jones, B. D., & Egley, R. J. (2004). Voices from the frontlines: Teachers' perceptions of high-stakes testing. *Education Policy Analysis Archives, 12*(39). Retrieved December 26, 2006, from http://epaa.asu.edu/epaa/v12n39/.

Jones, M. (2004). Policy legitimation, expert advice, and objectivity: "Opening" the UK governance framework for human genetics. *Social Epistemology, 18*(2–3), 247–270.

Kaestle, C. F. (1973). *Joseph Lancaster and the monitorial school system: A documentary history.* New York: Teachers College Press.

Kaestle, C. F. (1983). *Pillars of the republic: Common schools and American society, 1780–1860.* New. York: Hill & Wang.

Kane, M. T. (2001). So much remains the same: Conception and status of validation in setting standards. In G. J. Cijek (Ed.), *Setting performance standards: Concepts, methods, and perspectives* (pp. 53–88). Mahwah, NJ: Erlbaum.

Kane, T. J., & Steiger, D. O. (2002). Volatility in school test scores: Implications for test-based accountability systems. In D. Ravitch (Ed.), *Brookings papers on education policy 2002* (pp. 235–283). Washington, DC: Brookings Institution.

Kantor, H. A. (1988). *Learning to earn: School, work, and vocational reform in California, 1880–1930.* Madison: University of Wisconsin Press.

Katz, M. B. (1968). *The irony of early school reform.* Cambridge, MA: Harvard University Press.

Katz, M. B. (1975). *Class, bureaucracy and schools.* New York: Praeger

Katz, M. B. (1987). *Reconstructing American education.* Cambridge, MA: Harvard University Press.

Katznelson, I., & Weir, M. (1985). *Schooling for all: Class, race, and the decline of the democratic ideal.* New York: Basic Books.

Katznelson, I., & Zolberg, A. (Eds.) (1986). *Working class formation.* Princeton, NJ: Princeton University Press.

Kentucky Department of Education. (2006). *2006 CATS interpretive guide.* Frankfurt, KY: Author.

Kett, J. (1977). *Rites of passage: Adolescence in America, 1790 to the present.* New York: Basic Books.

Kiesling, J. B. (2005, July 3). Variations on a pledge. *Washington Post* [Online]. Retrieved July 6, 2006, from http://www.washingtonpost.com/wp-srv/opinion/2005/pledge/altpledge_kiesling.html.

Klausnitzer, D. (1996, November 15). Pupils need practice on that first "R." *Nashville Tennessean*, pp. 1A, 8A–10A.

Klein, S. P., Hamilton, L. S., McCaffrey, D. F., & Stecher, B. M. (2000, October). What do test scores in Texas tell us? *Education Policy Analysis Archives, 8*(49). Retrieved October 30, 2006, from http://epaa.asu.edu/epaa/v8n49/.

Kliebard, H. M. (1987). *The struggle for the American curriculum, 1893–1958.* New York: Routledge.

Koehler, P. (2001). *AIMS as a high school graduation requirement: Analysis of public survey data and recommendations.* San Francisco: Wested. Retrieved October 22, 2006, from http://www.ade.state.az.us/standards/aims/publicinput/SurveyFinal.pdf.

Kohn, A. (2004). *What does it mean to be well-educated? And more essays on standards, grading, and other follies.* Boston: Beacon Press.

Koretz, D. (1992). What happened to test scores, and why? *Educational Measurement: Issues and Practice, 11*(4), 7–11.

Koretz, D. (2005). Alignment, high stakes, and the inflation of test scores. In J. L. Herman & E. H. Haertel (Eds.), *Uses and misuses of data for educational accountability and improvement. The 104th yearbooks of the National Society for the Study of Education* (Part II, pp. 99–118). Malden, MA: Blackwell.

Koretz, D., & Diebert, E. (1993). *Interpretations of National Assessment of Educational Progress (NAEP) anchor points and achievement levels by the print media in 1991.* Santa Monica, CA: The RAND Corporation. (ERIC Document Reproduction Service No. ED 367 683).

Kossan, P., & González, D. (2000, November 2). Minorities fail AIMS at high rate: Some backers talking change. *Arizona Republic.* Retrieved December 30, 2006, from the LexisNexis Academic database.

Kossan, P. (2000a, November 27). By trying too much too quick, AIMS missed mark. *Arizona Republic.* Retrieved December 30, 2006, from the NewsBank database.

Kossan, P. (2000b, November 22). Keegan backs off AIMS requirement. *Arizona Republic.* Retrieved December 30, 2006, from the NewsBank database.

Kossan, P., & Flannery, P. (2001, March 4). Many favor AIMS delay. *Arizona Republic.* Retrieved December 30, 2006, from the NewsBank database.

Kovacs, P. (2006). *A petition calling for the dismantling of the No Child Left Behind Act.* Huntsville, AL: Educator Roundtable. Retrieved November 24, 2006, from http://www.petitiononline.com/1teacher/petition.html.

Krug, E. A. (1964). *The shaping of the American high school, 1880–1920* (Vol. 1). Madison: University of Wisconsin Press.

Krug, E. A. (1972). *The shaping of the American high school, 1920–1941* (Vol. 2). Madison: University of Wisconsin Press.

Kupermintz, H. (2003). Teacher effects and teacher effectiveness: A validity investigation of the Tennessee Value-Added Assessment System. *Educational Evaluation and Policy Analysis, 25*(3), 287–298.

Kyle, C., & Kantowicz, E. (1991, May). Bogus statistics. *Latino Studies Journal, 2,* 34–52.

Labaree, D. F. (1988). *The making of an American high school: The credentials market and the Central High School of Philadelphia, 1838–1939.* New Haven, CT: Yale University Press.

Labaree, D. F. (1997). *How to succeed in school without really learning: The credentials race in American education.* New Haven, CT: Yale University Press.

Lafferty, M. (2005, November 17). Intelligent design: Like Ohio, Kansas redefined science. *Columbus Dispatch.*

Lagemann, E. (1990). The plural worlds of educational research. *History of Education Quarterly, 29,* 185–214.

Lahsen, M. (2005). Technocracy, democracy, and U.S. climate politics: The need for demarcations. *Science, Technology, and Human Values, 30*(1), 137–169.

LaPlante, J. R., & Reddy, S. (1998, January 21). School survey wins friends, foes. *Providence Journal-Bulletin,* p. 1C. Retrieved December 30, 2006, from the LexisNexis Academic database.

Lazerson, M., & Grubb, W. N. (Eds.). (1974). *American education and vocationalism: A documentary history, 1870–1970.* New York: Teachers College Press.

Lee, J. (2006). *Tracking achievement gaps and assessing the impact of NCLB on the gaps.* Cambridge, MA: Civil Rights Project, Harvard University. Retrieved November 24, 2006, from http://www.civilrightsproject.harvard.edu/research/esea/nclb_naep_lee.pdf.

Lessinger, L. (1970). *Every kid a winner: Accountability in education.* Chicago: Science Research Associates.

Leung, S. O. (2003). A practical use of vertical equating by combining IRT equating and linear equating. *Practical Assessment, Research & Evaluation, 8*(23). Retrieved August 14, 2006, from http://PAREonline.net/getvn.asp?v=8&n=23.

Levin, H. M. (1998). Educational performance standards and the economy. *Educational Researcher, 27*(4), 4–10.

Licht, W. (1989). *Working for the railroad.* Princeton, NJ: Princeton University Press.

Lieberman, M. (2000). *The teacher unions: How they sabotage educational reform and why.* New York: Encounter Books.

Linn, R. L. (1978). Demands, cautions, and suggestions for setting standards. *Journal of Educational Measurement, 15,* 301–308.

Linn, R. L. (1979). Validity of inferences based on the proposed Title I evaluation models. *Educational Evaluation and Policy Analysis, 1*(2), 23–32.

Linn, R. L. (1994). Performance assessment: Policy promises and technical measurement standards. *Educational Researcher, 23*(9), 4–14.

Linn, R. L. (2000). Assessments and accountability. *Educational Researcher, 29,* 4–16.

Linn, R. L. (2003). Performance standards: Utility for different uses of assessments. *Education Policy Analysis Archives, 11*(31). Retrieved August 10, 2006, from http://epaa.asu.edu/epaa/v11n31/.

Linn, R. L. (2005). Conflicting demands of No Child Left Behind and state systems: Mixed messages about school performance. *Education Policy Analysis Archives, 13*(33). Retrieved October 22, 2006, from http://epaa.asu.edu/epaa/v13n33/.

Linn, R. L., & Werts, C. E. (1971). Considerations for studies of test bias. *Journal of Educational Measurement, 8*(1), 1–4.

Lippmann, W. (1922/1957). *Public opinion.* New York: Macmillan.

Lippmann, W. (1925). *The phantom public.* New York: Harcourt, Brace.

Lipsky, M. (1980). *Street-level bureaucracy: Dilemmas of the individual in public service.* New York: Russell Sage Foundation.

Little, R. J., & Rubin, D. B. (2002). *Statistical analysis with missing data* (2nd ed.). New York: Wiley.

Lockwood, J. R., Louis, T. A., & McCaffrey, D. F. (2002). Uncertainty in rank estimation: Implications for value-added modeling accountability systems. *Journal of Educational and Behavioral Statistics, 27*(3), 255–270.

Lowe, B. A. (1994). Payment by Results: An example of assessment in elementary education from nineteenth century Britain. *Education Policy Analysis Archives, 2*(1). Retrieved December 25, 2006, from http://epaa.asu.edu/epaa/v2n1.html

Lynn, J., & Jay, A. (1988, January 7). Power to the people. *Yes, Prime Minister* [Television series]. British Broadcasting Corporation.

MacLean S (2002). *2001 ENA national benchmark guide: Emergency departments.* Des Plaines, IL: Emergency Nurses Association.

Macris, G. (1999, September 13). Central High gets poor peer review. *Providence Journal-Bulletin,* p. 1C. Retrieved December 30, 2006, from the LexisNexis Academic database.

Madaus, G. F. (1988). The distortion of teaching and testing: High-stakes testing and instruction. *Peabody Journal of Education, 65,* 29–46.

Madaus, G. F. (1991). The effects of important tests on students. *Phi Delta Kappan, 73,* 226–231.

Maeroff, G. (1976, September 12). Aptitude test lag is puzzling experts. *New York Times,* p. 17.

Malone, K. (1925). A linguistic patriot. *American Speech, 1*(1), 26–31.

Manna, P. (2006). *School's in: Federalism and the national education agenda.* Washington, DC: Georgetown University Press.

Marchant, G. J., Paulson, S. E., & Shunk, A. (2006). Relations between high-stakes testing policies and student achievement after controlling for demographic factors in aggregated data. *Education Policy Analysis Archives, 14*(30). Retrieved November 15, 2006, from http://epaa.asu.edupeaa/v14n30/.

Marsden, D., & Belfield, R. (2006). *Pay for performance where output is hard to measure: The case of performance pay for school teachers* [Electronic version]. London: LSE Research Online. Retrieved November 19, 2006, from http://eprints.lse.ac.uk/archive/00000850.

Martin, D. T., Overholt, G. E., & Urban, W. J. (1975). *Accountability in American education: A critique.* Princeton, NJ: Princeton Book.

Martineau, J. A. (2006). Distorted value added: The use of longitudinal, vertically scaled student achievement data for growth-based, value-added accountability. *Journal of Educational and Behavioral Statistics, 31*(1), 35–62.

Martz, G., & Robinson, A. (2007). *Cracking the GMAT: 2007 edition.* New York: Random House.

Mathews, J. (2006a, February 20). Let's teach to the test. *Washington Post*, p. A21. Retrieved August 15, 2006, from http://www.washingtonpost.com/wp-dyn/content/article/2006/02/19/AR2006021900976.html.

Mathews, J. (2006b, September 3). National school testing urged. *Washington Post*, p. A1. Retrieved September 6, 2006, from http://www.washingtonpost.com/wp-dyn/content/article/2006/09/02/AR2006090201041.html.

Matus, R., & Winchester, D. (2006, April 1). Schools a weak link in poll for Gov. Bush. *St. Petersburg Times*. Retrieved June 15, 2006, from http://www.sptimes.com/2006/04/01/State/Schools_a_weak_link_i.shtml.

Mazzeo, C. (2001). Frameworks of state: Assessment policy in historical perspective. *Teachers College Record, 103*, 367–397.

McCaffrey, D. F., Lockwood, J. R., Koretz, D., Louis, T. A., & Hamilton, L. (2004). Models for value-added modeling of teacher effects. *Journal of Educational and Behavioral Statistics, 29*(1), 67–101.

McDonnell, L. M. (1994). *Policymakers' views of student assessment* (CSE Tech. Rep. No. 378). Los Angeles: University of California, Center for Research on Evaluation, Standards, and Student Testing (CRESST). Retrieved September 7, 2006, from http://www.cse.ucla.edu/Reports/TECH378.PDF.

McGuinn, P. J. (2006). *No Child Left Behind and the transformation of federal education policy, 1965–2005*. Lawrence, KS: University of Kansas Press.

McNeil, L. (2000). *Contradictions of school reform: Educational costs of standardized testing*. New York: Routledge.

Meier, D. (1995). *The power of their ideas: Lessons for America from a small school in Harlem*. Boston: Beacon Press.

Meier, D. (1999–2000, December/January). Educating a democracy: Standards and the future of public education. *Boston Review, 24*. Retrieved December 25, 2006, from http://bostonreview.net/BR24.6/meier.html.

Meier, D. (2004). NCLB and democracy. In D. Meier & G. Wood (Eds.), *Many children left behind: How the No Child Left Behind Act is damaging our children and our schools* (pp. 66–78). Boston: Beacon Press.

Meier, D., & Wood, G. (Eds.). (2004). *Many children left behind: How the No Child Left Behind Act is damaging our children and our schools*. Boston: Beacon Press.

Merrow, J. (1997). *Testing ... testing ... testing...* [Transcript]. Washington, DC: Public Broadcasting System. Retrieved September 27, 1997, from http://www.pbs.org/merrow/tttscript.txt.

Metz, M. H. (1990). Real school: A universal drama amid disparate experience in D. Mitchell and M. E. Goertz (Eds.), *Education politics for the new century: The twentieth anniversary yearbook of the Politics of Education Association* (pp. 75–91). Philadelphia: The Falmer Press.

Meyer v. Nebraska, 262 U.S. 390 (1922).

Michael, D., & Dorn, S. (2007). Accountability as a means of improvement: A continuity of themes. In K. M. Borman & S. Dorn (Eds.), *Education reform in Florida* (pp. 83–116). Albany: State University of New York Press.

Miller, M. (1997, November 17). Surprise! National school standards exist. *U. S. News and World Report* [Online]. Retrieved December 23, 1997, from http://www.usnews.com/usnews/issue/971117/17stan.htm.

Milliken v. Bradley, 418 U.S. 717 (1974).

Mintrop, H. (2004). *Schools on probation: How accountability works (and doesn't work)*. New York: Teachers College Press.

Mishel, L., & Roy, R. (2006). *Rethinking high school graduation rates and trends*. Washington, D.C.: Economic Policy Institute. Retrieved June 26, 2006, from http://www.epi.org/books/rethinking_hs_grad_rates/rethinking_hs_grad_rates-FULL_TEXT.pdf.

Missouri v. Jenkins, 515 U.S. 70 (1995).

Mitchell, K. J., Robinson, D. Z., Plake, B. S., & Knowles, K. T., (Eds.). (2001). *Testing teacher candidates: The role of licensure tests in improving teacher quality*. Washington, DC: National Research Council. Retrieved October 23, 2006, from http://fermat.nap.edu/books/0309074207/html/.

Monroe, W. S. (1918). Existing tests and standards. In G. W. Whipple (Ed.), *The measurement of educational products. The seventeenth yearbook of the National Society for the Study of Education*, Part II (pp. 71–104). Bloomington, IL: Public School Publishing Company.

Mooney, C. (2005). *The Republican war on science*. New York: Basic Books.

Moreau, J. (2003). *Schoolbook nation: Conflicts over American history textbooks from the civil war to the present*. Ann Arbor, MI: University of Michigan Press.

Murphy, M. (1990). *Blackboard unions: The AFT and the NEA, 1900–1980*. Ithaca, NY: Cornell University Press.

Murray, V. (2005, July 14). AIMS 2005: Everyone's passing, but is anyone learning? [Electronic version]. *Goldwater Institute Today's News*. Retrieved October 22, 2006, from http://www.goldwaterinstitute.org/article.php?/696.html.

Nagaoka, J., & Roderick, M. (2004). *Ending social promotion: The effects of retention*. Chicago: Consortium on Chicago School Research. Retrieved September 7, 2006, from http://www.consortium-chicago.org/publications/pdfs/p70.pdf.

Nash, G. B., Crabtree, C., & Dunn, R. E. (1997). *History on trial: Culture wars and the teaching of the past*. New York: Knopf.

Nation's Report Card. (2006). *State profiles* [Web site]. Washington, DC: National Center for Education Statistics. Retrieved October 23, 2006, from http://nces.ed.gov/nationsreportcard/states/profile.asp.

National Center on Education and the Economy. (1990). *America's choice: High skills or low wages*. Rochester, NY: Author.

National Commission on Excellence in Education. (1983). *A nation at risk*. Washington, DC: Government Printing Office.

National Education Association. (2005, November 21). *U.S. Education Dept. validates NEA's concerns* [Press release]. Washington, DC: Author. Retrieved August 14, 2006, from http://www.nea.org/newsreleases/2005/nr051121.html.

National Education Goals Panel (n.d.). *The National Education Goals Panel: Building a nation of learners* [Web site]. Retrieved October 21, 2006, from http://govinfo.library.unt.edu/negp/.

National Education Goals Panel. (1999). *The National Education Goals report: Building a nation of learners, 1999*. Washington, DC: U.S. Government Printing Office.

National Manpower Council. (1957). *Womanpower*. New York: Columbia University Press.

National Reading Panel. (2000). *Teaching children to read: An evidence-based assessment of the scientific research literature on reading and its implications for reading instruction.* Washington, DC: National Institute of Child Health and Human Development. Retrieved December 24, 2006, from http://www.nichd.nih.gov/publications/pubskey.cfm?from=reading.

National Vocational Education Act, Public L. No. 64–347, 39 Stat. 929 (1917).

Nebraska Department of Education. (2006). *S.T.A.R.S. and the U. S. Department of Education* [Web site]. Retrieved November 22, 2006, from http://www.nde.state.ne.us/1STARSNCLB/STARSandUSDE.htm.

Nelson, F. H. (2006, October). *The impact of collective bargaining on teacher transfer rates in urban high-poverty schools.* Washington, DC: American Federation of Teachers. Retrieved December 28, 2006, from http://www.aft.org/topics/teacher-quality/downloads/Teacher_Transfer_Rates.pdf.

Nelson, F. H., Rosenberg, B., & Van Meter, N. (2004). *Charter school achievement on the 2003 National Assessment of Educational Progress.* Washington, DC: American Federation of Teachers. Retrieved December 22, 2006, from http://www.aft.org/pubs-reports/downloads/teachers/NAEPCharterSchoolReport.pdf.

Newman, H. H., Freeman, F. N., & Holzinger, K. J. (1937). *Twins: A study of heredity and environment.* Chicago: University of Chicago Press.

Nichols, S. L., & Berliner, D. C. (2007). *Collateral damage: How high-stakes testing corrupts America's schools.* Cambridge, MA: Harvard Education Press.

Nichols, S. L., Glass, G. V, & Berliner, D. C. (2006). High-stakes testing and student achievement: Does accountability pressure increase student learning? *Education Policy Analysis Archives, 14*(1). Retrieved October 30, 2006, from http://epaa.asu.edu/epaa/v14n1/.

Nickerson, B. J., & Deenihan, G. M. (2003). From equity to adequacy: The legal battle for increased state funding of poor school districts in New York. *Fordham Urban Law Journal, 30,* 1341–1392.

No Child Left Behind Act of 2001, Pub. L. No. 107–110 (2002).

Norris, M. (2004, August 17). Students at charter schools lag peers. *All Things Considered.* Retrieved September 5, 2006, from http://www.npr.org/templates/story/story.php?storyId=3855679

North Carolina Public Schools. (2005). *ABCs Results: Nine-year summary chart, 1996–97 to 2004–05.* Raleigh, NC: Author. Retrieved July 30, 2006, from http://www.ncpublicschools.org/docs/accountability/reporting/abc/2004-05/abctrends.pdf

North Carolina Public Schools. (2006). *ABCs 2006 accountability report background packet.* Raleigh, NC: Author. Retrieved August 15, 2006, from http://www.ncpublicschools.org/docs/accountability/reporting/abc/2005-06/backgroundpacket.pdf.

Nye, D. E. (1996). *American technological sublime.* Cambridge, MA: MIT Press.

Odden, A., & Kelly, C. (2002). *Paying teachers for what they know and do: new and smarter compensation strategies to improve schools.* Thousand Oaks, CA: Corwin Press.

O'Donnell, S. (2001). *International review of curriculum and assessment frameworks: Thematic probe. Curriculum Review: An International Perspective.* London: Qualifications and Curriculum Authority. Retrieved October 22, 2006, from http://www.inca.org.uk/pdf/062001review.pdf.

Orel, S. (2003). Left behind in Birmingham: 522 pushed-out students. In R. C. Lent & G. Pipkin (Eds.), *Silent no more: Voices of courage in American schools* (pp. 1–14). Portsmouth, NH: Heinemann.

Orfield, G. (1969). *The reconstruction of southern education: The schools and the 1964 Civil Rights Act.* New York: Wiley.

Orfield, G. (1993). *The growth of segregation in American schools: Changing patterns of separation and poverty since 1968.* Alexandria, Va.: National School Boards Assocation, Council of Urban Boards of Education.

Orfield, G., Eaton, S. E., & Harvard Project on School Desegregation. (1996). *Dismantling desegregation: The quiet reversal of Brown v. Board of Education.* New York: New Press.

Owen, D., & Doerr, M. (1999). *None of the above: The truth behind the SATs* (2nd ed). Lanham, MD: Rowman & Littlefield.

Parkinson, J. (2004). Why deliberate? The encounter between deliberation and the new public managers. *Public Administration, 82*(2), 377–395.

Patterson, J. T. (2001). *Brown v. Board of Education: A civil rights milestone and its troubled legacy.* New York: Oxford University Press.

Pechman, E., & LaGuarda, K. (1993). *Status of new curriculum frameworks, standards, assessments, and monitoring systems.* Washington, DC: Policy Studies Associates.

Petrilli, M. J. (2006, July 27). Dropping acid. *Education Gadfly, 6*(29). Retrieved September 23, 2006, from http://www.edexcellence.net/foundation/global/page.cfm?id=379.

Phelps, R. P. (2003). *Kill the messenger: The war on standardized testing.* Somerset, NJ: Transaction.

Phenix, D., Siegel, D., Zaltsman, A., & Fruchter, N. (2005). A forced march for failing schools: Lessons from the New York City Chancellor's District. *Education Policy Analysis Archives, 13*(40). Retrieved November 21, 2006, from http://epaa.asu.edu/epaa/v13n40/.

Picus, L. O. (1994). *A conceptual framework for analyzing the costs of alternative assessment* (CSE Technical Report 384) Los Angeles: Center for the Study of Evaluation. Retrieved June 12, 2006, from http://www.cse.ucla.edu/CRESST/Reports/TECH384.PDF.

Pierce v. Society of Sisters, 268 U.S. 510 (1925).

Polichetti, B. (2000, March 14). SALT review: Western Hills is good, potentially excellent. *Providence Journal-Bulletin,* p. C1. Retrieved December 30, 2006, from the LexisNexis Academic database.

Polichetti, B. (2003, February 18). Rating team gives Park View Middle School dismal review. *Providence Journal-Bulletin,* p. C1. Retrieved December 30, 2006, from the LexisNexis Academic database.

Popham, W. J. (1972). *An evaluation guidebook: A set of practical guidelines for the educational evaluator.* Los Angeles: The Instructional Objectives Exchange.

Popham, W. J. (1978). As always, provocative. *Journal of Educational Measurement, 15,* 297–300.

Popham, W. J. (2004). *America's "failing" schools: How parents and teachers can cope with No Child Left Behind.* New York: Routledge.

Porter, T. M. (1995). *Trust in numbers: The pursuit of objectivity in science and public life*. Princeton, NJ: Princeton University Press.

Portner, J. (2002, July 30). California schools to receive bonuses for raising student test scores. *San Jose Mercury News*. Retrieved December 30, 2006, from the LexisNexis Academic database.

Potter, D. M. (1954). *People of plenty: Economic abundance and the American character*. Chicago: University of Chicago Press.

Powell, A. G., Farrar, E., & Cohen, D. K. (1985). *The shopping mall high school: Winners and losers in the educational marketplace*. New York: Houghton Mifflin.

Purdum, T. S. (1999, July 9). Clinton ends visit to poor with an appeal for support. *New York Times*, p. A10. Retrieved December 30, 2006, from the LexisNexis Academic database.

Rau, E. (1999, January 13). Report praises SALT. *Providence Journal-Bulletin*, p. 1B. Retrieved December 30, 2006, from the LexisNexis Academic database.

Raudenbush, S. W. (2004). What are value-added models estimating and what does this imply for statistical practice. *Journal of Educational and Behavioral Statistics, 29*(1), 121–130.

Ravitch, D. (1983). *The troubled crusade: American education, 1945–1980*. New York: Basic Books.

Ravitch, D. (1995). *National standards in American education: A citizen's guide*. Washington, DC: Brookings.

Ravitch, D. (2003). *Language police: How pressure groups restrict what students learn*. New York: Knopf.

Ravitch, D. (2006a, March). *The case for national curriculum, national standards, and national tests*. Paper prepared for the "Measuring Child Well-Being" conference, Foundation for Child Development and Brookings Institution, Washington, DC. Retrieved October 24, 2006, from http://www.fcd-us.org/pdfs/TheCaseforNationalCurriculumRavitch.pdf.

Ravitch, D. (2006b, January 18). *Reconsidering national standards, curricula, and tests* [Live chat transcript]. *Education Week*. Retrieved October 22, 2006, from http://www.edweek.org/chat/transcript_01_18_2006.html.

Reardon, S. F. (1996, April). *Eighth grade minimum competency testing and early high school dropout patterns*. Paper presented at the annual meeting of the American Educational Research Association, New York.

Reckase, M. D. (2004). The real world is more complicated than we would like. *Journal of Educational and Behavioral Statistics, 29*(1), 117–120.

Rees, J. (2001). Frederick Taylor in the classroom: Scientific testing and scientific management *Radical Pedagogy, 3*(2). Retrieved September 25, 2002, from http://radicalpedagogy.icaap.org/content/issue3_2/rees.html.

Reese, W. J. (1995). *The origins of the American high school*. New Haven, CT: Yale University Press.

Resnick, D. P. (1980). Minimum competency testing historically considered. *Review of Research in Education, 8*, 3–29.

Resnick, L. B., & Resnick, D. P. (1992). Assessing the thinking curriculum: New tools for educational reform. In B. R. Gifford & M. C. O'Connor (Eds.), *Changing assessments: Alternative views of aptitude, achievement, and instruction* (pp. 35–75). Boston: Kluwer.

Rhoades, K., & Madaus, G. (2003, May). *Errors in standardized tests: A systemic problem*. Boston: National Board on Educational Testing and Public Policy. Retrieved June 18, 2006, from http://www.bc.edu/research/nbetpp/statements/M1N4.pdf.

Rhoten, D., Carnoy, M., Chabrán, M., & Elmore, R. (2003). The conditions and characteristics of assessment and accountability: The case of four states. In M. Carnoy, R. Elmore, & L. S. Siskin (Eds.), *The new accountability: High schools and high-stakes testing* (pp. 13–54). New York: RoutledgeFarmer.

Rice, J. M. (1897a). The futility of the spelling grind I. *Forum, 23*, 163–172.

Rice, J. M. (1897b). The futility of the spelling grind II. *Forum, 23*, 409–419.

Richardson, J. G. (1999). *Common, delinquent, and special*. New York: Routledge-Falmer.

Richardson, K. (2000). *The making of intelligence*. New York: Columbia University Press.

Richardson, K. (2002). What IQ tests test. *Theory and Psychology, 12*, 283–314.

RMC Research Corporation. (1976). *Interpreting NCEs*. Technical Paper No. 2. Mountain View, CA: RMC Research Corporation Mountain View.

Rogosa, D. (2005). Statistical misunderstandings of the properties of school scores and school accountability. In J. L. Herman & E. H. Haertel (Eds.), *Uses and misuses of data for educational accountability and improvement. The 104th yearbooks of the National Society for the Study of Education* (Part II, pp. 147–174). Malden, MA: Blackwell.

Romano, L. (2005a, October 20). Test scores move little in math, reading. *Washington Post*. Retrieved December 30, 2006, from the LexisNexis Academic database.

Romano, L. (2005b, December 25). Literacy of college graduates is on decline. *Washington Post*, p. A12. Retrieved November 21, 2006, from http://www.washingtonpost.com/wp-dyn/content/article/2005/12/24/AR2005122400701.html.

Romano, L. (2006, August 31). Tweaking of "No Child" seen. *Washington Post*, p. A4. Retrieved November 24, 2006, from http://www.washingtonpost.com/wp-dyn/content/article/2006/08/30/AR2006083002914.html.

Rorabaugh, W. J. (1986). *The craft apprentice: From Franklin to the machine age in America*. New York: Oxford University Press.

Rose, L. C., & Gallup, A. M. (2005, September). The 37th annual Phi Delta Kappan/Gallup poll of the public's attitudes toward the public schools. *Kappan, 87*, 41–57. Retrieved June 15, 2006, from http://www.pdkintl.org/kappan/k0509pol.pdf.

Rose, L. C., & Gallup, A. M. (2006, September). The 38th annual Phi Delta Kappa/Gallup poll of the public's attitudes toward the public schools. *Kappan, 88*, 41–53. Retrieved August 28, 2006, from http://www.pdkmembers.org/e-GALLUP/kpoll_pdfs/pdkpoll38_2006.pdf.

Rosenshine, B. (2003). High-stakes testing: Another analysis. *Education Policy Analysis Archives, 11*(24). Retrieved January 7, 2004, from http://epaa.asu.edu/epaa/v11n24/.

Ross, D. (1972). *G. Stanley Hall*. Chicago: The University of Chicago Press.

Rotherham, A. (2005, December 13). Jenny D. on growth: What me worry? *Eduwonk* [blog]. Retrieved August 10, 2006, from http://www.eduwonk.com/archives/2005_12_11_archive.html#113449099550450685.

Rotherham, A. (2006a, February 1). Growth industry. *Eduwonk* [Blog]. Retrieved August 10, 2006, from http://www.eduwonk.com/archives/2006_01_29_archive.html#113879665704145232.

Rotherham, A. (2006b, May 18). A good day for edublogs or a bad day for newspapers? Eduwonk goes through the looking glass. *Eduwonk* [Blog]. Retrieved August 10, 2006, from http://www.eduwonk.com/archives/2006_05_14_archive.html#114791364921538329.

Rotherham, A. (2006c, May 19). Serious education journalist Alexander Russo slides into a fevered frenzy of malcontented grumbling. *Eduwonk* [Blog]. Retrieved August 10, 2006, from http://www.eduwonk.com/archives/2006_05_14_archive.html#114807357157835922.

Rothstein, R. (2004). *Class and schools: Using social, economic, and educational reform to close the Black–White achievement gap*. Washington, DC: Economic Policy Institute.

Rourke, F. E. (1957). The politics of administrative organization: A case history. *Journal of Politics, 19*(3), 461–478.

Rourke, F. E. (1984). *Bureaucracy, politics, and public policy* (3rd ed.). New York: Little, Brown.

Rousseau, J. -J. (1762). *Emile, ou de l'Education*. Retrieved December 22, 2006, from http://www.ilt.columbia.edu/pedagogies/rousseau/contents2.html.

Rubin, D. B., Stuart, E. A., & Zanutto, E. L. (2004). A potential outcomes view of value-added assessment in education. *Journal of Educational and Behavioral Statistics, 29*(1), 103–116.

Rudolph, J. (2002). *Scientists in the classroom: The Cold War reconstruction of American science education*. New York: Palgrave.

Ruggles, P. (1990). *Drawing the line: Alternative poverty measures and their implications for public policy*. Washington, DC: Urban Institute Press.

Rush, B. (1786/1965). A plan for the establishment of public schools and the diffusion of knowledge in Pennsylvania. In F. Rudolph (Ed.), *Essays on education in the early republic* (pp. 1–23). Cambridge, MA: Belknap Press.

Saltzman, J. (2004, August 24). Wages faulted in lawyer dispute. *Boston Globe*. Retrieved November 27, 2006, from http://www.boston.com/news/local/massachusetts/articles/2004/08/24/wages_faulted_in_lawyer_dispute/.

San Antonio v. Rodriguez, 411 U.S. 1 (1973).

Sanders, W. L., & Horn, S. P. (1994). The Tennessee Value-Added Assessment System (TVAAS): Mixed model methodology in educational assessment. *Journal of Personnel Evaluation in Education, 8*, 299–311.

Sanders, W. L., & Horn, S. P. (1995). Educational assessment reassessed: The usefulness of standardized and alternative measures of student achievement as *Education Policy Analysis Archives, 3*(6). Retrieved August 9, 2006, from http://epaa.asu.edu/epaa/v3n6.html.

Sanders model to measure "value added." (1991, May). *TEA News*, p. 5.

Sandler, M. (2001, April 11). Testing of pupils faulted at forum. *St. Petersburg Times*, p. 3B. Retrieved June 15, 2006, from http://www.sptimes.com/News/041101/Hillsborough/Testing_of_pupils_fau.shtml.

Sarason, S. B. (1993). *The predictable failure of educational reform: Can we change course before it's too late?* San Francisco: Jossey-Bass.

Schell, J. (1975). *The time of illusion*. New York: Knopf.

Scott, H. (1933). *Introduction to technocracy*. New York: John Day Company.

Scriven, M. (1967). The methodology of evaluation. In R. W. Tyler, R. M. Gagné, & M. Scriven (Eds.), *Perspectives of curriculum evaluation* (pp. 39–83). Chicago: Rand McNally.

Scriven, M. (1978). How to anchor standards. *Journal of Educational Measurement, 15*, 273–275.

Seijts, G. H., & Latham, G. P. (2001). The effect of learning, outcome, and proximal goals on a moderately complex task. *Journal of Organizational Behavior, 22*, 291–302.

Seijts, G. H., & Latham, G. P. (2005). Learning versus performance goals: When should each be used? *Academy of Management Executive, 19*(1), 124–131.

Selden, S. (1999). *Inheriting shame: The story of eugenics in America*. New York: Teachers College Press.

Serrano v. Priest, 5 C3d. 584 (1971).

Shelley, M. W. (1818/1869). *Frankenstein; or, the modern Prometheus*. Boston: Sever, Francis.

Shepard, L. A. (1991). Will national tests improve student learning? *Kappan, 73*, 232–238.

Shepard, L. A. (1995). Implications for standard setting of the National Academy of Education evaluation of the National Assessment of Educational Progress achievement levels. In *Joint conference on standard setting for largescale assessments: Proceedings* (Vol. 2., pp. 143–160). Washington, DC: U.S. Government Printing Office.

Shircliffe, B. J. (2006). *"The best of that world": Historically Black high schools and the crisis of segregation in a Southern metropolis*. Cresskill, NJ: Hampton Press.

Sirotnik, K. A., (Ed.). (2004). *Holding accountability accountable: What ought to matter in public education*. New York: Teachers College Press.

Sizer, T. R. (1992). *Horace's school: Redesigning the American high school*. Boston: Houghton Mifflin.

Sizer, T. R. (1995). Will national standards and assessments make a difference? In D. Ravitch (Ed.), *Debating the future of American education: Do we need national standards and assessments?* (pp. 33–39). Washington, DC: Brookings Institution.

Skocpol, T. (1991). Targeting within universalism: Politically viable policies to combat poverty in the United States. In C. Jencks & P. E. Peterson (Eds.), *The urban underclass* (pp. 411–436). Washington, DC: Brookings Institution.

Skocpol, T. (1992). *Protecting soldiers and mothers: The political origins of social policy in the United States*. Cambridge, MA: Belknap Press.

Smith, M. L. (1991a). Meanings of test preparation. *American Educational Research Journal, 28*(3), 521–542.

Smith, M. L. (1991b). Put to the test: The effects of external testing on teachers. *Educational Researcher, 20*(5), 8–11.

Smith, M. L., Edelsky, C., Draper, K., Rottenberg, C., & Cherland, M. (1989). *The role of testing in elementary schools*. Los Angeles: Center for Research on Educational Standards and Student Tests.

Smith, M. S., & Scoll, B. W. (1995). The Clinton human capital agenda. *Teachers College Record, 96*, 389–404.

Smith, S. S., & Mickelson, R. A. (2000). All that glitters is not gold: School reform in Charlotte-Mecklenburg. *Educational Evaluation and Policy Analysis, 22*(2), 101–127.

Smith, S. W. (1990). Individualized education programs (IEPs) in special education—from intent to acquiescence. *Exceptional Children, 57*, 6–14.

Snider, K. F. (2000). Expertise or experimenting? Pragmatism and American public administration, 1920–1950. *Administration and Society, 32*(3), 329–354.

Snijders, T. A. B. (2003). Multilevel analysis. In M. Lewis-Beck, A.E. Bryman, and T.F. Liao (Eds.), *The SAGE encyclopedia of social science research methods* (pp. 673–677). Thousand Oaks, CA: Sage.

Social Security Act, Pub. L. No. 74-271 (1935).

Somerby, B. (2006, January 19). How to read literacy (part 3). *The Daily Howler: Caveat Lector* [blog]. Retrieved November 21, 2006, from http://www.dailyhowler.com/dh011906.shtml.

Southern Governor's Conference. (1973). *Summary of proceeding, thirty-ninth annual meeting of the Southern Governor's Conference, September 23–26*. Atlanta, GA: Council of State Governments.

Spearman, C. (1904) General intelligence. *American Journal of Psychology, 15*, 201–293

Spring, J. (1989). *The sorting machine revisited: National educational policy since 1945* (updated ed.). New York: Longman.

Starr, P. (1982). *The social transformation of American medicine*. New York: Basic Books.

Starr, P. (1987). The sociology of official statistics. In P. Starr & W. Alonso (Ed.), *The politics of numbers* (pp. 7–57). New York: Russell Sage Foundation.

Stecker, P. M., Fuchs, L. S., & Fuchs, D. (2005). Using curriculum-based measurement to improve student achievement: Review of research. *Psychology in the Schools, 42*, 597–819.

Steiny, J. (1998, July 19). Grudgingly, school says SALT helped. *Providence Journal-Bulletin*, p. 1H. Retrieved December 30, 2006, from the LexisNexis Academic database.

Stern, M. J. (1987). *Society and family strategy: Erie County, New York, 1850–1920*. Albany: State University of New York Press.

Stoel, R. D. (2003). *Issues in growth curve modeling*. Amsterdam: TT-Publikaties. Retrieved August 14, 2006, from http://home.medewerker.uva.nl/r.d.stoel/bestanden/Stoel%20(2003).pdf.

Stonehill, R. M., & Groves, C. L. (1983). U.S. Department of Education policies and ESEA Title I evaluation utility: Changes in attitudes, changes in platitudes. *Educational Evaluation and Policy Analysis, 5*(1), 65–73.

Strober, M. H., & Tyack, D. (1980). Why do women teach and men manage? A report on research on schools. *Signs, 5*, 494–503.

Stronge, J. H., Gareis, C. R., & Little, C. A. (2006). *Teacher pay and teacher quality: Attracting, developing, and retaining the best teachers.* Thousand Oaks, CA: Corwin Press.

Taylor, F. W. (1911). *Principles of scientific management.* New York: Harper Bros.

Tekwe, C. D., Carter, R. L., Ma, C.-X., Algina, J., Lucas, M. L., Roth, J., et al. (2004). An empirical comparison of statistical models for value-added assessment of school performance. *Journal of Educational and Behavioral Statistics, 29*(1), 11–36.

Tennessee Department of Education. (1996). *21st century report card.* Retrieved September 27, 1997, from http://www.state.tn.us/education/rptcrd96/index.html.

Terman, L. M. (1930). Autobiography of Lewis M. Terman (1930). In C. Murchison (Ed.), *History of psychology in autobiography* (Vol. 2, pp. 297–331). Worcester, MA: Clark University Press.

Thum, Y. M. (2002). *Measuring student and school progress with the California API.* CSE Technical Report 578. Los Angeles: National Center for Research on Evaluation, Standards, and Student Testing. Retrieved July 30, 2006, from http://cresst96.cse.ucla.edu/CRESST/Reports/TR578.pdf.

Tilly, C. (1998). *Durable inequality.* Berkeley: University of California Press.

Tobin, T.C., & Winchester, D. (2004, October 4). New FCAT push accelerates teaching pace. *St. Petersburg Times.* Retrieved June 6, 2006, from http://www.sptimes.com/2004/10/04/Southpinellas/New_FCAT_push_acceler.shtml.

Toch, T. (2006a). *Margins of error: The testing industry in the No Child Left Behind era.* Washington, DC: Education Sector. Retrieved August 16, 2006, from http://www.educationsector.org/research/research_show.htm?doc_id=346734.

Toch, T. (2006b, March 27). Less is not more. *The Quick and the Ed* [Blog]. Retrieved September 5, 2006, from http://www.quickanded.com/2006/03/less-is-not-more.html.

Tong, E. (2003, March 2). Awards fade with economy. *Los Angeles Daily News.* Retrieved December 30, 2006, from the LexisNexis Academic database.

Tracey, C. (2005). Listening to teachers: Classroom realities and NCLB. In G. L. Sunderman, J. S. Kim, & G. Orfield (Eds.), *NCLB meets school realities: Lessons from the field* (pp. 81–104). Thousand Oaks, CA: Corwin Press.

Turner, S. (2003). *Liberal democracy 3.0: Civil society in an age of experts.* Thousand Oaks, CA: Sage.

Tyack, D. B. (1974). *The one best system: A history of American urban education.* Cambridge, MA: Harvard University Press.

Tyack, D. B., & Cuban, L. (1995). *Tinkering toward utopia: A century of public school reform.* Cambridge, MA: Harvard University Press.

Tyack, D. B., & Hansot, E. (1982). *Managers of virtue: Public school leadership in America, 1820–1980.* New York: Basic Books.

U.S. Department of Education. (2005). *Digest of education statistics, 2004.* Washington, DC: Author.

U.S. Department of Education. (2006). *Growth models: Ensuring grade-level proficiency for all students by 2014.* Washington, DC: Author. Retrieved August 14, 2006, from http://www.ed.gov/admins/lead/account/growthmodel/proficiency.pdf.

Urban, W. J. (2000). *Gender, race, and the National Education Association: Professionalism and its limitations.* New York: Routledge Falmer.

Van Buuren, A., Edelenbos, J., & Klijn, E.-H. (2004). *Managing knowledge in policy networks: Organising joint fact-finding in the Scheldt Estuary.* Paper presented at the International Conference on Democratic Network Governance, Copenhagen, Denmark. Retrieved November 24, 2006, from http://www.ruc.dk/demnetgov_en/conference/int_conf/papers/Erik-HansKlijn_paper/.

vanderPloeg, A. J. (1982). ESEA Title I evaluation: The service of two masters. *Educational Evaluation and Policy Analysis, 4*(4), 521–526.

Vinovskis, M. A. (1999). Do federal compensatory education programs really work? A brief historical analysis of Title I and Head Start. *American Journal of Education, 107*(3), 187–209.

Vinovskis, M. A. (1999). *The road to Charlottesville: The 1989 education summit.* Washington, DC: National Education Goals Panel. Retrieved October 21, 2006, from http://govinfo.library.unt.edu/negp/reports/negp30.pdf.

Virginia Board of Education. (1995). *History and social science standards of learning for Virginia public schools.* Richmond, VA: Author. Retrieved October 21, 2006, from http://www.pen.k12.va.us/VDOE/Superintendent/Sols/home.shtml.

Warren, J. R. (2005). State-level high school completion rates: Concepts, measures, and trends. *Education Policy Analysis Archives, 13*(51). Retrieved December 24, 2005, from http://epaa.asu.edu/epaa/v13n51/.

Weaver, R. (2006, July 2). *Keynote speech delivered to Representative Assembly of the National Education Association.* Washington: National Education Association. Retrieved August 6, 2006, from http://www.nea.org/annualmeeting/raaction/RegKeynote.html.

Webster, N. (1789/1992). Declaration of linguistic independence. In J. Crawford (Ed.), *Language loyalties: A source book on the Official English controversy* (pp. 33–36). Chicago: University of Chicago Press.

Weiss, C. H. (1988). Interview study. In C. H. Weiss & E. Singer (Eds.), *Reporting of social science in the national media* (pp. 21–171). New York: Russell Sage Foundation.

Weiss, J. A., & Gruber, J. E. (1987). The managed irrelevance of federal education statistics. In P. Starr & W. Alonso (Eds.), *The politics of numbers* (pp. 363–391). New York: Russell Sage Foundation.

Werum, R. (1997). Sectionalism and racial politics: Federal vocational policies and programs in the predesegregation South. *Social Science History, 21*, 399–453.

Westbrook, R. (1991). *John Dewey and American democracy.* Ithaca, NY: Cornell University Press.

Westhoff, L. M. (1995). The popularization of knowledge: John Dewey on experts and American democracy. *History of Education Quarterly, 35*, 27–47.

Wiebe, R. H. (1967). *The search for order, 1877–1920.* New York: Hill and Wang.

Williams, J. (2005). *Cheating our kids: How politics and greed ruin education.* New York: Palgrave Macmillan.

Wilson, N. (1998). Educational standards and the problem of error. *Education Policy Analysis Archives, 6*(10). Retrieved August 10, 2006, from http://epaa.asu.edu/epaa/v6n10/.

Wilson, T. A. (1996). *Reaching for a better standard: English school inspection and the dilemma of accountability for American public schools.* New York: Teachers College Press.

Winerip, M. (2006, April 5). No Child Left Behind? Ask the gifted. *New York Times,* p. B7. Retrieved December 22, 2006, from http://select.nytimes.com/gst/abstract.html?res=F00917FC3B540C768CDDAD0894DE404482.

Winters, D., & Latham, G. (1996). The effect of learning versus outcome goals on a simple versus a complex task. *Group and Organization Management, 21,* 236–250.

Wise, A. E. (1979). *Legislated learning: The bureaucratization of the American classroom.* Berkeley, CA: University of California Press.

Wong, K. K., & Shen, F. X. (2001, August-September). *Does school district takeover work? Assessing the effectiveness of city and state takeover as a school reform strategy.* Paper prepared for delivery at the annual meeting of the American Political Science Association, San Francisco. (ERIC Document Reproduction Service No. ED 468 271).

Wood, R., Mento, A., & Locke, E. (1987). Task complexity as a moderator of goal effects. *Journal of Applied Psychology, 17,* 416–425.

Worthen, B. R., & Sanders, J. R. (1991). The changing face of educational evaluation. *Theory into Practice, 30*(1), 3–12.

Wuerz, R. C., Milne, L. W., Eitel, D. R., Travers, D., & Gilboy, N. (2000). Reliability and validity of a new five-level triage instrument. *Academic Emergency Medicine,* 7(3), 236–242.

Wuerz, R. C., Fernandes, C. M., & Alarcon, J. (1998). Inconsistency of emergency department triage. Emergency department operations research working group. *Annals of Emergency Medicine, 32*(4), 431–435.

Wynne, E. (1972). *The politics of school accountability: Public information about schools.* Berkeley, CA: McCutchan.

Yen, W. M. (1986). The choice of scale for educational measurement: An IRT perspective. *Journal of Educational Measurement, 23,* 299–326.

Yishai, Y. (1992). From an iron triangle to an iron duet? *European Journal of Political Research, 21,* 91–108.

Zelizer, V. (1985). *Pricing the priceless child.* New York: Basic Books.

Ziebarth, T. (2002). *State takeovers and reconstitutions.* Denver: Education Commission of the States. Retrieved November 19, 2006, from http://eric.ed.gov/ERICDocs/data/ericdocs2/content_storage_01/0000000b/80/28/0c/45.pdf.

Zimmerman, J. (2002). *Whose America?* Cambridge, MA: Harvard University Press.

INDEX

Printed in the United States
105991LV00001B/161/A

9 781593 116231